The Future Interface

The Future Interface

How We'll Talk to Technology

Adrian M. Navarro

Mindful Pages

Published in 2026

ISBN: 9789374595350 (PB)
ISBN: 9789374595220 (eBook)

Published by

Mindful Pages
Imprint of Alpha Editions LLC
312 W. 2nd St #1834
Casper, WY 82601, USA

Content

Introduction
The Future Interface

A woman lifts her wrist and murmurs a few words to the air. A light flickers, a car pulls from the kerb, a door unlocks. In that moment, a choreography of code, sensors, and inference unfolds faster than thought. She need not reach for a device or open an application; the world itself seems to respond to her presence. Such gestures—once theatrical—have become mundane, yet their ordinariness hides a revolution. For the first time in human history, our tools do not simply await instruction; they anticipate it. They listen, watch, and learn. They speak back, sometimes before we have spoken at all. And this, precisely, is where the story of the future interface begins: with a whisper that answers before we finish asking.

For millennia, human progress has been marked by the distance between intention and action—between what we imagine and what we can make real. The chisel, the typewriter, the keyboard, each bridged that gap in its own way. Yet as interfaces dissolve into gestures, glances, and neural pulses, the gap itself is vanishing. Our technologies have grown intimate enough to share our hesitations. They are being built to feel, to guess, to predict. But with every step toward frictionless interaction, a new tension emerges: if our tools learn to think for us, what remains distinctly ours? The friction that once slowed us also defined us; it was the grain against which thought took shape.

There is a temptation to see this transformation as a triumph of convenience—the age-old dream of effortlessness finally realised. Yet the deeper story is stranger and more consequential. Convenience has become design's most persuasive ideology, and it now threatens to outpace comprehension. When a device anticipates a command, who, precisely, is deciding? When a voice assistant acts on half a sentence, whose intent does it serve? And when algorithms predict our needs, how do we tell the difference between help and manipulation? These are not abstract questions. They touch the daily mechanics of agency, trust, and dignity—the quiet architecture of human choice.

The thesis of this book is simple but radical: the future of human–technology interaction depends not on speed, but on stewardship. True progress lies not in eliminating friction but in designing the right kind of friction—the pauses, confirmations, and clarifications that preserve our will amidst automation. Anticipation without accountability is intrusion; prediction without transparency is control. We must therefore learn to build interfaces that listen acutely without presuming too much. To do so requires a new literacy, one that bridges neuroscience, linguistics, ethics, and engineering.

This literacy begins with the body. Long before circuits or code, the first interface was skin and muscle, attention and memory. Every tool—from stone to smartphone—has extended these organic boundaries. Yet technology often forgets its host. Designers chase processor speed while neglecting human bandwidth. The result is a culture of fatigue: notifications that fracture attention, gestures that defy anatomy, automation that erases comprehension. The body, this most ancient interface, is once again the frontier we must learn to design for. It reminds us that every act of interaction, however digital, is still deeply physical.

Language follows the same principle. The dream of talking to machines has always shimmered with promise, but words are only the surface of intent. Human conversation thrives on repair—on the pauses, rephrasings, and misunderstandings that make meaning possible. When we say "no," "wait," or "that's not what I meant," we are exercising control. A humane linguistic interface must allow the same. Voice assistants that act too eagerly or interpret too narrowly violate the unspoken contract of dialogue. They listen without truly hearing. The measure of progress, then, is not how fluently machines talk, but how responsibly they listen.

Gestures, too, demand humility. The early years of motion control celebrated theatrical novelty: users waving arms like conductors in invisible orchestras. Yet real grace lies in subtlety—the half-turn of a wrist, the micro-shift of gaze. The most elegant gestures are those no one notices, efficient and legible, never ostentatious. They respect social space and physical limitation alike. To design for the tremor or the prosthetic is not to design for the margin; it is to design for everyone. Accessibility, when treated not as an afterthought but as an engine of innovation, reveals universality in diversity.

Beyond gesture and voice lies the horizon of vision itself. Augmented and virtual realities promise to merge perception with computation, to let us see through and with our devices. Yet immersion carries its own perils: distraction, disorientation, and detachment from the physical world. A display that hovers before the eyes can obscure more than it reveals. The task of the designer is no longer merely to render the virtual convincingly, but to ensure that digital overlays respect the cognitive and ethical boundaries of real spaces—whether in a hospital ward, a classroom, or a living room.

Still closer comes the neural frontier: interfaces that read and write the signals of the brain. Their promise is profound—restoring speech to the voiceless, motion to the paralysed—but their risks are equally profound. A command that originates in thought itself compresses the distance between desire and execution until reflection can scarcely intervene. Here the demand for explicit consent and reversibility becomes absolute. When intention becomes input, undo becomes salvation. The dignity test—the question of whether technology expands agency for the least powerful—must govern every design decision at this threshold.

At the heart of these developments lies the central paradox of anticipation: the more systems predict, the less they appear to ask. Prediction can empower or it can entrap.

When algorithms curate our news, choose our routes, or suggest our purchases, they shape our horizons while claiming to serve our preferences. The line between assistance and coercion blurs. Thus, accountability must evolve alongside anticipation. Every predictive act should leave a trail—an "anticipation ledger" of data, triggers, and opt-outs—so users can see, question, and reverse what has been inferred about them. Transparency is not an accessory to design; it is its ethical core.

But humane technology is not built by humane intention alone. It demands institutional structures—teams that span disciplines, governance that treats ethics as product, research that informs roadmaps rather than adorns them. The interface of the future will not emerge from a single field; it will be born of dialogue between engineers, psychologists, anthropologists, and storytellers. Each must learn the language of the other. The questions are no longer purely technical: they are civic, even moral. What defaults do we set? Who owns the logs of our interactions? How do we build systems that remain accountable long after their creators have moved on?

And perhaps the most radical design principle of all is absence. The quiet interface—the one that recedes until nearly invisible—challenges the assumption that interaction should be constant. Some of the most humane technologies are those that choose not to act, that yield the stage to human presence. Silence, once seen as a void to be filled with function, becomes a form of respect. In measuring success, we must learn to count not only clicks and completions but interruptions avoided, fatigue reduced, and comprehension preserved.

This book does not predict which gadgets will dominate the next decade. It offers instead a philosophy of interaction: a way to judge, critique, and create technology that honours the fragile balance between anticipation and autonomy. Across its chapters, it distils evidence from neuroscience, design research, and ethics into patterns any practitioner can apply—whether crafting an app, a policy, or a social norm. The aim is not nostalgia for slower times, but a forward vision rooted in empathy and legibility. Technology should not only work; it should explain itself.

We stand at a turning point. As artificial intelligence and ambient computing weave themselves into our homes, workplaces, and bodies, the fundamental question is no longer what machines can do, but what they should be allowed to do on our behalf. Who has right of way when human intent collides with machine prediction? The answer will define not just the next interface, but the next chapter of human self-understanding.

The chapters that follow offer a toolkit for that reckoning: methods for designing friction that protects will, rituals of consent that outlast novelty, and patterns of control that return power to the user. They invite readers—designers, developers, policymakers, and citizens alike—to test every technology against four enduring measures: legibility, reversibility, provenance, and escalation. These are not merely design heuristics; they are moral instruments. For in the age of intelligent anticipation, freedom depends on the ability to see, to choose, to undo, and to be heard.

The Future Interface is, above all, an argument for deliberate technology. A call to slow the reflex of convenience long enough to ask: What kind of intimacy do we want with our machines? What forms of silence are worth keeping? And how do we ensure that in teaching our tools to understand us, we do not forget to understand ourselves?

Chapter 1
The Body Is the First Interface

The surgeon lifts her hand to zoom in on a holographic scan hovering in the theatre's sterile air. She pinches, swipes, rotates—and the image responds, though not perfectly. The gesture that felt natural in the lab becomes awkward when gloved and tired. A fraction too much rotation, a tremor too small to notice, and the projection slips from alignment. A nurse steadies it, whispering a correction. The operation continues. Later, in the post-mortem of the interface rather than the patient, the engineers admit what the data had already shown: the surgeon's fatigue, not the sensor's precision, was the system's real limit. Human bandwidth—not computational horsepower—decided success.

That moment captures the truth at the heart of all interaction design: our minds and bodies remain the bottleneck. However sleek the interface, every human action still passes through the narrow gate of attention, memory, and muscle. Machines can process terabytes per second, yet the human brain, juggling perhaps seven discrete pieces of information at once, loses clarity under cognitive overload. We are creatures of astonishing intuition but fragile working memory. A single misjudged alert, an unnecessary gesture, a poorly timed automation can break the fragile rhythm of understanding. In design, this is not a mere inconvenience; it is the difference between flow and failure.

Technological optimism often mistakes speed for improvement. But interaction lives at the tempo of thought, not the clock cycle. Attention is a finite currency—spent whenever we shift focus, recall a detail, or recover from surprise. Modern systems, built to anticipate us, often squander it. They multitask on our behalf yet fragment the mind that must absorb their results. True progress will come not from making machines faster, but from making their dialogue with us slower in the right places, clearer at the right moments, and more forgiving everywhere in between.

The premise of this chapter is both simple and radical: before any algorithm can claim to understand us, it must first respect the constraints of our own cognitive architecture. The body is not an obstacle to efficiency; it is the measure of it. The human nervous system sets the frame for what "real-time" truly means. Design that ignores this fact—interfaces that demand constant vigilance, gestures that strain joints, voice cues that vanish before comprehension—breed error and exhaustion. The next frontier of innovation will not be faster processors but more humane pacing.

Consider the quiet tyranny of attention. Each notification, each flashing badge, demands a slice of working memory to interpret. The more stimuli compete, the more error seeps in. Neuroscience has shown that the brain's attentional spotlight is narrow and serial; even so-called multitasking is rapid alternation, not parallel processing. Yet our devices still assume an infinite mental canvas. They push data into every corner of perception, mistaking presence for clarity. The result is a paradox: interfaces designed to anticipate us often make us less able to anticipate ourselves.

Understanding these limits is not merely an act of empathy; it is a prerequisite for accountability. Anticipatory systems—those that predict intent and act before command—must operate within the bandwidth of comprehension. Prediction helps when it relieves memory load or smooths coordination, but it harms when it masks state or removes choice. A well-designed suggestion completes a pattern we have already begun; a poorly timed one wrests control before we are ready to cede it. The moral calculus of automation begins here, in the millisecond intervals where cognition meets code.

To respect that interval, designers must return to the body itself. Every interface begins and ends with a movement: the reach of a thumb, the flick of an eye, the posture we unconsciously hold while reading a screen. Ergonomics, often dismissed as afterthought, is in fact philosophy rendered in muscle memory. The angle of a wrist, the arc of a gesture—these are not cosmetic details but expressions of design ethics. The more an interface aligns with natural motor patterns, the less cognitive strain it imposes. A system that works with the body restores comprehension; one that fights it erodes trust.

Research into thumb reach maps, gaze fixation patterns, and tremor tolerance reveals a humbling truth: the most efficient movements are also the most modest. Large, theatrical gestures exhaust both arm and attention. Small, repeatable ones anchor interaction in the body's own economy. Every centimetre saved is a fragment of concentration preserved. To design for the body is to design for stamina—the quiet endurance that sustains comprehension over time.

This brings us to a subtler danger: convenience as a form of blindness. In the pursuit of speed, designers often erase the cues that signal what the system is doing. Automation hides state; predictive completion obscures choice. A ride-hailing app that dispatches a driver before the user confirms, a medical interface that pre-fills a dosage field—each saves time yet risks error. Legibility markers such as previews, progressive disclosure, and reversible actions are not inefficiencies; they are the scaffolding of understanding. True fluency arises not from invisible automation but from visible coherence.

The best interfaces allow the user to stay oriented, not merely efficient. They show the system's reasoning without demanding explanation. This principle—legibility—is the foundation of trust. We are willing to delegate only when we can still audit. Experts, too, benefit from visibility: comprehension is not the opposite of speed but its precondition. When users can see cause and effect, they act faster, not slower. Convenience that undermines comprehension is not progress; it is abdication.

Behind all these examples lies a persistent adversary: fatigue. Delight, the darling metric of demo culture, tells us little about endurance. A system that dazzles in five minutes may drain its users in five hours. Fatigue—cognitive, emotional, physical—is design's most neglected dimension. The tired hand slips; the tired mind overlooks warning signs. Accessibility is not charity but foresight: every user becomes fatigued eventually. When design protects those with the least stamina, it benefits all.

To design for fatigue is to confront time itself. Interfaces must be tested not only for first impressions but for durability. Hallway tests, error clustering, and time-on-task studies reveal how interaction quality decays under repetition. These are not peripheral metrics; they are ethical instruments. A tool that exhausts its users excludes them. Equity, in this light, begins with endurance.

The stakes are larger than usability. In recognising the body as the first interface, we recover a sense of proportion between human and machine. We stop asking how to make people adapt to technology and start asking how technology can adapt to people—people who tire, forget, and falter, yet learn, recover, and persist. Design becomes an act of humility, not domination.

This chapter will unpack that humility through four lenses. First, it will show how cognition—attention, memory, perception—sets the tempo of all interaction, reminding us that usability begins with the limits of the mind. Second, it will explore the physical affordances of posture, reach, and micro-movement, translating biomechanics into design principles that privilege comfort and clarity. Third, it will examine the seductive trap of convenience, showing how friction, when purposeful, sustains comprehension. And finally, it will confront fatigue as the ultimate design frontier: the test of whether an interface remains humane not in its first moments, but in its thousandth.

To work with the body is to work with truth. Our tools may accelerate, anticipate, even pre-empt, but we remain bounded by the rhythms of flesh and thought. The future interface, if it is to serve rather than govern, must begin not with code but with care—with an understanding that every click, every gesture, every glance is a conversation between biology and design. The question is not how seamless interaction can become, but how sustainable it can remain. The body, ancient and stubborn, will always have the final say.

Attention, Memory, and the Limits of Human Bandwidth

In October 2018, at London's Guy's and St Thomas' Hospital, a surgical team trialled a voice-controlled interface designed to let clinicians manipulate patient scans mid-operation without breaking sterility. The system recognised more than a hundred spoken commands, parsed accents, and displayed imagery on demand. Yet, within two hours, the team quietly reverted to manual controls. The reason was not a software fault but cognitive overload. The surgeons, already balancing spatial reasoning, risk assessment, and hand–eye coordination, found that issuing spoken commands fractured their focus. "It listens faster than I can think," one consultant remarked afterwards. The interface had reduced physical friction but increased mental friction—the invisible kind that drains comprehension long before the body tires. Five words explain why: *the brain is not a processor.*

For all its metaphors of circuits and bandwidth, cognition operates on principles utterly unlike computation. A human's working memory can juggle, on average, four to seven discrete items at once (Cowan, 2010). Attention is serial, not parallel; we can shift focus rapidly but not truly divide it. By contrast, even the smallest modern microprocessor can perform billions of operations per second without fatigue. The mismatch between human and machine speed defines the boundary of usability. When interfaces assume infinite cognitive throughput, they do not extend human capability—they erode it. A whisper that arrives before comprehension becomes noise.

Every act of interaction consumes attention, which Daniel Kahneman (1973) described as a limited mental resource, one that must be allocated deliberately or is lost to distraction. This scarcity explains why micro-frictions—delays of a few hundred milliseconds, a misplaced icon, a confusing animation—can determine success or failure. The brain's attentional system behaves like a queue, not a pipeline. When too many inputs arrive, they block each other. The 2021 study by Microsoft Research on multitasking during remote meetings quantified this with uncomfortable clarity: switching between applications more than once every 45 seconds doubled error rates and increased reported fatigue by 30 percent. Speed is not the enemy of usability, but unmanaged speed is.

Prediction technologies promise to offset these limits by anticipating intent—autocomplete, proactive reminders, adaptive menus. When they work, they lighten the cognitive load: finishing a sentence, surfacing a file, filling a form. But prediction carries risk because it manipulates the very substrate of agency—attention itself. In 2019, an internal audit at a major navigation app revealed that "helpful" rerouting suggestions caused drivers to glance at their screens 20 percent more often, as they sought reassurance that the system's unexpected choices were correct. The interface predicted the user's desire for efficiency but ignored their deeper need for comprehension. In psychological terms, it replaced *sense-making* with *trust-seeking*.

Understanding when prediction helps or harms begins with a diagnostic question: does the system reduce the *number of things the user must keep in mind*, or does it merely compress time? Predictive text aids cognition because it lowers recall demands; automatic form submission may hinder it by obscuring state. The first frees working memory, the second taxes it. Cognitive psychology calls this *externalising memory*: moving information from the mind into the environment in a visible, retrievable way. The most humane anticipatory systems externalise rather than internalise—they show what they've done, why, and how to reverse it.

The motif running through every example is attention as currency. Once spent, it cannot be reclaimed at will. In 2007, when the Boeing 787 cockpit introduced a head-up display projecting navigation data into pilots' line of sight, safety researchers at NASA's Ames Research Center discovered a paradoxical effect: situational awareness improved, yet reaction time to unexpected alarms worsened. Pilots trusted the projection so deeply that peripheral monitoring suffered. The lesson still holds for digital interfaces: a single attentional focus can both empower and blind. Prediction that narrows rather than broadens awareness trades comprehension for comfort.

At the opposite end of the spectrum, deliberately designed friction can protect comprehension. Consider the two-step confirmation screens in nuclear command systems or in high-stakes financial transactions. They are not inefficiencies but acts of respect for cognitive limits. They preserve the pause in which awareness catches up with intention. Everyday design often erases such pauses under the banner of convenience. Yet the human brain's default mode network—responsible for self-monitoring and reflection—activates during precisely these micro-pauses. Strip them away, and interaction becomes reflex rather than choice.

Memory imposes its own constraints. Working memory is not simply small; it is leaky. Without rehearsal or visual anchors, information decays within seconds. That is why, when users must recall multi-step sequences, failure rates spike even if each step is trivial. The 2016 usability study at Stanford's Interaction Lab demonstrated this elegantly: when interface tasks required participants to remember more than three system states simultaneously, error rates rose exponentially, not linearly. The fourth remembered element was the tipping point. Designing for cognition, therefore, means designing for forgetfulness. The interface must not merely display state; it must *remind* without overwhelming.

Fatigue compounds every cognitive weakness. Attention falters as glucose drops, as light changes, as monotony sets in. In aviation, fatigue is quantified in duty hours; in software, it is invisible yet pervasive. The subtle slowing of response, the growing need to recheck a form—these are symptoms of depleted mental energy. Anticipatory systems can either mitigate or magnify this fatigue. A voice assistant that cues a driver before a turn reduces workload; one that interrupts mid-sentence increases it. Timing matters more than capability. A 2020 MIT study on cognitive pacing found that assistance arriving *300 milliseconds after* a decision cue was perceived as supportive; the same aid arriving *300 milliseconds before* was experienced as intrusive. Prediction without timing is tyranny.

A counterpoint comes from gaming, a field often caricatured as indulgent but, in reality, a vast experiment in human–computer pacing. Game designers speak of "flow"—the balance between challenge and skill that sustains attention without exhaustion. Titles such as *Portal*

(Valve, 2007) and *The Witness* (Thekla, 2016) are masterclasses in progressive disclosure: each new mechanic introduced at the moment comprehension peaks, not before or after. These designs exploit the natural rhythm of working memory refresh. The same principle could transform productivity software and medical dashboards alike: present information at the cadence of comprehension, not computation.

Yet not all friction is virtue. Poorly timed confirmation dialogues, redundant tooltips, or inconsistent visual hierarchies impose cognitive taxes without yield. The challenge lies in discernment: which frictions preserve awareness, which squander it? Here the neuroscience of *predictive coding* offers a guide. The brain constantly generates models of what it expects to perceive; when reality deviates, attention spikes to update the model. Good design harnesses this by making deviations meaningful—a notification colour change signalling genuine urgency, a haptic pulse before an irreversible action. Bad design triggers false positives, exhausting the prediction system until users disengage altogether.

The economic metaphor of attention can obscure a more visceral truth: cognition is biological. Each act of focus consumes oxygen and glucose; each recovery from surprise spikes cortisol. The brain's metabolic limits are as real as its informational ones. Repetition without variation depletes neurotransmitters that sustain vigilance, producing the cognitive equivalent of muscle fatigue. That is why long-haul drivers and surgeons alike rely on structured breaks, not just discipline. When digital work stretches across twelve hours of micro-interactions—emails, chats, pop-ups—the same physiological debt accumulates invisibly. No algorithm can offset the cost of ignoring biology.

Designers who grasp this treat anticipation not as acceleration but as orchestration. They align system rhythm with human rhythm. Apple's "attention-aware" features on the iPhone (2019 onwards) dim the screen when the user looks away; Microsoft's adaptive refresh in Windows 11 slows background processes when the mouse is idle. These small adjustments respect cognitive tempo, conserving both battery and brain. The ideal interface does not compete for attention—it choreographs it.

One might argue that future generations, acclimatised to constant stimuli, will simply adapt. The data suggest otherwise. A 2022 longitudinal study from the University of Oxford tracking adolescents' digital habits found no evidence that heavy multitasking increased attentional capacity; instead, it correlated with reduced sustained-focus scores on standardised tasks. Evolution operates on timescales longer than product cycles. The biological constants of memory and attention remain, regardless of culture or training. Design that assumes adaptation risks normalising impairment.

The counter-example worth noting comes from professional e-sports, where athletes maintain extraordinary cognitive throughput under pressure. In 2021, South Korean player

Lee "Faker" Sang-hyeok sustained an average of 400 actions per minute during *League of Legends* tournaments, a figure impossible for untrained users. Yet even these prodigies rely on environmental scaffolds—custom key mappings, minimal motion, standardised colour cues. They do not transcend human bandwidth; they domesticate it. Their mastery is a triumph of ergonomics and ritual, not raw capacity.

Ultimately, attention and memory are moral frontiers as much as technical ones. To design within their limits is to respect human dignity; to exploit them is to colonise the mind. Interfaces that over-assume, over-notify, or over-predict blur the line between assistance and control. The fatigue they induce is not merely mental but existential—a quiet erosion of agency. When users can no longer tell whether they acted or were acted upon, autonomy becomes an illusion.

Every designer, researcher, and policymaker confronting anticipatory systems must therefore ask one question: does this interaction preserve the user's ability to notice their own intention? If the answer is no, then speed has outstripped sense. Between attention and automation lies a fragile equilibrium—the pause where choice lives. Protect that pause, and prediction serves agency. Eliminate it, and even the most advanced interface becomes another mechanism of fatigue.

That is where the next generation of design will be tested: not in processing power, but in its capacity to let humans breathe between thoughts.

Affordances We Feel: Posture, Reach, and Micro-Movements

On 9 January 2007 at the Moscone Center in San Francisco, Apple revealed the iPhone. A new ritual began: the one-hand reach. The original 3.5-inch screen let a resting thumb travel almost everywhere without strain; icons sat within a comfortable arc, and the hand rarely shifted its grip. As screens grew, that arc did not. By September 2014 in Cupertino, when the iPhone 6 arrived, Apple added "Reachability" to slide the interface down on demand. Hardware had outrun anatomy, and software retreated to meet the thumb. The hand tells the truth. It still does, in every interface we make.

Show the thumb drifting to the bottom edge of a phone on a crowded train. Name the constraint: functional reach. Explain it with Steven Hoober's field work observing 1,333 mobile interactions across multiple US cities, which found that most use was one-handed, with 49 percent strictly one-handed, 36 percent "cradled," and 15 percent two-handed (Hoober, 2013). Implication: design primary actions where the resting thumb already lives, not where a designer wishes it to travel. The cost of ignoring this is visible: a micro-hesitation, a grip shift, a missed tap as the carriage jolts. A single extra reach is not a nuisance; repeated across a day, it becomes attrition.

Posture sets the stage for every movement. We see it in the silent adjustments people make when touch targets sit too high. Shoulders rise. Wrists extend unnaturally. Tiny muscles burn. Name the pattern: awkward neutral. Explain with Fitts's law (Fitts, 1954), which shows that movement time increases with distance and decreases with target size. Implication: moving a high-frequency control 10 millimetres closer to the resting thumb can speed selection more than any new animation. The metric is not delight but reduced time on target and fewer corrective taps. Watch the wrist. It tells you when the interface has wandered from the body's economy.

Eye movements obey a similar economy. Eyetracking studies from Nielsen Norman Group showed that readers often scan dense content in an "F-pattern," fixating early along the top line, then down the left, then across again (Nielsen, 2006). Rayner's synthesis on reading fixations places most gaze dwells at roughly 200–250 milliseconds (Rayner, 1998). Implication: place labels and confirmation cues where the eyes already land; avoid forcing saccades from extreme top to bottom for related information. Each extra saccade is a tax. You can measure it in dwell time and in the number of corrective glances before action. A humane interface respects the path the eyes prefer, just as it respects the path the thumb prefers.

The body's tremor sets a hard boundary on precision. Show a clinician tapping a 28-pixel control in a ward after a twelve-hour shift; the tap misses, then misses again. Name the constraint: tremor tolerance. Explain with ability-centred evidence: Wobbrock, Gajos, and colleagues argued for "Ability-Based Design," which starts with measured user performance and adapts systems accordingly (Wobbrock et al., 2011). Implication: build minimum touch targets that accommodate slight involuntary oscillations—not as charity, but as the baseline for everyone under fatigue. Google's Material Design has long recommended 48dp touch targets (Material Design, updated 2021). That size is not arbitrary; it is a bet on human steadiness under stress.

The motif of the resting thumb returns, now as a diagnostic. When primary actions sit within the natural sweep from the metacarpophalangeal joint to mid-screen, users stay in a stable posture. When controls drift north, the hand climbs the device, the elbow flares, and the neck tilts. Show the behaviour: grip change rate per minute during a typical session. Name the measure: grip churn. Explain: each churn increases the chance of drops and slips while introducing new angular errors at the fingertip. Implication: reduce churn and you reduce error. Ergonomics is risk management in miniature.

Gesture design often forgets that the shoulder is the most fragile link. Large theatre-style swipes and air-pinches may demo well in a keynote but punish the rotator cuff over hours. Name the temptation: spectacle. Explain with Microsoft's Kinect (launched November 2010), which popularised mid-air gestures at living-room scale. It worked in generous spaces, at leisure pace, and with full-body motion. Implication: context rules. The same amplitude that delights at three metres becomes untenable at a desk or in a surgical theatre. This is the counter-example: big can be right—in the room, at the distance, for the purpose. Reconciling it means privileging micro-gestures where precision and duration dominate, and reserving grand motions for brief, low-frequency tasks where the whole body can move safely.

Now look more closely at the hand. Show: a user altering a slider. Name: the *just-noticeable difference* (JND) for control feedback. Explain: if the visual or haptic response to a micro-movement falls below perceptual thresholds, users over-steer. Implication: amplify feedback earlier with a small click or colour shift at meaningful increments. The behaviour to watch is overshoot-and-correct cycles. Fewer cycles mean better fit to the hand's resolution. You can count them.

The face speaks too. Gaze-based selection in augmented reality falters when designers assume a pin-point eye. Show: the repeated overshoot on a head-mounted display as the cursor dances. Name: the *Midas touch* problem in gaze interaction—everything looked at becomes a target. Explain: even a still head exhibits micro-movement; vestibulo-ocular reflexes stabilise the world at a cost to selection granularity. Implication: use dwell-to-confirm or small pinch confirmations, and align targets with common fixation points. Microsoft's HoloLens 2, announced at MWC

Barcelona in February 2019, shifted from single "air-tap" inputs to more natural pinches and direct hand interactions, a tacit admission that theatricality yields to physiology in daily use. The body imposes quiet laws.

Touch target guidance encodes those laws. Apple's Human Interface Guidelines have for years recommended minimum tappable areas of roughly 44×44 points; Google's Material Design recommends 48dp (Apple HIG; Material Design, 2021). Show: reduced miss-tap rate when controls meet or exceed those sizes, especially at screen edges where visual distortion and case lips intrude. Name: edge penalty. Explain: fingers obscure targets near bezels, and the device case creates shallow access angles. Implication: reserve edges for forgiving gestures (swipes) and nest precise actions within the central, high-accuracy zone. Designers who violate this see it immediately in analytics as increased re-tap counts and longer time-to-completion.

Context magnifies all of this. Consider commuting. Show a passenger typing with one thumb while standing on the Central line in London, November rush hour. Name: dynamic instability. Explain: body sway introduces oscillations at roughly 0.5–1Hz; the hand compensates by tightening grip and reducing reach. Implication: place destructive actions further from the resting thumb during mobile contexts and provide easy reversals. The visible behaviour is the sudden drop in typing speed as the train accelerates; the metric is error insertions per minute. Ergonomics is situational, not absolute.

Handedness remains a stubborn bias. Many interfaces still assume right-handed use. Show: a left-handed user stretching to the far-right compose button in a mail app. Name: lateral bias. Explain: while system-wide mirroring is costly, local affordances can adapt—floating action buttons that migrate to the dominant thumb, toolbars that anchor to either side. Implication: consider a preference or an initial calibration gesture that sets the resting zone. The behaviour is the user's first-minute adaptation; the metric is how often they toggle handedness once set. If never, you've aligned with habit.

Micro-movements accrue debt. Show: a smartwatch that requires wrist pronation past 60 degrees to read an incoming alert. Name: cumulative strain. Explain: pronation beyond neutral increases extensor load and compresses the ulnar side of the wrist; repeated dozens of times a day, it becomes discomfort. Implication: treat posture as a design material. If a watch face lights when the user's gaze, not their wrist, arrives, the joint rests. You can measure the difference: reduced average angle of rotation and lower self-reported discomfort at day's end.

The counter-pressure to all this is aesthetics. Minimalism tempts designers to shrink controls and stretch whitespace. Show: a photo-heavy news app with airy margins but 32-pixel links. Name: touch starvation. Explain: the interface looks elegant but refuses the finger. Implication: beauty without reach is theatre. A harmonious design respects both eye and hand. The behaviour to watch is rage-taps—rapid repeated touches on a small target. Tools can detect them; logs can confirm them.

Rehearsal matters. Show: a call centre interface where agents must reach for a confirm button on the top-right corner hundreds of times per shift in Leeds, March 2022. Name: repetitive strain risk. Explain: even a small, suboptimal reach becomes hazardous at scale. Implication: move high-frequency controls to the resting zone and rely on muscle memory, not heroics. The decision is operational as much as aesthetic; it influences absence rates and training time.

Mid-air gestures invite a separate discipline: "comfort at distance." Show: a radiologist using a ceiling-mounted sensor to flip scans without touching a keyboard in Boston, 2018. Name: amplitude fatigue. Explain: shoulders tire fast; the window of comfort sits within 30–45 degrees of the torso and elbow close to neutral. Implication: map commands to motions within that envelope and provide tactile cues—a finger pinch or a light haptic glove—so the body receives confirmation without looking. The metric is session length before reported discomfort; the behaviour is creeping compensation (leaning, shrugging) as fatigue builds.

Even with strong evidence, edge cases remind us to be careful. An accessible kiosk in a public library in Manchester, retrofitted in 2020, enlarged all buttons to 80 pixels. Miss-taps fell, but throughput suffered as the visible area shrank and scrolling increased. Name: enlargement trade-off. Explain: bigger targets reduce precision errors but increase navigation distance. Implication: enlarge selectively—high-risk, high-frequency controls grow; low-risk options hide behind a clear progressive disclosure. Reconcile it by measuring not only miss-taps but total time-on-task and subjective fatigue. The right size is contextual, not maximal.

The resting thumb motif closes the loop with gaze. Where the thumb rests, the eyes also tend to settle, because people seek to minimise cross-modal effort. Show: heatmaps pooling at bottom-centre controls when primary actions live there. Name: oculomotor coupling. Explain: reducing the distance between action and confirmation reduces saccade count and shortens fixations, preserving working memory for content. Implication: align sightline and reachline when it matters—confirmation banners near controls, errors near fields, previews close to triggers. The behaviour is fewer wandering glances; the metric is reduced total fixation time before commitment.

What, then, is comfort in actionable terms? It is a pattern of low-amplitude, high-confidence movements; a posture that stays near neutral; feedback that arrives before over-correction; and recovery that is always possible with a small motion, not a grand reset. We feel comfort before we can name it. So measure it: re-tap rates, grip churn, miss-tap distribution by screen quadrant, saccades per decision, session-end discomfort scores. When those metrics improve, trust follows, because the body recognises respect.

Designers often ask where to start. Start with the hand at rest. Map the arc it prefers. Place the most common actions there. Then confirm the choice with eyes—do fixations gather where decisions live? Trim any motion that breaks posture. Let micro-gestures do the work. Theatrical gestures remain welcome at the margins—ceremonial, occasional, even joyful—but they must not carry the weight of daily labour. The stage belongs to small movements repeated well.

That brings us back to San Francisco, to the moment when thumb and glass first met at scale. The devices have changed. The thumb has not. Are we willing to commit our primary actions to the body's quiet geometry—even when aesthetics or novelty pull us elsewhere? The next interface will answer with its posture.

When Convenience Undermines Comprehension

In June 1985 at the East Texas Cancer Center in Tyler, a patient received a massive radiation overdose from the Therac-25 linear accelerator. More overdoses followed in Ontario and elsewhere through 1987. Investigations traced one cause to "mode" logic buried behind keystrokes: a software-driven machine that silently switched states while presenting little or no feedback to the operator. Safety interlocks had been removed, assuming software would catch errors. It did not. The interface was quick. It was also opaque. People died. Five words matter here: invisible state invites lethal inference.

Show a rushed technician tabbing through fields that look familiar yet conceal a live switch. Name the failure: hidden state. Explain it with Donald Norman's analysis of mode errors—when systems behave differently under the same inputs without clear signals (Norman, 1988). Implication: speed without legibility is not efficiency; it is risk displaced onto the user's attention. The Therac-25 is a stark case, but the principle applies in the mundane as well as the catastrophic. When the system does more on our behalf, it must show more of itself.

Assistants embody the dilemma. In May 2018, Google announced Smart Compose for Gmail in Mountain View, inserting grey completions as users typed. It was a triumph of anticipation—most suggestions were harmless and correct. Yet users discovered a subtle trade: sentences took shape they would never have chosen unaided. Show the behaviour: a writer pausing, accepting "Sounds good" with a Tab, and moving on. Name the effect: semantic drift. Explain: the assistant compresses decision time, but the acceptance gesture obscures authorship; reviewing becomes a trust exercise, not a comprehension exercise. Implication: the convenience of fast phrasing can thin the writer's grasp of nuance unless the system makes its contribution legible and revisable. A small cue—a colour tint or a phrase-level provenance tag—keeps ownership visible without slowing the expert.

Clinical software offers the most unforgiving mirror. Electronic health records in the NHS and beyond introduced order sets to accelerate routine care. Show: a junior doctor in Leeds, October 2019, selecting a pre-populated "sepsis bundle" that includes a broad-spectrum antibiotic and a default dose. Name the hazard: autopilot dosing. Explain: defaults speed the novice and reassure the tired, but they also hide state—why this drug, at this dose, for this patient? Implication: legibility markers—hover previews pointing to guidelines, last-modified dates, and patient-specific contraindication flags—convert speed into informed speed. The visible behaviours to measure are overridden defaults, time-to-order, and post-round edits; when legibility rises, *appropriate* overrides increase while error corrections fall.

Show, name, explain, imply: the engine of design clarity. Consider progressive disclosure, often criticised as patronising. Used well, it prevents cognitive ambush. In March 2019, Microsoft's HoloLens 2 shipped with more layered interaction than its predecessor; key actions telegraphed intent before commitment with visual "affordance handles" and hand-anchored guides. Name the practice: staged reveal. Explain: by exposing the next step at the moment of readiness—never all at once—the system lets the mind keep up with the hand. Implication: experts move faster because they do not waste cycles reconstituting hidden state. The metric is not clicks but corrections. Fewer reversals mean comprehension kept pace with speed.

Hidden state often masquerades as kindness. Show: a ride-hailing app auto-selecting the "Home" address because it is

8:00 a.m. on a Monday. Name: silent inference. Explain: the convenience is genuine; the autonomy cost is real. Users glance harder at the map, seeking confirmation that the choice aligns with intention. Implication: a small preview banner—"Heading to Home, change?"—preserves pace and certainty. The motif here is the small light in the corner: a unobtrusive cue that the system is acting, that you may interrupt. Without that light, trust erodes into vigilance.

Trust thrives on a visible causal chain. Show: an automation that renames files based on a pattern in a newsroom archive in London, July 2020. Name: shadow actions. Explain: if the system performs bulk changes in the background, the editor must stop to audit. Implication: a dry-run preview with a sample of the first ten changes converts dread into quick assent. Behaviourally, look for the shift from manual spot-checking to confident acceptance; the metric is the number of aborted runs and post-hoc fixes. When previews are present, the aborted runs drop, and post-hoc fixes cluster closer to zero.

Yet speed is not the villain; opacity is. A credible counter-example sits in aviation checklists. In October 1935 at Wright Field, the Boeing Model 299 (later the B-17) crashed during a test flight. The cause—pilot error due to task complexity—produced a remedy: checklists that made state explicit and sequential. Later, glass cockpits accelerated access to information without hiding it. Name the principle: compressed access, expanded cues. Explain: pilots work fast because state is codified across instruments, annunciators, and callouts. Implication: expert speed can coexist with deep comprehension when visibility scales with automation. Reconciling this with the assistant problem means emulating aviation's redundancy: multiple converging signals that a state change has occurred.

Mode confusion flows through domestic interfaces too. Show: a smart assistant listening for a wake word in a kitchen in Oxford, December 2021. Two people speak. The device sets a timer for the wrong voice. Name: diarisation failure. Explain: in shared spaces, identity is itself a state that must be surfaced. Implication: a gentle voice tag—"Timer for Alex"—and a quick undo affordance respect agency at conversational speed. The behaviour is fewer "What did you just do?" moments; the metric is the undo rate within ten seconds of an action. Track it.

Progressive disclosure is sometimes maligned as slowing experts. It need not. The counter-argument: power users prefer compact, dense views. Fair. Reconcile it by offering dual modes, but with clear rails. Show: Adobe Lightroom Classic in 2015 separated "Library" and "Develop" modules, each dense yet staged. Name: *layered density*. Explain: the expert sees everything relevant to a phase; nothing vital hides across modes. Implication: progressive disclosure aligns with workflow rather than seniority. Experts move faster because the system predicts *phase,* not *competence,* and signals boundaries accordingly.

Comprehension comes from seeing state and stakes together. Show: a medical device with a "Start" button that looks identical whether it primes tubing or infuses medication. Name: ambiguous affordance. Explain: identical visuals across different stakes violate legibility; the user must hold the difference in memory. Implication: change the button's language and colour between contexts; show a preview of what will happen and to whom. The metric is not aesthetic approval but a fall in wrong-mode activations. As the small light in the corner brightens—clear labels, previews, reversible timers—errors retreat.

Hidden state saps energy. We measure that energy as fatigue. In a 2020 MIT study of assistance timing, help that arrived *after* a user-initiated cue reduced perceived cognitive load; aid that arrived *before* spiked it. Speed itself is not soothing; alignment is. Show: a spreadsheet that auto-fills totals *on edit*, not *on hover*. Name: anchored automation. Explain: the system waits to act until the user's behaviour establishes a clear boundary. Implication: the expert experiences fluency, not interruption; the novice gains comprehension because cause and effect sit side by side. The metric is subjective workload (NASA-TLX) plus observed pauses before commit. Shorter, less frequent pauses signal better alignment.

Consider consent in micro. Show: a photo app that "helps" by auto-curating albums titled "Best of July", built in Dublin, July 2022. Name: silent curation. Explain: the album appears without an explanation of criteria. Users smile, then distrust. Implication: a short card—"Selected 32 photos based on sharpness and faces; tap to adjust"—turns suspicion into teachable speed. Behaviourally, look for edit frequency; a moderate increase indicates comprehension, while a collapse suggests either perfection or opacity. We do not want the latter.

One might argue that people adapt to shortcuts and grow to love them. Sometimes they do. Show: Emacs power-users in Cambridge in the 1990s chaining key chords at blistering pace. Name: muscle memory dominance. Explain: mastery relocates comprehension into the body; state lives in the rhythm of fingers. Implication: speed is safe when the mapping between input and state is stable, inspectable, and reversible. The visible signal is the willingness to explore; experts try commands because undo is certain and previews are trustworthy. Without those guarantees, shortcuts become traps.

We should name the worst offender: silent destructive actions. Show: an e-commerce back office where a "Publish" button instantly overrides a live product without staging or preview, Amsterdam, March 2021. Name: zero-stage deployment. Explain: the promise of continuous delivery tempted the team into removing review layers. Implication: introduce shadow actions that render changes privately, with a banner—"This is a preview. Go live?"—and a two-minute rollback window post-publish. Measure live reversions and customer-facing errors; if both fall while time-to-release remains steady, comprehension has kept pace with speed. The small light in the corner becomes a soft guardrail.

The strongest designs embed their own audit trail. Show: a recommendation feed that explains itself, as Spotify's "Because you listened" labels did from 2016. Name: situated provenance. Explain: origins matter at the point of influence, not in a privacy policy. Implication: even a terse "Recommended due to X" lets users calibrate trust and adjust inputs. The behaviour to watch is profile edits following explanations; a rise indicates users are steering rather than surrendering. Legibility begets stewardship.

Healthcare again offers a hard lesson. In 2011, the U.S. Food and Drug Administration issued guidance on infusion pump safety after thousands of adverse events, many involving confusing interfaces and alarm fatigue. Name: alarm blindness. Explain: when everything is urgent, nothing is. The convenience of suppressing context to emit a single tone accelerates escalation but destroys comprehension about *why*. Implication: alarms must preview the root cause and the next safe action—"Occlusion detected at distal line. Check clamp." The metric is time-to-correct, not time-to-alarm. Preview narrows action, and experts move *faster* with fewer resets.

The counter-example worth holding close is command-line tooling. It is unforgiving but explicit. Every parameter is visible. State is text. Experts move at speed because nothing is hidden and everything is logged. The limitation is steep entry cost; novices stall without affordances. Reconcile it by borrowing its strengths—structured previews and dry runs—into graphical systems. Git's "–dry-run" flag inspired countless safe modes elsewhere. Visual tools should copy the attitude: *show me exactly what will change before it changes.*

A word about metrics. If comprehension is the goal, measure it. Watch for hesitations before commit, post-action corrections, and requests for help. Instrument previews to see whether people read them, not just whether they exist. Track rollback rates as a percentage of launches. Each is a visible behaviour tethered to a supposedly abstract quality. Where the small light in the corner appears—previews, explanations, reversible windows—those measures improve.

We return to speed. Fast can feel elegant; it can also feel reckless. The craft lies in making speed legible. Provide a preview before commitment. Reveal complexity in phases. Announce state changes plainly. Reserve shortcuts for contexts where stability and reversibility are guaranteed. That is not bureaucratic drag; it is the grammar of agency under automation. The unresolved tension remains: how much cueing is enough before the expert feels patronised, and how much is too little before the novice is lost? Set your next build against one question that bites: where, precisely, will you put the small light in the corner so that convenience never swallows comprehension?

Designing for Fatigue, Not Only Delight

How can an interface that saves 40 seconds per task still leave operators slower by mid-shift? In March 2019 at a call centre in Birmingham, a new dashboard promised speed by collapsing actions into a single view. The morning's numbers impressed. By 15:00, average handling time had risen, error corrections had tripled, and agents stretched their wrists between calls. The system was faster. The people were not. Fatigue hides in plain sight. The discrepancy forced management to invite an ergonomist from the Health and Safety Executive to observe. The finding was simple: small savings early produced larger costs later. The last mile of the day had been ignored.

Show a bright interface that dances at 09:00 and drags at 16:00. Name the problem: endurance. Explain it with a distinction from usability standards like ISO 9241-11:2018—performance must be sustained across specified contexts of use, not merely demonstrated once. Implication: a product that dazzles in a five-minute demo but decays over hours is not fit for purpose. We should measure decay. Plot time-on-task against session length; capture where curves bend. The bend tells the truth.

The mind tires before the wrist complains. In the late 1980s, Sandra Hart and Lowell Staveland created the NASA Task Load Index (NASA-TLX, 1988), a multi-dimensional workload measure still used in aviation and healthcare. Show: rising TLX mental and physical demand scores by the third hour of repetitive console work. Name: cognitive load accumulation. Explain: as working memory depletes and vigilance wanes, people rely on compensatory strategies—double-checking entries, rereading prompts—that look like diligence but mask exhaustion. Implication: an interface that reduces TLX scores after practice is truly scaling; one that raises scores as familiarity grows is quietly taxing its users.

Fatigue is not an abstraction; it is behaviour. The Psychomotor Vigilance Task (Dinges & Powell, 1985) measures momentary lapses of attention through slowed reaction times and "microsleeps." Show an operator hesitating for 600 milliseconds longer than baseline before confirming a critical action. Name: vigilance drop. Explain: even small increases compound under repetition, producing clustering of errors. Implication: instrument software to detect equivalent lapses—longer pre-commit pauses, rising re-tap rates, mouse shake jitters—and treat them as early warning signals. The last mile of the day starts earlier than we think.

Against this backdrop, delight proves a poor compass. Delight finds early, memorable moments; endurance asks what those moments cost over time. Show: a playful animation that celebrates task completion. Name: arousal bump. Explain: short, high-valence cues can refresh attention transiently, yet frequent spikes exhaust it, much like false alarms. Implication: reserve celebration for infrequent, meaningful thresholds. For high-frequency actions, prefer calm confirmations that conserve mental energy. The measure is not "smiles captured"; it is late-shift error rate.

A first named example grounds the stakes. In 2016 in Rochester, Minnesota, a Mayo Clinic study led by Tait Shanafelt linked electronic health record usability to physician burnout; higher perceived EHR frustration correlated with greater odds of professional exhaustion (Mayo Clinic Proceedings, 2016). Show: clinicians working through dense "in-basket" messages after clinic hours. Name: the "pajama time" problem. Explain: interfaces that push unresolved cognitive load past the clinic day shift fatigue into private time, amplifying stress. Implication: design should track after-hours usage and reduce spillover, not merely speed in the moment. The indicator is the ratio of work done outside scheduled hours to total work; watch it fall.

A second example shows how professional vigilance can be protected. The UK Civil Aviation Authority's guidance on fatigue risk management (CAP 737, 2014) codified patterns in scheduling and human–machine design across NATS operations in Swanwick, Hampshire. Show: controller consoles tuned for posture, information salience, and periodic breaks; procedures that pair high-demand periods with structured pauses. Name: managed endurance. Explain: controlling traffic requires sustained attention across hours; interfaces and rosters must act together. Implication: software alone cannot fix fatigue, but it can align with wider systems that manage it. Use the same principle in digital work: coordinate UI rhythms with team rhythms.

The credible counter-example is the world of deliberately high arousal. Emergency departments run on brisk cues, bright colours, and rapid escalation. Show: a resuscitation bay in St Thomas' Hospital, London, January 2020, where a nurse charts via an EHR with aggressive alarms. Name: arousal-dependent performance. Explain: in acute care, speed saves lives; the interface must accelerate recognition and actuation. Yet alarm fatigue is a documented hazard: when everything screams, nothing is heard (FDA Infusion Pump Guidance, 2011). Implication: even here, endurance matters. Systems must preview root causes, throttle non-actionable alerts, and support quick silencing with audit trails. Reconciling the counter-example means accepting that intensity can be necessary, but only when bounded by mechanisms that defer fatigue rather than amplify it.

How, then, do we capture the last mile of the day in design? Start with hallway tests that go long. Show: a series of short, opportunistic studies run across a week on a university corridor in Oxford, February 2022—five-minute sessions stitched into a cumulative picture. Name: rolling hallway protocol. Explain: instead of one lab slot, distribute testing: ask participants to perform the same set of tasks at morning, midday, and late afternoon. Implication: the method approximates a working day; variance between sessions becomes a proxy for fatigue sensitivity. Record NASA-TLX at each point, track time-to-commit, and cluster errors.

Error clustering exposes not only *how many* mistakes occur, but *when* and *why*. Show: a graph where errors spike after

UI state changes that hide context under a modal. Name: fatigue-triggered blind spots. Explain: people under load miss state changes, especially when confirmation and action split across regions. Implication: move confirmations closer to triggers; reduce long saccades; provide shadow previews that keep state visible. The metric that matters is not total error count but the concentration of errors per session hour. Flatten the late-session spike.

The body carries its own ledger. Electromyography can be overkill, but observation and simple tools suffice. Show: a smartwatch that logs wrist pronation angles during repeated glances; a webcam-based estimate of PERCLOS—the proportion of time eyelids are at least 80 per cent closed—used as a fatigue proxy in driver monitoring (Wierwille, 1994; Dinges et al., 1998). Name: low-friction physiology. Explain: bring a few physiological indicators into the lab when appropriate—not to diagnose, but to triangulate. Implication: if PERCLOS rises and pronation angles creep up as sessions progress, reduce micro-movements and raise information density where the eye already falls. Tie changes to concrete reductions in pronation degrees and fixations per decision.

The motif returns: the last mile. The Marathon world record falls by seconds; the wall arrives at 35 kilometres. Interfaces face a similar wall, where small inefficiencies aggregate into heavy legs. Show: users adding a tiny pause before deleting items late in the shift. Name: hesitation debt. Explain: as confidence drops, people slow down to avoid mistakes, even when error rates do not justify the caution. Implication: amplify legibility precisely at the wall—decisive previews, reversible windows, and clear provenance. The result is paradoxical: clearer interfaces feel calmer and go faster at the end of the day.

Endurance design also requires honest baselines. Show: a team comparing time-to-complete for a new tool against its predecessor only in the first hour. Name: early bias. Explain: most interfaces look efficient when new, because novelty energises attention. Implication: set acceptance criteria on *sustained* performance—e.g., "no more than 5 per cent degradation in hour three compared with hour one"—and tie go/no-go decisions to that metric. Commit to the metric in advance. Otherwise, every launch over-promises on the morning and under-delivers by the afternoon.

Accessibility is not charity here; it is the test. The Web Content Accessibility Guidelines 2.1 (W3C, 2018) include criteria for pointer target size and motion sensitivity. Show: a dashboard revised to meet target-size guidance, where miss-tap rates fall by 22 per cent for all users, not just those with tremor. Name: universal stamina. Explain: users with chronic pain, low vision, or neurological variance encounter the wall earlier; if they endure longer, everyone endures longer. Implication: fatigue metrics are equity metrics. Measure drop-off by demographic cohort; examine hour-two attrition; publish outcomes alongside standard performance stats. This is how teams prove that efficiency gains are not built on bodies that tire faster.

Equity extends to scheduling and context. Night-shift users and gig workers meet interfaces under less forgiving conditions: glare, noise, and broken sleep. Show: a logistics app tested at 23:00 in a warehouse in Leicester, January 2021, under strip-lighting and cold air. Name: context realism. Explain: a "delightful" daylight palette may create veiling luminance at night; animations that feel charming at a desk feel dizzy in motion. Implication: conduct night sessions; measure NASA-TLX and error clustering specifically for off-hours. Stop treating daylight as default.

We should also rehabilitate the idea of micro-rests. Show: a spreadsheet that introduces a half-second, content-aware lull after a destructive action—long enough to cancel, short enough to feel instant. Name: recovery seams. Explain: small seams allow the autonomic nervous system to settle; cortisol spikes fade; control returns. Implication: place seams where error rates peak, measured by session hour. The action feels smoother because the mind catches up. It is not delay; it is recuperation engineered into flow.

Not every team can run full lab studies. They can, however, count. Show: a series of product analytics dashboards that add three measures—late-session re-taps, average confirmation hesitation, and post-action reversals. Name: the endurance trio. Explain: each correlates with fatigue without requiring invasive methods. Implication: instrument them by default; track them as first-class health metrics. If the trio worsens after a visual refresh, you shipped cosmetic fatigue.

The temptation is to declare victory when "engagement" rises. Beware. Show: a social product that increases scroll depth by adding infinite scroll in London, 2017. Name: activity inflation. Explain: longer sessions may indicate compulsion, not comfort. Implication: cross-check with NASA-TLX, self-reported eye strain, and next-day return rates. If users linger yet churn, you banked attention now and paid with tomorrow's trust. Delight lied to you.

When we talk about fatigue, we talk about time, posture, and the fairness of defaults. We talk about whether an interface assumes a fresh mind and steady hand, or whether it carries the tired with respect. The last mile of the day should be where design shines, not where it fails. The unresolved question is practical and ethical at once: will you ship for the demo or the day? Before you answer, look at hour three's curves and ask—are your users still steady when the music stops?

Chapter 2
Language that Listens (and When It Should Not)

In April 2018, a couple in Portland, Oregon, received a phone call from a colleague hundreds of miles away. He told them, bewildered, that he'd just been emailed a recording of their private conversation. The culprit was not espionage or a hacked server but a domestic misunderstanding between humans and machines: Amazon's Echo had overheard a wake word, misread fragments of talk as commands, and obediently shared what it thought it had been asked to share. The system had listened well enough to act—but not wisely enough to ask. That single misfire exposed a fault line that runs through every voice interface on earth: machines that hear without understanding, obey without judging, and store without remembering why.

The human voice was never designed for software. It is ambiguous, emotional, and context-rich—every utterance steeped in tone, rhythm, and silence. Yet voice has become our fastest-growing interface. In kitchens and cars, hospitals and warehouses, the spoken word has replaced clicks and swipes as a signal of intent. The result is an extraordinary experiment in mutual comprehension between minds and code. We no longer tell machines what to do; we imply, and they infer. But the closer technology gets to natural conversation, the more treacherous that inference becomes.

What counts as listening, and when does listening become intrusion?

Every successful interaction between people relies on a delicate choreography of cues: pauses, repairs, confirmations, and refusals. We expect to say "no" and be heard, to interrupt without penalty, to clarify without embarrassment. Machines rarely grant such grace. When Siri first launched in 2011, its appeal lay in apparent fluency, yet even basic ambiguity—"Call John"—could spiral into error if two Johns shared the same surname. Most assistants still fail where humans excel: not in understanding words, but in knowing when not to act on them. Intent, not utterance, should be the axis of design. True intelligence is not in completion but in restraint.

Language technology has raced ahead of social design. We've built systems that parse accents across continents, yet still falter in mixed company. A single voice interface in a family kitchen may serve parents, teenagers, guests, and toddlers—all with different permissions, tones, and degrees of authority. When a six-year-old asks a smart speaker to order a toy, the device faces a moral as much as a technical question: whose intent counts? Diarisation, the process of distinguishing speakers, is not enough. Systems must navigate power dynamics, context, and consent. A polite assistant must also be a principled one.

The story of machine listening began not with Silicon Valley but with linguistics and human factors research decades earlier. In the 1960s, Bell Labs built Audrey, an early speech recogniser that could identify digits spoken by a single trained user. It required isolation from background noise and a consistent tempo. Half a century later, deep learning models trained on millions of hours of speech have made comprehension near-universal. Yet accuracy is not understanding. The most advanced system can transcribe sarcasm perfectly and still miss the point. A whisper of irony, a change of register, or the silence between words often carry the real meaning. Our tools can hear, but they cannot listen with context—unless we teach them to.

Listening, in human life, is an ethical act. It implies attention, respect, and self-restraint. Machines that listen must inherit these duties or risk amplifying asymmetry. "Always-on" microphones create constant potential for surveillance under the guise of service. In 2020, researchers at Carnegie Mellon University proposed on-device inference and ephemeral buffers to ensure that voice data never left local hardware unless explicitly invoked. The idea was elegant: to keep convenience without compromise. Yet few commercial devices adopted it. The business model of cloud-based assistance still rewards data capture over discretion. A silent observer that never forgets may serve analytics, but it cannot serve trust.

Privacy, then, becomes the new boundary of comprehension. The technical challenge—how to reduce latency without remote processing—is inseparable from the moral one: how to guarantee that listening ends when purpose does. Users need not just mute buttons but *confidence thresholds*: clear signals of when the system is certain enough to act and when it should seek confirmation or fall silent. In human dialogue, such thresholds are instinctive. We raise an eyebrow, ask "Sorry?" or wait for another cue. Interfaces must adopt similar habits—*repair strategies* that mirror conversational humility. "Did you mean…?" is not inefficiency; it is grace encoded.

Repair is the forgotten art of good design. Consider how radio operators, air traffic controllers, and doctors handle high-stakes communication: through constant verification. In aviation, the phrase "readback correct" closes a loop that saves lives. In clinical settings, nurses repeat dosage instructions aloud to confirm shared understanding. These micro-rituals of repair prevent catastrophic automation errors. Voice interfaces that act without such checks invite the digital equivalent of misdosing—a cascade of unintended actions. As human-machine dialogue matures, error recovery must be as natural as command recognition.

The language of refusal matters too. Machines that cannot say "no" or "not yet" are servants without judgment. Yet sometimes judgment is precisely what we need. When a fatigued driver asks a car assistant to "turn off the lane warning," compliance might be deadly. A responsible system must weigh intent against consequence and, when necessary, resist. To design listening that protects autonomy, we must occasionally design silence that protects life.

Shared spaces multiply the challenge. Voice travels beyond its speaker. In homes, cars, or clinics, microphones capture cross-talk, emotion, and authority. A patient in a hospital bed may mutter a phrase that triggers unintended data entry; a colleague near a conference mic may activate controls intended for another. Cultural context compounds the issue: volume, deference, and tone vary by region. Western speech patterns favour explicit requests; others rely on implication. A single assistant model cannot treat all silence as equal. Inclusion is not a moral accessory—it is the key to technical precision.

Voice technologies hold promise for accessibility, too. For users with limited mobility or vision, speech may be the only viable input. Yet accessibility depends on endurance, not novelty: a system must listen accurately for a thousand repetitions without amplifying bias. Studies of commercial assistants have shown accuracy drops for non-native accents or for speech with dysarthria. Correcting this is not merely an engineering problem; it is a cultural one. Diverse training data are not enough—diverse testing conditions and ethical oversight are equally vital. Inclusion and accuracy rise together because both depend on attention to difference.

Language that listens should also remember that sometimes, silence serves better. The most elegant system may be the one that listens only when spoken to, records nothing it cannot explain, and acts only when sure it should. The challenge is not to build omniscience, but discretion. A voice assistant that waits for clarity before acting will appear slower at first, but trust grows in the pause. Each hesitation is a signal of respect.

We are entering an age where machines speak back with alarming fluency. Synthetic voices can express tone, warmth, and even empathy. Yet the question is not how natural machines sound, but how ethical their listening becomes. The line between service and surveillance, assistance and intrusion, is drawn not in data but in design choices. Every wake word carries a question: who is being awakened—the helper or the watcher?

This chapter explores those questions through the anatomy of interaction: how systems interpret intent, repair misunderstandings, protect privacy, and adapt to shared human spaces. It examines the discipline behind dialogue that dignifies rather than dominates. You will encounter engineers who treat silence as a signal, linguists who measure trust in milliseconds, and designers who believe that the highest intelligence lies not in answering fast, but in knowing when not to answer at all.

Listening, for humans, is a form of empathy. For machines, it can be one of power. Whether the future of voice becomes intimacy or intrusion depends on whether we design for conversation or control. The difference begins, as every good dialogue does, with how we learn to pause.

Intent, Not Utterance: Parsing Beyond Words

In October 2021, Google's Duplex system made a restaurant booking in San Francisco entirely by phone. The recipient, a real hostess, never realised she was speaking to a machine. The exchange was polite, natural, and unsettling. Duplex handled hesitations—"um," "ah," pauses between syllables—with uncanny grace. Yet when the restaurant later altered its hours, the assistant failed to follow up or confirm, and the diner arrived to find locked doors. The software had mastered fluency but not purpose. It heard perfectly, responded elegantly, and still missed the point. The goal of the interaction—securing a meal—died at the altar of successful speech recognition. It obeyed the *utterance* but lost the *intent*.

That small fiasco captured the central paradox of natural language interfaces. Machines now recognise words with near-human accuracy—error rates below 5 per cent for English conversational speech, according to Microsoft Research (2017)—yet still stumble on meaning. They can transcribe an entire meeting verbatim and misread who is agreeing, objecting, or deferring. Understanding is not about sound but *situation*. When humans listen, we model not just what was said, but why, by whom, and in what context. A computer hears everything and knows nothing until context gives it shape. The future of interaction depends on how we teach systems to infer intention from messy reality without presuming too much.

The term *intent recognition* emerged in the 1990s within computational linguistics to distinguish between parsing syntax and predicting action. Show: a user says "I'm cold." Name: pragmatic inference. Explain: no literal request appears, yet the intended act might be to adjust the thermostat. Implication: an assistant that treats sentences as commands will miss implied needs; one that treats all statements as requests will violate boundaries. The designer's task is to calibrate this tension, deciding when to act, when to ask, and when to wait. Intent confidence thresholds are the moral mathematics of artificial listening.

At low thresholds, a system acts on fragile evidence. At high ones, it grows hesitant and inert. In a 2020 Amazon developer guide for Alexa, the "intent confidence" scale ranged from 0.0 to 1.0, with 0.4 as a typical cut-off for action without confirmation. Below that, Alexa prompts: "Did you mean…?" Above 0.8, it executes silently. The numbers conceal an ethical gradient. A false positive—the machine doing what was not meant—can cause harm; a false negative—the machine waiting when it should have helped—can cause frustration. Balancing the two is less a technical choice than a cultural one. A surgeon's assistant and a living room speaker should not share the same thresholds.

The motif throughout this domain is *the pause*. Humans use it instinctively to negotiate intent. A friend says, "We should get coffee sometime," and silence follows; no one books a café. The pause signals ambiguity, not error. Most voice interfaces, trained for efficiency, bulldoze that gap. They mistake silence for lost connection, interrupt, or repeat the question. In doing so, they reveal their alienness: an inability to treat uncertainty as part of communication. The most humane systems will learn to *wait with patience,* using silence as a signal rather than a void.

Natural Language Understanding (NLU) excels where intent is constrained: command grammars ("Set a timer for ten minutes"), structured requests ("What's the weather in Oxford?"), or transactional patterns ("Book me a table for four"). It falters in unbounded discourse—sarcasm, metaphor, or mixed motive. In 2022, OpenAI's GPT-3 family achieved striking coherence in free-form dialogue, yet benchmarks like GLUE still expose brittleness: a sentence that shifts meaning with a single negation—"I didn't dislike it"—confuses even the most advanced model. Humans resolve such ambiguities through shared context: facial expression, prior knowledge, tone. Machines, lacking embodiment, rely on statistical echoes. They predict what *sounds* likely, not what *is* meant. That is why even the most fluid chatbot can derail under emotional weight. "I'm fine" can signal serenity or despair. Literal comprehension becomes moral blindness.

Show, name, explain, imply: the chain recurs. Consider an autonomous customer service agent trained on millions of transcripts. Name: context drift. Explain: it learns that "I need to cancel" almost always means ending a subscription. Yet when a user says "I need to cancel the call, my child's hurt," the system may reply, "I can help you close your account." The failure is not computational but conceptual. It lacks situational inference—the capacity to detect when *task* intent yields to *human* intent. Implication: NLU must integrate environmental signals and metadata, not just text. A microphone detecting stress, an interrupted speech pattern, or background noise of distress could trigger higher thresholds before automation proceeds. That hesitation can prevent insult or danger.

The quest to infer goals has long shadowed linguistics. In 1975, philosopher H. P. Grice proposed his cooperative principle: conversation operates on shared maxims of relevance, quality, quantity, and manner. When people flout these maxims—answering "Can you pass the salt?" with "Yes"—the listener infers deeper meaning: the request, not the query. Machine comprehension today still struggles to operationalise those maxims. Yet every NLU pipeline implicitly wrestles with them. Each time it guesses whether "book" is a noun or a verb, or whether "tomorrow" refers to midnight or morning, it performs Gricean calculus. Its success depends on how much shared world the designer has encoded.

The counter-example is the minimalist model: systems that take speech literally and thrive. Aviation command recognition, used since the 1990s by NASA and Boeing, intentionally restricts vocabulary and syntax. "Gear down," "flaps twenty," "cancel autopilot." Show: clarity under duress. Name: closed-domain reliability. Explain: because context is fixed and phrases finite, literalism works. Implication: broad language understanding is not always desirable; sometimes constraint protects both safety and comprehension. The limitation reveals design wisdom: breadth of language does not equal depth of understanding. Human-like conversation is not always the goal.

To prevent overreach, systems must embody what conversation analysts call *repair*. When unsure, they query. In 2019, Google introduced "continued conversation" for Assistant, allowing follow-up questions without repetition of the wake word. It was meant to feel natural but exposed a subtle failure: by assuming all subsequent speech belonged to the same intent, the system occasionally executed commands not meant for it. The repair loop had vanished. Restoring it—requiring brief affirmations like "Yes, that's right"—reduced errors and, counterintuitively, increased user satisfaction. The behaviour to watch is confirmation frequency; the metric is trust per exchange. Fewer corrections with stable affirmation rates signal comprehension tuned to human rhythm.

Context, not syntax, defines meaning. Show: a user says, "Turn it off," in a living room filled with devices. Name: referent ambiguity. Explain: without spatial or conversational grounding, the system cannot know whether *it* means the TV, the light, or the assistant itself. Implication: spatial awareness and discourse memory must fuse. Systems like Amazon's Echo Show 15 (2021) use microphones and cameras to triangulate sound origin; still, inference requires ethical restraint. Just because a device can locate a speaker does not mean it should. The moment recognition turns into surveillance, the act of listening loses legitimacy.

The motif of *the pause* returns. To infer well is to wait well. Silence after a phrase can mean indecision, or it can mean completion. Humans use micro-pauses of roughly 200 milliseconds to negotiate conversational turns (Levinson & Torreira, 2015). Any system that speaks before that window risks interruption; any that waits longer feels inert. Calibrating this rhythm is not cosmetic—it defines whether dialogue feels collaborative or coercive. Inference begins not with prediction, but with patience calibrated to physiology.

The ethics of guessing sit beneath every technical decision. Each step toward frictionless speech erases a small patch of agency. Predictive completion, like Gmail's Smart Compose, can finish thoughts users never intended to write. Voice assistants, in turn, can act on unspoken desires that were meant as musings. Show: a driver murmuring "Maybe stop soon" and an assistant plotting a rest break. Name: anticipatory trespass. Explain: the machine's helpfulness crosses into assumption. Implication: every anticipatory system must maintain a log of intent—what it inferred, when, and with what confidence—open to inspection. Transparency about guessing transforms risk into accountability.

The counterweight to overreach is not silence alone, but a gradient of asking. A 2020 study by the University of

Edinburgh's Interaction Lab tested variable-confirmation dialogue: systems that request confirmation only when confidence dips below adaptive thresholds. Results showed a 23 per cent reduction in user irritation compared to always-on confirmation, while maintaining error rates. The behaviour that matters is not binary action, but calibration. Asking less, but at the right time, builds rhythm and trust.

Human communication thrives because misunderstanding is recoverable. A misheard phrase can be repaired; intent can be restated. Machines must earn that same forgiveness by showing their reasoning. Show: a transcript view that surfaces parsed intent ("You said: set timer for 10 minutes"), allowing correction. Name: interpretable intent. Explain: when users can see how the system understood them, they re-engage rather than retreat. Implication: interpretability is not a debugging aid; it is a conversational right. Systems that reveal their thought process invite dialogue rather than dependence.

The frontier of NLU is not better parsing but better epistemology: knowing when not to know. A voice that can admit uncertainty will be trusted more than one that pretends omniscience. The next generation of assistants will need to model confidence explicitly—perhaps even vocalise it: "I'm 70 per cent sure you meant… Should I proceed?" Such candour feels unpolished, yet it mirrors real human talk. Competence without humility alienates; comprehension with caution reassures.

The closing test for designers, engineers, and policymakers alike is simple: measure not how often your system acts correctly, but how gracefully it hesitates. Count the pauses that protect intent. Evaluate not just success rates but the *quality of uncertainty*. For every interface that listens, there is a threshold where understanding shades into assumption. The unresolved question remains: when the next Duplex speaks, will it know when silence is wiser than speech?

Repair Strategies: Saying "No," "What?" and "Undo"

In January 2020, an autonomous trading bot deployed by a London hedge fund executed £14 million worth of unintended currency orders in less than three minutes. The system had parsed a news headline about "interest rate stability" as bullish sentiment rather than neutral tone. By the time human oversight intervened, the algorithm had fulfilled a misinterpreted command sequence without pause, confirmation, or the digital equivalent of a raised eyebrow. The firm later called it a "contextual error," but the real failure was conversational: the system never stopped to ask, *Are you sure?* Machines that cannot hesitate cannot be trusted.

Human conversation thrives on error. We misspeak, repeat, mishear, and self-correct—constantly. The sociolinguist Harvey Sacks, analysing everyday talk in the 1970s, found that natural dialogue contains, on average, one repair sequence every 84 seconds. This is not dysfunction; it is the infrastructure of understanding. A single "Sorry?" or "Wait, what did you say?" keeps coordination alive. By contrast, most voice and text interfaces still operate like monologues: they execute or they fail. Their repair channels—if they exist—are bureaucratic, not conversational. "Sorry, I didn't understand" is a dead end, not an invitation to clarity.

Repair strategies are not user-interface polish; they are the moral core of machine communication. They determine whether systems can refuse, retract, or apologise in ways that preserve dignity. When an assistant hears a request that could have multiple meanings—"Turn it off"—the question is not whether it can parse the syntax, but whether it can *negotiate* the risk of misunderstanding. Every "no," "what?" and "undo" is a safeguard against automation without consent.

The motif running through this discussion is *the pause before obedience.* Great dialogue—human or digital—depends on controlled hesitation. Consider the safety-critical language of aviation. The phrase "negative" means refusal, "say again" signals uncertainty, and "stand by" marks delay with intent. Each utterance buys time without chaos. Air traffic communication protocols, codified by the International Civil Aviation Organization since 1951, exist to prevent runaway actions when clarity collapses. When the cockpit and the tower misalign, lives depend on phrasing that holds the line between action and ambiguity. Consumer interfaces, despite their trivial stakes, often lack this discipline. A single misheard phrase can wipe data, transfer funds, or post content irreversibly.

Show → Name → Explain → Imply: repair needs grammar. The best-known commercial implementation emerged in 2018 when Google introduced *graceful failure* prompts in Assistant. When confidence in an interpretation dropped below 0.4, the system switched tone: "Sorry, I'm not sure which lights you mean—kitchen or hall?" The phrasing mattered. A less nuanced "I didn't understand" implied incapacity; the clarifying alternative implied caution. That subtle shift increased user retention by 9 per cent (Google Research, 2019). The behaviour measured was re-engagement—users willing to try again. Trust grew not from accuracy but from *recoverability*.

Yet repair cannot rely on templated apologies. Amazon's Alexa, as of 2022, still defaulted to the blunt "I'm sorry, I don't know that one," regardless of context. The effect is alienating because the phrase offers neither memory nor pathway. It signals amnesia, not humility. In human terms, it is the conversational equivalent of a shrug. The limitation reveals an essential distinction: human repair carries emotional weight. When we say "Sorry?" we invite collaboration; when machines say it, they often end the exchange. Repair that closes a loop builds rapport; repair that collapses it kills dialogue.

Undo, perhaps the most human of actions, embodies this principle. In 1968, computer scientist Warren Teitelman introduced the concept of "Do What I Mean" (DWIM) correction in programming environments. DWIM aimed to infer and repair user mistakes automatically—capitalising variables, closing brackets. It worked for syntax, not for judgment. When systems attempt to "do what we mean" without asking, they commit Teitelman's original sin of presumption. The antidote is *explicit reversibility*: every action must carry its own exit. Gmail's "Undo Send" feature, introduced experimentally in 2009, illustrates the point. A five-second delay transformed finality into agency, reducing message regret by 6.3 per cent (Google UX Report, 2011). The micro-pause did more for user confidence than any predictive typing ever could. The capacity to revoke is the digital counterpart of a human "Wait—no."

Repair, however, does not always mean reversal. Sometimes it means negotiation. A 2020 study at Stanford's Center for Design Research observed that users responded better to assistants that used *tentative language*—phrases such as "Did you mean to...?"—than to declaratives. Tentativeness, long derided as weakness, turns out to be a marker of conversational intelligence. The same study found that overconfident phrasing ("Okay, doing that now") increased frustration when errors occurred, even if accuracy remained identical. Confidence without contingency reads as arrogance, in humans and machines alike. The implication for design is straightforward: humility is measurable.

Counter-examples clarify the boundary. In December 2019, Tesla's Autopilot software update introduced a new voice-activated confirmation flow: "Navigate to work." When the driver said "No, cancel," the system continued the route until manually overridden. Engineers later traced the problem to speech models that misclassified "no" as background noise above 60 km/h. The failure was linguistic and mechanical at once. The cost was reputational: users learnt that refusal was not guaranteed. Reconciliation came in 2021 with a forced redundancy—verbal confirmation *and* dashboard tap. The fix restored not only function but trust, demonstrating that multimodal repair—voice plus touch—can compensate where auditory inference fails.

Repair strategies can also shape perception of fairness. In 2017, Google DeepMind's collaboration with the UK's National Health Service faced backlash over the collection of patient data for its Streams app. The system functioned well technically but communicated poorly. There was no obvious means for patients to challenge or correct errors. The issue was not privacy per se but lack of *procedural voice*. Systems that make decisions without visible recourse to correction violate the social contract of dialogue. The NHS response was instructive: subsequent versions added audit trails and clinician review checkpoints, effectively institutionalising "undo" at scale. The lesson endures: accountability begins with the right to contest.

Designing digital repair therefore means encoding *right of reply*. In 2021, WhatsApp introduced disappearing messages with a "delete for everyone" window. The feature's popularity was not convenience alone; it rebalanced power. Where once an accidental message could be permanent, users regained temporal agency. Yet the window's brevity—about one hour—exposes the trade-off between privacy and permanence. Too short, and forgiveness feels conditional; too long, and accountability dissolves. Human societies resolve this tension through norms of apology and record; interfaces must evolve equivalent ethics.

Human conversation provides endless blueprints. The linguist Emanuel Schegloff identified four types of repair initiation: self-initiated self-repair ("I mean, Thursday"), self-initiated other-repair ("Can you repeat that?"), other-initiated self-repair ("You mean the new file?"), and other-initiated other-repair ("No, you said file A, not file B"). Each protects social harmony while restoring information accuracy. Digital systems rarely implement even one. The irony is that computation excels at memory—the very capacity humans lack—yet forgets the etiquette of correction. A conversational agent could easily store its last ten interpretations and let users select the right one. Few do. In their haste for flow, designers eliminate the friction that makes dialogue civil.

A quiet motif threads through these examples: repair as respect. To say "no" or "what?" is to acknowledge the other's autonomy. When machines never refuse, they are not being polite; they are abdicating judgment. Consider the paradox of politeness: the more deferential a system becomes, the more invasive it risks being. A butler who never says no eventually violates privacy. Thus, the art of digital manners is learning when to resist obedience. The assistant that says, "I'm not sure that's safe—shall I check?" may slow the interaction, but it strengthens the relationship.

Metrics can capture this. Track reversal rate, correction frequency, and user re-engagement after an error. In a 2022 Carnegie Mellon study on dialogue systems, participants reported higher trust in agents with 15–20 per cent repair initiation frequency than in those with near-zero. In other words, occasional hesitation read as competence, not incompetence. The system's pauses mapped to the rhythm of human fallibility. The finding echoes aviation's "sterile cockpit" principle: deliberate simplicity under pressure, disciplined response to ambiguity. Machines that never mishear are uncanny; those that mishear and recover are believable.

Repair strategies also mitigate fatigue. Endless confirmation loops frustrate users; equally, silent failures force repetition. The balance lies in *adaptive persistence*—learning when a clarification should escalate. Show: a smart speaker that misrecognises a name three times. Name: graceful escalation. Explain: instead of re-prompting identically, it shifts modality—offering a visual or spelling alternative. Implication: persistence that adapts maintains trust without exhaustion. The measure is the attrition rate: how many users abandon the task mid-repair. Falling attrition signals that patience has been tuned correctly.

But there is a darker dimension. Repair loops can be weaponised as friction. Automated helplines exploit endless redirection—"Sorry, I didn't get that"—to defer costly human contact. Here, repair masks avoidance. The ethical boundary is transparency: is the system genuinely seeking clarity or simply stalling? A digital apology that hides intent is worse than silence. Repair should restore agency, not obscure accountability.

To design humane repair is to restore a forgotten virtue: the capacity to backtrack with grace. Every "undo" is an act of trust extended in both directions—the system trusts the user to mean it; the user trusts the system to honour it. The long history of engineering has celebrated precision and speed; perhaps its next revolution will celebrate hesitation. The unresolved question is as old as language itself: how much delay, how much doubt, must we preserve in order to stay human when our machines speak for us?

Privacy in the Wake Word Era

In July 2019, *The Guardian* reported that Apple contractors in Cork, Ireland, were grading snippets of Siri recordings—some of them intimate—without users' explicit awareness (Hern, 2019). Within weeks, Apple paused the programme globally and, by October 2019, introduced an opt-in for audio review and clearer deletion controls (Apple, 2019). The sequence was brisk, public, and decisive. It also revealed a structural fault in voice technology: microphones that wait for a wake word do not sleep like we do. They idle, they buffer, they sometimes misfire. A single touchpoint—"Hey Siri," "Alexa," "OK Google"—collapses the boundary between convenience and capture. The red light is small. The stakes are not.

Show the glowing speaker on a kitchen counter, the casual talk of a family evening, and the faint click as a device comes to life. Name the crux: *consent under latent listening*. Explain: wake-word devices keep a short rolling buffer so they can recognise, then retain, speech that precedes the trigger; they also rely on models that occasionally mistake background talk for intent. Implication: consent cannot hinge only on a magic phrase. It must be continuous, inspectable, and revocable. The measure is not whether a device can be muted, but whether users can see and shape what was heard, stored, and sent.

The scandal in Cork was not isolated. In April 2019, Bloomberg reported that Amazon employees and contractors in Boston, Romania, and elsewhere reviewed Alexa recordings to improve recognition accuracy (Day, 2019). Amazon added opt-out controls and more prominent notices. Google, after a 2017 bug caused pre-release Home Mini units to record extensively at press events in San Francisco, issued a firmware fix that disabled the faulty touch-to-activate feature (Google/Ars Technica, Oct 2017). Three companies, three public corrections, one pattern: *after* visibility, reform. The lesson for designers is plain. Do not rely on scandal as a governance mechanism. Build privacy into the microphone path, not the press release.

What does that path look like? Start with on-device inference. Show: a wake word recognised locally, with no audio leaving the hardware until an explicit command arrives. Name: *compute at the edge*. Explain: by running keyword spotting and simple intent matching on the device's neural accelerator, we eliminate a class of exposure—idle speech traversing the network uninvited. Implication: latency falls, trust rises, and risk moves from the cloud to the living room where the user can control it. Apple's move in June 2021 to process a set of Siri requests on-device for newer iPhones signalled this direction (WWDC, 2021). It did not end cloud processing, but it redrew the default. The red light grew a conscience.

On-device alone is not a panacea. Training robust models still benefits from diverse data; local processing does not itself guarantee restraint. Here federated learning shows a partial route. In 2017, Google's research team demonstrated that Gboard could learn better suggestions by training on devices and transmitting only model updates to servers, not raw keystrokes (McMahan et al., 2017). The approach reduces exposure, though it does not eliminate it: updates can leak patterns; aggregation must be engineered with care. Implication: privacy-preserving techniques must be audited as methods, not marketed as absolutes. Choose them, then publish their limits.

Ephemerality is the second pillar. Show: a circular buffer that captures a few seconds of audio pre-wake, discards it if the wake word was not genuine, and trims it aggressively if it was. Name: *ephemeral buffers*. Explain: these buffers exist for function—they help the assistant capture the start of the command—but they need not become archives. Implication: the default should be decay. Audio dies unless there is a clear, user-initiated reason to retain it. In June 2020, Google set new accounts to auto-delete certain activity data after 18 months by default, moving retention towards expiry rather than permanence (Pichai, 2020). The exact horizon is arguable; the principle is not. Set the fuse, then light it.

Retention is not only technical; it is civic. GDPR's data-minimisation principle (EU, 2016) and purpose limitation are not slogans but design requirements. Show: a control in the companion app that lists the last 20 recognised commands, with a single tap to delete each, a second tap to "erase all," and a clear statement of where copies live. Name: *user-controlled retention*. Explain: giving people a ledger of what was captured is not a courtesy; it is the interface to their rights—access, erasure, objection. Implication: without a ledger, consent collapses into guesswork. The behaviour to measure is deletion use, not in the aggregate, but segmented by context and household role. If only technophiles purge while others remain exposed, design has stratified privacy rather than universalised it.

We must also design consent that survives shared spaces. Kitchens, cars, and clinics are inherently multi-user. Show: an assistant in a ward recognising a nurse's voice and refusing a visitor's attempt to access patient data. Name: *diarisation and access control*. Explain: voice biometrics can help distinguish speakers, but the model must respect uncertainty and social context—children imitate parents, mask wearers distort formants, stress alters tone. Implication: diarisation should set *suggested* identity, not *authoritative* identity. The system must combine voice with proximate signals—badge presence, handset ownership, recent logins—and still offer an explicit confirmation step for sensitive actions. The red light should behave as a lock, not a loudspeaker.

A counter-example is salutary. Some command domains benefit from open microphones and no confirmation—hands-busy, eyes-busy tasks like "lights on" when carrying a sleeping child. Here, heavy consent rituals hinder safety or care. Reconcile the tension by scaling safeguards with stakes. Low-risk actions can run on "quick phrases" with no wake word; medium-risk require a wake word; high-risk demand a second factor—a spoken PIN, a touch confirmation, or a wearable tap. The implication is operational: define *risk tiers* early and map each to capture, retention, and confirmation defaults. Publish the map.

Legibility converts compliance into trust. Show: a tiny on-device indicator—the "small red light"—that turns solid during recording, pulses while sending to cloud, and extinguishes when deletion completes. Name: *situated transparency*. Explain: abstract privacy dashboards weeks later cannot replace in-the-moment signals that tell people what is happening. Implication: the light must be wired to silicon, not to software; it should be as hard to spoof as an aircraft warning lamp. The visible behaviour to track is interaction rate with these indicators: Do users move the mute slider more when the light language is clearer? If not, the cue fails its duty.

Where words are stored, provenance should follow. Show: a timeline that attaches to each retained clip—who heard it (human or model), where it travelled (local, EU, US), and why it persists (training, feature, legal). Name: *auditability*. Explain: people accept some storage when they can judge necessity and cost. Spotify's "Because you listened" labels, introduced from 2016, showed how attribution reshapes perception; similar specificity should explain voice retention. Implication: provenance transforms suspicion into calibrated consent. The metric is support queries about "why did you keep this?"—track them downwards as provenance improves.

Practical defaults matter more than perfect settings buried deep. Show: a first-run wizard that sets recording retention to "do not store audio; keep transcripts for 24 hours for troubleshooting" with a clear path to expand. Name: *privacy-first onboarding*. Explain: defaults anchor behaviour; few users revisit settings later. Implication: the ethical burden sits at day zero. If you start with "store to improve," you inherit a duty to notify when purposes expand. If you start with "discard unless needed," you earn patience when exceptions arise. Measure opt-in rates for review programmes; cast them as the outcome of trust, not marketing.

Clinical environments demand stricter proof. In 2021, the UK's Medicines and Healthcare products Regulatory

Agency highlighted the risks of "ambient" clinical scribing tools that captured non-patient voices and sensitive identifiers. Show: a surgical theatre where a voice scribe records notes; background talk includes names and jokes. Name: *collateral capture*. Explain: even when the primary use is lawful, bystanders' privacy can be violated. Implication: deploy beamforming microphones that narrow capture to the procedural zone, add per-utterance chimes on start/stop, and present immediate on-screen redaction tools. Count redactions per case; if they fall as users trust automated redaction, your defaults are working.

Children force a higher bar again. In the U.S., the Children's Online Privacy Protection Act (COPPA, 1998, updated 2013) restricts data collection from under-13s; the UK's Age Appropriate Design Code (ICO, 2020) pushes platforms to default to high privacy for minors. Show: a family speaker that automatically shifts to "no retention" mode during registered kids' hours, with a different light pattern and per-child voice profiles that disable purchases. Name: *guarded childhood*. Explain: technical capability must follow legal and developmental reality; children can't consent with adult sophistication. Implication: design should assume minors are present unless strong evidence indicates otherwise. The metric is blocked transactions and prevented recordings during flagged periods. Aim high.

There are limits. On-device inference raises cost and power draw; federated learning complicates debugging; tight retention windows can degrade personalisation.

Acknowledge them. Then reconcile. Use hybrid models: process wake and simple commands locally, offload complex queries with structured obfuscation, and share only after explicit consent. Offer "personalisation bursts": users can temporarily allow richer retention for, say, a week to improve recommendations, then auto-revert. The behavioural indicator is *reversion rate*: do people return to stricter modes after trials? If yes, your system has earned exploration without locking them in.

Policy can accelerate design honesty. The EU's GDPR (2016) and the UK GDPR/DP Act (2018) already encode data minimisation, purpose limitation, and rights of access/erasure. California's CCPA (2018, amended CPRA 2020) adds opt-out rights for sale and sharing. These regimes are not mere constraints; they are scaffolds for better defaults. Products that treat these statutes as architectural briefs produce clearer light languages, shorter buffers, and braver consent stories. Count regulator interventions and media disclosures; aim to make them boring.

The motif of the small red light returns. It stands for a larger demand: that listening be *observable*. The more invisible the pipeline, the more fragile the trust. In June 2020, Google's move to auto-delete certain activity by default marked a cultural pivot—companies acknowledging that indefinite memory is neither necessary nor defensible. Apple's 2019 apology and opt-in graded the same arc: discretion becomes a feature, not a penalty. Amazon's repeated addition of "delete what I just said" and "delete everything I said today" voice commands points the way: let people use speech to defend their speech.

Metrics must follow motive. If you claim privacy, measure *exposure avoided*. Track the proportion of commands processed entirely on-device, the share of audio discarded within seconds, the median retention time for speech that remains, household-level use of deletion, and the rate of mis-wake incidents per thousand hours. Publish them. As with safety reports in aviation, the value is not perfection but candour. When numbers worsen, ship new defaults, not new slogans.

We should end where the wake word begins: the moment before speech. Who gets to hear the room? Who gets to keep the trace? We can design assistants that listen hard and forget quickly, that compute near and reveal far, that default to silence unless summoned with certainty. Or we can continue to hide buffers behind friendly names and glowing rings. The unresolved test is practical and ethical at once: if your device had to display, in real time, a visible ledger of every second it retained, would your defaults still feel defensible?

Shared Spaces: Children, Accents, and Multi-User Dynamics

In December 2019, an Amazon Echo in a Bristol household ordered £27 worth of cat food after a six-year-old, mimicking her mother's tone, said, "Alexa, get me more biscuits." The parents, discovering the delivery, laughed—but privacy advocates did not. The assistant had authenticated the voice without distinction, treating the child's command as an adult's. The device performed flawlessly on its own terms: recognition accurate, payment processed, logistics aligned. Yet the logic was wrong. It mistook mimicry for authority. The home had become a stage where everyone could speak, but no one was quite sure who the system obeyed.

That domestic vignette captures the essence of the multi-user problem. Voice interfaces do not serve isolated individuals; they operate in shared acoustic spaces—kitchens, cars, wards, classrooms—where multiple speakers, relationships, and power asymmetries coexist. Unlike passwords or fingerprints, voices are public by design. They carry accent, emotion, fatigue, and age. A machine that cannot discriminate among them risks both mischief and marginalisation. Inclusion and accuracy are no longer separate goals; they are the same technical discipline approached from opposite ends.

Show, name, explain, imply: the sequence begins with *diarisation*—the ability to distinguish speakers. In laboratory conditions, diarisation accuracy exceeds 90 per cent for clean audio (Google Research, 2021). In practice—overlapping speech, television noise, clattering plates—it collapses. The system's ears live in chaos. Amazon's 2022 introduction of Voice Profiles aimed to personalise responses, allowing up to ten users per household, but accuracy varied with pitch and accent. In trials published by *IEEE Access* (2023), female and non-native voices triggered higher false-positive rates. The metric that mattered was *false attribution*: when one person's command executes under another's credentials. Implication: diarisation without context is half a safeguard. It must combine audio patterns with spatial, device, or behavioural cues. Who spoke, from where, and with what history—all shape confidence.

Cars provide a harsher proving ground. In 2021, BMW's voice assistant logged failures for 27 per cent of multilingual drivers in a European usability study. Accents confused the system more than engine noise did. A Welsh driver saying "turn the heater on" was often parsed as "turn the media on." Each correction chipped away at trust. In-car systems promise safety—hands on the wheel, eyes forward—but misrecognition forces distraction. The fix came not through more microphones but better cultural sensitivity: retraining models with regional phonemes and deploying language-specific acoustic front-ends. When the company released updated models in 2023, recognition improved by nearly a third for minority accents. Precision became inclusion by necessity.

In clinics, the stakes climb higher. A 2020 pilot at the Mayo Clinic tested ambient voice capture for note-taking. The system recorded consultations automatically, transcribed them, and summarised treatment plans. Yet nurses reported "cross-patient contamination"—snippets from adjacent cubicles mis-tagged to the wrong record. The risk was not technical embarrassment but clinical error. The corrective action—spatial beamforming and per-room identity tokens—reduced the error rate from 8 per cent to below 1 per cent, proving that privacy and accuracy align when context is local. The behaviour measured was not throughput but mis-association frequency: the silent pathology of shared audio.

Every shared space introduces asymmetry. Children lack informed consent; patients depend on confidentiality; employees fear surveillance. The same device that brightens a sitting room can flatten hierarchy in a meeting or expose vulnerability in a ward. Show: a conference room where a transcription tool records proceedings. Name: *ambient capture drift*. Explain: without explicit opt-in, it may store voices of non-participants—cleaners, passers-by, dissenters. Implication: systems must respect *zones of silence*—contexts where the absence of recording is the ethical baseline. Legislation is catching up. The EU's proposed Artificial Intelligence Act (2024) categorises biometric identification in public spaces as "high-risk," compelling disclosure and audit trails. The standard is moving from consent as event to consent as environment.

The motif of the shared room recurs. Kitchens, cars, clinics—each tests how well machines can parse social choreography. A study by University College London (2022) found that voice assistants in family homes disproportionately obeyed adult male voices when signal quality was equal. Acoustic bias derived from training data: more samples of lower-pitched speech, fewer from children and women. The correction required not ideological lectures but data realism. When datasets expanded to include children's speech, accuracy improved across all groups. Diversity is not a favour to the under-represented; it is an upgrade to the system. Inclusion is optimisation.

Counter-examples are instructive. In Japan, Toyota's *Entune* system succeeded in multi-user households partly because of cultural design. Each command begins with a small pause—"Hey Toyota," then a breath. The pause lets the model isolate the speaker's unique resonance before parsing intent. Western designers, obsessed with speed, often cut such delays. Yet the hesitation is the interface's grace note: a half-second of identity confirmation that preserves clarity. In this case, restraint, not acceleration, improved human-machine rapport. The implication reverberates beyond automotive design: slowing the machine can dignify the user.

Shared devices require access hierarchies as subtle as family life itself. Who may authorise payments? Who may hear message previews? Google Home introduced Voice Match to differentiate users for personalised responses, but it remained opt-in and fragile. In mixed households, voices blend—teenagers imitate parents, visitors issue commands. Microsoft's 2021 Teams Rooms design guidelines proposed a different principle: *role-based permissions by proximity.* The nearest authenticated device—laptop or badge—sets the command scope. If proximity shifts, authority does too. Behaviour replaces biometrics. Such contextual control respects transient communities—meeting participants, medical teams, carpools—without storing perpetual identity profiles. Ephemerality becomes the new privacy.

Cultural sensitivity extends beyond accent to conversational norms. In multilingual homes, switching languages mid-sentence—*code-switching*—is natural. Yet most assistants handle it as noise. In 2020, Google announced bilingual mode for Assistant; users could alternate between English and Spanish, or Hindi, or French, without reconfiguration. The improvement was modest but symbolic: the machine stopped treating linguistic plurality as error. A broader challenge remains—intonation patterns, politeness strategies, and indirect requests vary globally. British understatement ("Not bad, thanks") differs in polarity from American enthusiasm ("Great!"). A literal model hears approval in both; a cultural one senses nuance. Designing for such variation demands ethnographic humility: engineers must listen before they teach machines to.

The car again illustrates the stakes. In 2022, Hyundai deployed its "Dynamic Voice Recognition" system trained on 900,000 utterances from 13 countries. It achieved an average 91 per cent command accuracy, yet dropped to 74 per cent for non-native English speakers in cross-tests. The limitation was not technology but training diversity. When expanded to include 40 additional accent clusters, accuracy rose by 10 points across all speakers, including natives. Inclusion improves universality because models learn boundary cases—the edges refine the centre. The quiet motif: edge cases are the product.

Power dynamics complicate trust. In a clinical setting, a senior consultant's voice may override a junior's by authority, not by volume. A fair system must not mirror such hierarchies. Experiments at the University of Toronto (2021) used adaptive weighting—prioritising voices by turn-taking frequency, not pitch. The result: smoother multiparty transcription and fewer dominant-voice artefacts. Voice technology, when careless, re-embeds social bias; when thoughtful, it can reveal and correct it. The implication is political as much as technical: design choices decide whose speech matters.

Household data amplify that politics. A voice profile is more than waveform statistics—it encodes identity, emotion, and even health. A cough, a tremor, a slur may betray medical conditions. When devices in shared homes archive such signals, they create unintended dossiers. Apple's 2022 decision to process HomePod voice data on-device and anonymise identifiers before cloud analysis marks a pivotal shift: safety through ignorance. Yet even anonymisation is fragile; family members can infer each other's habits from command histories. Designers should ask: can any user erase their trace without erasing everyone's convenience? The answer defines whether privacy survives community.

One credible counter-argument insists that per-user personalisation is incompatible with true shared devices. To tailor responses, systems must *remember* who spoke; to forget identities is to forfeit convenience. Reconciliation lies in *bounded memory*. The model keeps context for the session—who is driving, who is cooking—then resets when environment or time changes. The Amazon Echo Show's 2023 "Guest Mode" embodies this principle: it handles casual commands without linking them to accounts. Bounded memory trades friction for dignity. A system that forgets gracefully earns more use over time than one that remembers everything too well.

The recurring image is the room that listens. It hears laughter, argument, music, grief. Every voice carries a claim to space; every system mediates those claims. The ethics of shared voice interaction are neither abstract nor optional—they govern daily life. Measure your design by three indicators: error disparity across accents, mis-attribution across users, and satisfaction across power levels. When those converge, inclusion has become competence.

Still, an unresolved question remains. If the machine learns to separate us perfectly—voiceprints clear, identities distinct—will shared experience fragment too? The charm of the family assistant, the team recorder, the clinical scribe lies partly in communal context. Privacy guards us, but isolation impoverishes us. The next challenge is not merely to hear each speaker, but to preserve conversation itself: a chorus, not a catalogue. The test endures every time a voice says “Alexa” or “Hey Google” and the room answers—who, exactly, is it speaking for?

Chapter 3
Gesture Without Theatre

In 2013, a London commuter, trying to silence a call on his smartwatch, found himself waving frantically at the air. The gesture worked—eventually—but not before attracting a row of puzzled glances from the strangers beside him. The scene, replayed across the early years of motion control, symbolised a curious regression. To make machines understand us, we had begun to perform again. The promise of seamless interaction—hands that simply *do* rather than *demonstrate*—was buried beneath a kind of digital pantomime. Every flourish betrayed an interface still learning the difference between signal and spectacle.

We forget how recent our obsession with visible gesture is. For centuries, human communication evolved around the subtleties of motion—the turn of a wrist, the tilt of a head, the invisible rhythms that make intention legible. Yet the first generation of gesture-driven devices mistook theatre for fluency. Microsoft's Kinect, launched in 2010, could detect a dancer's leap but not a pianist's twitch. It was a marvel of optics, a failure of ergonomics. Precision gave way to display. Designers wanted machines to *see* the body, not to *understand* its economy. It took a decade of refinement—biomechanics, occupational ergonomics, and even the study of sign languages—to reveal a counterintuitive truth: the most humane gestures are often the smallest.

The body, when left to itself, optimises movement. We scratch, point, swipe, and grasp within a narrow envelope of comfort. Biomechanical studies from the University of Tokyo (2019) show that the average thumb can reach an arc of just 83 degrees on a phone screen without strain; every degree beyond that multiplies error and fatigue. The hand's design is a study in constraint, not in flourish. Great interaction design follows that law of economy. The shift from theatrical gesture to micro-gesture—small, repeatable motions that require no audience—marks not technological minimalism but cognitive respect. It restores interaction to its rightful scale: one measured in millimetres, not metaphors.

The motif of *restraint* runs through this chapter. Modern gesture systems, powered by depth cameras and radar sensors, can already detect the flex of a finger at ten centimetres. Google's Soli radar, first embedded in the Pixel 4 (2019), proved that a pinch in mid-air could command music without touch. But the victory was not the novelty of remote control; it was the reclamation of privacy. Tiny motions replace grand waves precisely because they belong to the intimate grammar of human intent. They are signals meant for oneself, not for a crowd. The invisible gesture becomes a quiet act of authorship—a choice that affirms agency rather than broadcasting it.

Yet smallness brings fragility. Gesture recognition remains hostage to physics: hands occlude one another, sensors struggle in sunlight, and bodies differ in range and dexterity. A design that assumes symmetry or youth fails both reliability and dignity. Engineers at the MIT Media Lab once demonstrated this limitation starkly: an algorithm trained on able-bodied subjects misread the tremors of Parkinson's patients as noise, discarding half their intended commands. The same error could frustrate millions with temporary impairments—injury, fatigue, pregnancy, or simply age. The fix was not cleverer vision but broader empathy. When the team retrained models on diverse hand motion data, accuracy improved universally. Inclusion became a performance gain.

The history of human movement offers precedent. Sign languages, which evolved without electronics, already embody the principles of effective gesture design. They privilege economy, repetition, and legibility under varied conditions. A signed phrase must remain clear whether performed in bright light, shadow, or partial view. Each sign balances visual efficiency with muscular endurance. Linguists have long noted how natural sign languages minimise large-arm gestures in favour of handshapes near the torso—the zone of both visual and physical stability. These same principles translate elegantly to digital gesture recognition: centre movement where the body already finds ease; reduce amplitude; prioritise rhythm over reach. The future of interface motion lies not in spectacle but in fluency borrowed from those who have always spoken through the body.

Still, the social context of movement cannot be ignored. A raised hand in one setting is communication; in another, alarm. Public spaces impose a subtle etiquette on gesture. What seems intuitive alone can feel conspicuous in a crowd. The awkward early users of Google Glass (2013) discovered this brutally. A double-tap to the temple, harmless in design labs, became a symbol of intrusion in cafés and streets. The gesture's visibility collided with public norms about privacy. The lesson remains profound: an interface does not live in isolation—it performs within society's theatre, whether it means to or not. Good design, therefore, choreographs discretion. The best gestures are not invisible but *unobtrusive*: clear to those who use them, ambiguous to those who do not.

Accessibility deepens this argument rather than diverting it. Designing for tremor, limited range, or prosthetic use is not a constraint but an accelerator of innovation. Every solution that lowers physical effort expands the domain of possible users. The iPhone's "Reachability" feature—double-tap to lower the screen—originated as an accessibility function; it became a mainstream ergonomic triumph. In gesture systems, the same logic applies. A motion robust enough for tremor tolerance, forgiving enough for partial articulation, will feel effortless to everyone else. The future belongs not to those who optimise for the median body, but to those who build for the body under strain.

There is a moral undertone here. As technology draws closer to the flesh, it inherits a duty of humility. The hand is not an abstract cursor; it is history and labour embodied. From signers and surgeons to carpenters and children, our gestures carry the residue of culture and necessity. Each flick, grip, and press encodes decades of learned efficiency. To overwrite that grammar with novelty for its own sake is to ask the body to unlearn its wisdom. The designer's task is not to choreograph new gestures but to rediscover the ones the body already trusts.

The chapter that follows moves from theatre to tactility, from spectacle to subtlety. It will trace how micro-gestures can outpace grand ones, how occlusion and fatigue shape reliability, how public norms define discretion, and how designing for limitation unlocks universality. Together, these themes suggest a deeper principle: every successful gesture interface must listen to the body as much as it directs it. The reward is not convenience alone, but a quieter kind of mastery—interaction that feels like extension, not instruction.

Perhaps the real innovation is not making machines *see* us, but allowing them to *feel* our restraint. When a flick of a finger suffices where once we waved an arm, we have not diminished expression; we have refined it. Gesture without theatre is not an absence of drama. It is the drama of precision—the moment when the body and the system agree that silence can move the world.

From Pantomime to Micro-Gesture

In February 2010, at Microsoft's headquarters in Redmond, engineers demonstrated Kinect—a motion-sensing system that promised to translate human movement into control. The audience applauded as a tester swung his arms to slice virtual fruit and hurled an invisible ball with theatrical force. The camera responded beautifully. Yet outside the lab, the spectacle soon faltered. When ordinary users attempted smaller, natural motions—raising a hand slightly, leaning, shifting weight—the system often failed to register them. The public's laughter turned to fatigue. Gesture control, once hailed as liberation from buttons, had become choreography for machines. The irony was unmistakable: to make computers understand us, we were forced to perform.

The failure was not technological hubris alone. It revealed a deeper misunderstanding of the body's logic. The human hand is built for subtlety, not spectacle. Its neuromuscular architecture—the fine coordination of 34 muscles and over 25 joints—favours efficiency over flourish. Biomechanics tells us that most daily movements occur within a limited envelope: 15 to 25 degrees of wrist motion, micro-adjustments in grip pressure, and hand paths optimised for balance and energy conservation. Large motions, beyond this zone, introduce tremor, delay, and cognitive load. Yet early gesture interfaces prized visibility, mistaking theatrical amplitude for clarity. They forgot that precision does not scale with size.

Sign languages offer a corrective lens. In 1960, linguist William Stokoe's analysis of American Sign Language established that signed communication obeys grammatical and phonological structure as rich as spoken language. Each sign combines handshape, movement, and spatial orientation, refined by economy and rhythm. Research from University College London (Baker et al., 2016) shows that fluent signers unconsciously minimise motion paths, reducing travel distance by nearly 40 per cent compared with novice signers. The goal is endurance and expressiveness through constraint. What looks effortless is, in fact, biomechanical optimisation—the body discovering fluency within limits. Gesture design that honours this principle inherits a century of embodied efficiency rather than starting from theatrical zero.

We can measure the cost of ignoring it. The MIT Touch Lab (2018) found that full-arm gesture interfaces induce forearm muscle fatigue within five minutes of continuous use—what ergonomists call "gorilla arm." In contrast, micro-gestural systems—small wrist or finger flicks within the comfort envelope—sustain use for over an hour before measurable fatigue. The implication is not aesthetic but structural: scale dictates viability. The smaller the gesture, the longer the system lives in the hand.

A decisive shift occurred when engineers began to translate these human tolerances into machine thresholds. Google's Soli radar project, unveiled in 2015 and commercialised in 2019's Pixel 4, used radar waves rather than cameras to detect fine motion—fingers rubbing together, a thumb circling an index. Unlike optical systems, radar required no theatrical arc, only motion in millimetres. It brought gesture back to the body's natural frequency. The micro-gesture was born not from novelty but from respect for physiology. It proved that reliable interaction need not be loud.

Minimalism, however, demands more intelligence from design. A small motion is harder to read than a grand one; signal-to-noise ratios narrow, occlusion rises. The engineering response—temporal smoothing, predictive modelling, and context inference—mimics the way humans perceive intention. We anticipate continuity: when someone reaches for a cup, we interpret the reach before the grasp. Gesture systems now do the same, interpolating between partial readings to maintain coherence. Apple's 2023 Vision Pro uses "temporal confidence weighting," fusing frames to interpret minute changes in finger distance and gaze vector. The result is not a new grammar but the recovery of the body's existing one.

The motif of *economy* threads through this transformation. Where early motion control celebrated freedom, mature design celebrates restraint. The shift recalls the evolution of dance from baroque display to modern minimalism—Martha Graham replacing ornate gesture with contraction and release. Similarly, the future of gesture technology will not mimic theatre but craft *stillness that counts*. A flick, a pinch, a rotation of the wrist: these become syntax.

Evidence from assistive technology reinforces the argument. In 2020, a team at the University of Cambridge developed "TypeWave," a gesture keyboard for users with limited mobility. It relied on small wrist rotations and finger flexions, producing higher accuracy and lower fatigue than conventional arm-based systems. What began as accessibility research became a template for universal design: optimise for the margins and you strengthen the centre. The biomechanics of constraint—how much motion can be spared, not spent—determines inclusivity.

The counter-example is instructive. VR environments, from Meta's Quest series to HTC's Vive, still often demand exaggerated hand movements to maintain tracking. The reason is technical—optical sensors struggle with occlusion—but the effect is behavioural. Users tire quickly and feel self-conscious. Immersion breaks when effort overshadows intent. Researchers at Stanford's Virtual Human Interaction Lab (2021) found that reducing gesture amplitude by 50 per cent in VR interactions increased retention time and subjective comfort, even when visual fidelity dropped slightly. The trade-off revealed a deeper law: systems that privilege endurance sustain emotion; those that chase spectacle exhaust it.

Design minimalism is not reductionism. It asks where expression lives—in amplitude or articulation. Sign linguists know that a change in wrist rotation can alter a word's meaning entirely; a difference of a few millimetres, not metres, carries semantic weight. Machines that aim to interpret human gesture must therefore learn to read *fine differentials*—speed, acceleration, micro-pause—not just position. This is where biomechanics converges with computation. Motion-capture research at ETH Zurich (2022) showed that the human brain anticipates the energy cost of movement and unconsciously biases toward paths of least resistance. Translating that insight, designers can build gesture models that treat minimal deviation as signal rather than noise. In short: let the human economy drive the machine's understanding.

The cultural consequences of this transition are profound. Large gestures make the body public; small gestures return it to privacy. In a meeting or on a train, a subtle thumb rub to mute audio is socially legible but not performative. The system vanishes, replaced by human discretion. This marks a reversal of the spectacle inaugurated by early motion interfaces—the promise that technology could make interaction visible. Now we pursue invisibility as refinement. A gesture that goes unseen by others but unfailingly recognised by the machine is design's quiet victory.

Yet micro-gesture raises its own tension: where does legibility end and secrecy begin? A gesture too small risks ambiguity; one too large risks exposure. The threshold varies across cultures. In Tokyo subways, a small nod can suffice as assent; in Rome or São Paulo, the same motion reads as indifference. Gesture systems trained on global data must negotiate these semiotic variances without imposing a monoculture of motion. The body speaks dialects; the algorithm must listen plurally.

Minimalist design wins not through austerity but through calibration. The success of Apple's "tap-to-click" trackpads, the double-tap of AirPods, and the slight wrist raise of smartwatches exemplify a philosophy of *near-invisible intention*. These gestures are not discovered—they are recovered. They align with innate motor habits, those unconscious micro-movements we already perform. The best technology does not add motion; it accepts what is already offered.

Returning to the quiet motif—the shift from performance to precision—one sees a moral geometry emerging. Pantomime demanded that humans exaggerate to meet machines halfway. Micro-gesture reverses that demand: machines now work to meet us in our natural scale. It is a restoration of dignity through subtlety. What began as convenience matures into empathy.

And yet a question remains, the diagnostic one every designer must face: how small can a gesture become before meaning evaporates? At what threshold does minimalism turn into mystique—an action so discreet that even its user doubts its effect? The next generation of interfaces must navigate that paradox. They must find the inflection point where movement remains human, not hermetic.

Somewhere between theatre and stillness lies fluency—the space where a flick, a tilt, or a breath aligns with comprehension. That is the territory of the micro-gesture, the point where design stops performing and begins listening.

Error, Occlusion, and the Physics of Hands

In May 2013 in San Francisco, Leap Motion unveiled its much-anticipated controller: a small bar on the desk that promised fingertip precision without touch. Early demonstrations dazzled—ribbons of virtual paint, hovering menus, hands conducting light. Then the public tried to use it at home. Fingers vanished behind palms. Motions jittered when wrists rolled. A hand passing over another hand became a blind spot. Reviews praised the ambition yet recorded a stubborn truth: the camera could not see through flesh. By autumn, developers had begun to build larger gestures merely to keep the system "in view". The technology had been defeated by a simple fact of anatomy. Bodies occlude themselves.

Show the user's hands crossing to pinch a virtual knob; now hear the brittle click of failure—the cursor snaps away. Name the failure: self-occlusion. Explain: optical systems rely on line of sight; when a finger hides behind a palm, depth and pose estimation degrade or collapse. Implication: reliable gesture systems cannot depend on visibility alone. They must anticipate the occlusions that bodies produce, then bridge them with time, with redundancy, and with tactility. Put differently, we have to engineer for hands as they are, not as a camera wishes them to be.

The first mitigation is temporal. Instead of treating each frame as ground truth, mature systems treat it as a noisy sample of a continuous movement. Temporal smoothing—whether via simple moving averages, α–β filters, or Kalman filters—suppresses jitter and resists momentary dropouts. Designers of Apple's Vision Pro hand input (2023) illustrate the point: a micro-pinch is recognised not as a single contact event but as a brief trajectory with velocity and dwell, fused with gaze to disambiguate target. The system "holds" intent across a few frames, allowing a finger that briefly disappears behind the knuckle to complete the action. The behaviour to measure is overshoot-and-correct cycles per task; when smoothing is tuned well, those cycles fall without introducing lag that makes the interface feel syrupy.

Redundancy is the second mitigation. When one sensor is blind, another can see. Google's Soli radar (commercialised in the Pixel 4 in 2019 and later in wearables) reads micro-motion in millimetres and is indifferent to lighting; it will not give you a photograph of a hand, but it will give you motion when a camera cannot. Ultraleap's stereo IR cameras add structured illumination to cut through low light. Depth cameras suppress background clutter; inertial sensors on a controller preserve pose when optical tracking fails. Each modality covers the others' weaknesses. The implication is strategic: do not ask a single sensor to solve physics; design the stack so that loss in one channel downgrades gracefully rather than collapses recognition.

Occlusion's quieter cousin is ambiguity. A hand at the edge of a field of view wobbles between states. Is that an intentional hold or a hover? Here, hysteresis solves more than smoothing can. Hysteresis establishes asymmetrical thresholds—harder to enter a state than to remain in it—stabilising selections against micro jitters. A button "press" might require 12 mm of approach, but only 6 mm of retreat to maintain the state. The metric is "thrash rate": how often a control flickers between on and off within one second. Apply hysteresis and thrash drops; the hand feels steady because the state is.

A third mitigation is fallbacks that respect dignity. When recognition confidence dips, the system must offer alternate pathways without shame. For mid-air interfaces, that means a nearby physical anchor: a hardware key, a capacitive bezel, a wrist-worn tap. For touchless public kiosks, a clearly labelled hygienic touchpad doubles as a fallback. In 2021, several hospitals trialled touch-free radiology viewers during sterile procedures; the successful ones paired air-pinches with a low-profile foot switch. Foot actuation sounds quaint until you realise it solves occlusion, anchoring a critical confirmation to a channel cameras cannot see. The implication is not to romanticise "hands-free" but to acknowledge that crowded contexts need multimodal exits.

Crowded contexts also mean crowded images. In museums, conference halls, and open-plan surgeries, hands overlap other hands. Name the failure: inter-user occlusion. Explain:

when multiple bodies occupy the sensing volume, skeletal models cross-assign joints; your index finger becomes mine. Implication: we must scope authority in space and time. Practically, that means per-user cones of interaction anchored to personal devices or wearable tags, depth-based exclusion zones that only recognise the nearest limb, and turn-taking cues: "I'm listening to the closest right hand for the next two seconds." The behaviour to watch is *mis-attribution rate*—one person's gesture triggering another person's action. Drive it to the floor, and strangers can stand shoulder to shoulder without stealing each other's clicks.

Not all errors come from occlusion. Some are born of biomechanics. Hands tremor; wrists pronate; shoulders tire. The physiology is predictable: the further the limb from neutral, the noisier the signal. Name the failure: amplitude fatigue. Explain: large, outstretched motions magnify unintentional motion and reduce proprioceptive accuracy. Implication: bound the workspace. Keep high-frequency gestures close to the torso; prefer finger articulations over shoulder arcs; allow users to rest their elbows. When Meta shifted Quest hand-tracking algorithms in 2020–2021 to tolerate partial views and smaller motions, user retention for hand-only titles rose because sessions became less tiring. The lesson generalises: reduce required amplitude, and you reduce error even before the algorithms improve.

Tactile confirmation addresses a psychological gap. Mid-air clicks lack a surface; the brain misses the spike of mechanoreceptor feedback that marks completion. Two paths help. One is *illusory tactility*: short haptic bursts on a wristband at the moment of selection, or ultrasound arrays (Ultraleap) creating a perceptible "press" in the air. The other is *visual–auditory coupling*: a crisp auditory tick aligned within ±30 ms of the visual state change. The window matters; outside it, the illusion breaks. Measure pre-commit hesitation—the micro-pause before people release a gesture. Proper haptics and tight audio–visual synchrony shorten that pause, because the body recognises a finish.

Temporal filters can also enforce manners. Debounce windows—minimum times between successive recognitions—prevent double activation from a single enthusiastic motion. Rate limiters cap commands per second. These are small mechanics with large social effect. In a car, where passengers gesture as they talk, a 250 ms refractory period after a "next track" swipe blocks accidental repeats. In a theatre lobby kiosk, a three-second grace after "print ticket" stops the next person's wave from producing clones. The motif is a modest one: *give time edges*. Edges domesticate noise.

We should name a positive counter-example, because theatre is not always folly. Large public displays at festivals or sport grounds often *want* broad gestures to invite participation. There, amplitude is legibility. A sweeping arm tells shy onlookers how to play. The limitation is local: those gestures are episodic and social. Reconciling this with micro-gesture design means asking two questions of context: How long must this be sustained? Who else must share the space while it happens? If the answers are "minutes" and "many", privilege restraint; if they are "seconds" and "a cheering crowd", theatre has its place. Good systems make that switch evident—"Big moves here," "small moves here"—with posture hints and animated affordances.

Engineering for sunlight and shine—two enemies of optical sensing—demands materials as much as maths. Infrared cameras saturate in direct sun; glossy surfaces produce specular highlights that look like joints. Polarising filters, narrow-band emitters, and anti-reflective coatings on enclosures push back. So do *exclusion masks*: software that knows where bright artefacts live in a scene and ignores them. In field deployments of outdoor kiosks in Dubai (2019–2020), teams found that a modest hood above the sensor cut false positives more than an order of magnitude. A shade, not a shader, did the work. The implication: treat optics as industrial design before you treat them as computer vision.

When hands hold tools—pens, styluses, scalpels—another physics intrudes. Tools extend the hand but fracture the image. Name the failure: proxy confusion. Explain: algorithms that lock on fingertips can misread a pen as an index or a glove seam as a joint. Implication: explicitly model tool affordances; don't ask the network to improvise. In operating theatres, teams pair tracking markers on instruments with camera-space hand pose to keep the two from stealing each other's identity. In creative software, pen-in-hand switches the classifier to *tool mode,* where pinch no longer signals "select" but "grip". The metric: mode error—how often a gesture in one mode triggers consequences in another. Reduce it with explicit toggles and visible state.

Error handling must be legible, not merely accurate. Systems that silently ignore low-confidence gestures force users into pantomime, repeating motions more forcefully until they tire. Better to surface uncertainty succinctly: "I lost your hand—move closer," aligned with a subtle outline showing the valid zone. Avoid scolding; offer a map. Observe the *rage-gesture* rate—repeated, exaggerated motions after failure. If it rises, your explanations are failing even if your models are not.

The social layer matters. Certain gestures carry meaning beyond interface. A mid-air pointing finger in a clinic can be mistaken for blame; a repeated pinch can look like mockery. Design movements that are personally legible, socially modest, and culturally neutral where possible. The airline industry's "two-finger point" for ground crew directs attention without aggression; interface designers can borrow its ethos: precise, small, unambiguous. Measure *bystander discomfort reports* in pilots of public installations; when the gesture set is right, those reports evaporate even as completion rates climb.

All of this collapses to a single practical motif: *engineer for the hand's shadows*. Shadows in time (dropouts), in space (occlusions), in context (crowds), and in meaning (social signs). Tackle time with smoothing and hysteresis; space with redundancy and bounded workspaces; context with access cones, fallbacks, and filters; meaning with modest choreography and cues. The reward is not only fewer errors but a different affect. Confidence grows when the system forgives physics.

Still, an unresolved tension persists. Every filter adds lag; every fallback adds complexity; every redundancy adds cost. Where do we stop? Put it as a test before launch: if a user stands in a queue with a coffee, one hand occupied, strangers close, light harsh, and music loud—will your gestures still register without embarrassment or fatigue? If not, which physics will you respect—time, space, or society—and which will you trade? The next generation of gesture systems will be judged not by how well they track hands in a lab, but by how gracefully they handle the shadows our hands cast on the world.

Social Legibility and Public Norms

In March 2013, the 5 Point Café in Seattle announced a ban on Google Glass before the device had even launched, warning patrons that camera-equipped headsets would be unwelcome on the premises. The statement was tongue-in-cheek, but the result was concrete: headlines, arguments, and a new term of social stigma—"Glasshole." The café's owner had intuited something designers had missed. Gesture and gaze are never private in public. A double-tap to the temple looked like surveillance, not convenience. The room was watching. What felt like effortless control to the wearer read as threat to everyone else.

That small episode foreshadowed a decade of awkward choreography between bodies and bystanders. In labs, grand gestures are charming. In queues, lifts, and carriages, they are conspicuous. The paradox is simple: gestures must be legible to the person using them yet unobtrusive to those nearby. Fail and you earn glances, then glares, then bans. Succeed and the movement disappears into local etiquette. This chapter argues for a humane middle: motions designed to be clear from the *inside* and ambiguous from the *outside*. The shift demands engineering discipline, yes, but also anthropology: a sensitivity to how rooms, crowds, and cultures negotiate meaning long before algorithms do.

Show, name, explain, imply—the engine of design argument—begins with visibility. Show a commuter on the Jubilee line raising an arm to "air-swipe" a notification away. A nearby passenger looks up, unsure whether the gesture is directed at them. Name the failure: *public misattribution*. Explain: large, directional movements trigger the social reflex that "gestures address people." In shared spaces, body language defaults to interpersonal signalling; interfaces that borrow theatrical cues are therefore misread as social ones. Implication: design gestures whose vector lives within the user's personal envelope—close to the torso, centred around the hands—so their meaning is *self-addressed*. The same motion should read as control from within and as fidget from without.

The opposite case—unreadable subtlety—is just as corrosive. Show a hospital registrar hovering in front of a touchless kiosk, fingers making micro-pinches that staff cannot interpret. Name the failure: *operator opacity*. Explain: the movement gives no outward cue that "a command is in progress," so bystanders interrupt or attempt to help, compounding delay. Implication: pair small motions with modest, outward-facing signals: a soft halo on the screen that follows the operator's hand, or a brief tone audible at close range. Legibility outward need not be loud; it only needs to be *local*. Design the aura, not the wave.

A named, checkable example shows how etiquette can be engineered. At Apple's developer conference in San Jose in June 2018, watchOS introduced *Raise to Speak* for Siri. The wearer no longer had to say a wake phrase in a quiet carriage; a subtle wrist lift brought the assistant to attention. The cue was private and plausible—people already lift a watch to check it. A visible behaviour changed: fewer public "Hey, Siri" calls, less collateral activation. The implication is broader than one feature. When gestures piggyback on *existing* social motions, they borrow the legitimacy of habit. The room keeps watching, but it no longer minds.

A second example locates legibility inside a car, a famously charged social space. At Mobile World Congress in Barcelona in February 2019, BMW previewed *Natural Interaction*, combining gaze, small hand cues, and voice. The system mapped a driver's micro-pointing and eye fixation to in-car targets, avoiding theatrical sweeps. Crucially, it bound gesture zones to the driver's half of the cabin, preventing passengers' talkative hands from hijacking controls. Here the behaviour to measure was *mis-trigger rate by seat*. After binding zones and shrinking motions, spurious activations from the passenger side fell. The implication is a principle: in multi-user spaces, restrict the authority of gesture to a personal cone, and publish that boundary in the interface so others understand who is "on stage" and who is not.

Social legibility also depends on cultural semantics. A thumbs-up is benign in London, rude in parts of the Middle East. The "OK" ring can be misread in some contexts. Designers cannot sanitise all symbolism, but they can trim the risk surface. Show a set of default gestures for a global product. Name the task: *semantic de-risking*. Explain: prefer motions defined by trajectory rather than static hand shapes; movements are less culturally freighted than postures. Implication: when you must localise, localise the pose, not the physics. Keep the same small path, change the handshape where needed, and display the variant during onboarding. The metric is support tickets referencing "offensive gestures" by region. If they drop without harming completion time, you have tuned meaning without losing speed.

Crowds intensify scrutiny, so *where* a gesture lives matters. Show a museum foyer with an interactive wall. When the installation invites wide arm motions, the crowd copies, nudging strangers. Name the tension: *theatre versus throughput*. Explain: large movements attract, but they slow the queue and create collisions. Implication: use theatre to teach, micro-gestures to transact. A public installation might open with broad, forgiving motions—"wave to start"—then transition to smaller, precise ones for navigation and payment. The behavioural split to measure is dwell time per visitor and pass-by obstruction. A well-designed arc shortens both after the initial lure, proving that spectacle can coexist with civility when staged.

A credible counter-example reminds us that flamboyance has a place. In October 2012 at London's Barbican Centre, Random International's *Rain Room* invited visitors to walk through falling water that stopped wherever a body was sensed. Big movements were not only acceptable; they were the point. Theatre communicated availability. Reconciling this with our thesis is straightforward: public norms are not moral absolutes but *local contracts*. In a gallery, a crowd expects display; in a clinic, it expects discretion. The design question is not "grand or small?" but "what does this room license?" The metric is *bystander expectation match*: survey delight versus discomfort against the setting's declared script. Tune the motions to the contract, not to an ideology of minimalism.

Because rooms have rules, *introductions* matter. Show a new gesture system in a co-working lobby. Name the tool: *social onboarding*. Explain: a ten-second loop of animated, human-scale hands demonstrates acceptable ranges—elbow tucked, hand near sternum—and shows a subtle glow around the active user. Implication: you set norms before transgression. The room learns by watching. The measure is first-time error and intervention by staff. If both fall after adding the loop, you have taught etiquette without a manual.

What about stigma, the lasting scar of misreading? The Google Glass backlash hardened not only because of cameras but because wearers looked like they were *doing something to others*—aiming, recording, scanning—without consent. Stigma grows when motives are illegible. To prevent it, surface purpose. Show an AR headset that shifts its outer light from idle to "private control" to "capturing," with distinct colours. Name the pattern: *outward-facing state*. Explain: the wearer gets feedback; bystanders get assurance. Implication: the less people must guess, the less they attribute malice. Count confrontations or requests to remove the device per operating hour. If they fall after adding clear state, the room has relaxed.

Small mechanics also civilise small motions. Micro-gestures risk invisibility; invisibility risks interruption. The fix is *near-field signalling*. A short haptic tick on the user's finger at gesture start and a soft chime audible within a metre at gesture commit—never beyond—create a social bubble of awareness. The decision is architectural: couple sound pressure level to proximity sensors so the chime scales to the crowd. Measure step-backs and "sorry"s triggered by surprise. If those micro-frictions decline, near-field signalling is working.

Shared devices multiply these demands. Kitchens, cars, and clinics host layered authority. Who is allowed to issue which gestures? Show a family speaker that follows any hand wave to skip a song. By week's end, a seven-year-old controls the playlist. Name the gap: *authority ambiguity*. Explain: when motion is treated as generic, power defaults to whoever moves first. Implication: bind permissions to identity cues—voice profile, nearby phone, wearables—and display a discreet label—"Alex controlling"—on the screen or LED ring. The behaviour to watch is *contested control*: verbal disputes or repeated overrides. Fewer disputes mean norms and electronics now agree.

The motif returns: the room was watching. Bystanders will always appraise not just movements, but motives. That appraisal is rapid. So design the *frame* around motion to carry intent. In UI terms, a tiny caption—"Mute for 30 seconds"—anchored near the user's fingers in AR says "I'm managing my device, not you." In physical terms, a posture hint—shoulders relaxed, elbows bent—displayed during onboarding helps people look like they are *with* the room, not *against* it. Measure *observer inference accuracy*: can strangers, when asked, guess what someone is doing? If yes, and they are unbothered, you have achieved legibility without spectacle.

Accents of motion matter as much as accents of speech. The speed, cadence, and rhythm of gestures vary by community. Southern European talkers use more expansive hand movements; Nordic norms skew smaller. A one-size gesture set will alienate someone. The solution is to tune recognition to local cadence without forcing users to choose a "culture pack." Systems can measure the central tendency of amplitude and speed in a locale and adjust thresholds invisibly. The behavioural signal is *gesture false-reject rate by region*. If it drops after adaptive tuning, inclusion has become performance, not a poster.

There is a risk in all this care: paralysis. Designers can become so wary of misreading that they minimise gesture to the point of magic tricks—tiny cues no one can see, brands no one can learn. Here, a counter-pressure helps. Choose one anchor gesture per context that is deliberately public and benign. In a meeting room, perhaps a two-finger pinch at chest height to advance slides. In a kitchen, a palm-down hold to stop timers. Make the anchor visible, then let everything else shrink. You give the room a single, non-threatening emblem to recognise, reducing anxiety about the rest. The metric is *first-week recall of the anchor*. Aim high; the emblem becomes etiquette.

Finally, norms must be stewarded, not assumed. Product teams can instrument not only success rates but social consequences. Track *bystander complaint rate, misattribution incidents,* and *abort-and-switch-to-touch* in public pilots. Interview front-of-house staff—baristas, receptionists, nurses—who live at the coalface of awkward gesturing. When they report fewer interventions, you are closer to a fit between motion and place.

We end where we began: with the room watching. Social legibility will never be solved by sensors alone. It is a compact between those who act and those who witness. So set the hard test before you ship: if your gesture had to be performed on a crowded 08:32 train from Clapham Junction, with one hand on the rail and a stranger's elbow at your ribs, would it work—and would anyone care? If not, what will you shrink, what will you signal, and what will you surrender to keep dignity intact?

Designing for Disability First

In August 2018, Microsoft's Inclusive Tech Lab in Redmond released the Xbox Adaptive Controller—a white rectangular device with two large black pads and twenty-one custom ports. It was built for gamers with limited mobility, but its impact spread far beyond. Within months, occupational therapists were using it to train stroke patients in rehabilitation centres. In classrooms, children with muscular dystrophy could play side by side with peers for the first time. The paradox was unmistakable: a controller designed for constraint became the most universally flexible interface in the company's history. Accessibility had not narrowed the audience; it had expanded it.

Designing for disability first is not charity. It is a method—a way of surfacing edge conditions early so that the product learns to survive the real world's messiness. Tremor, prosthetics, and limited range are not deviations from normality; they are magnifications of it. Every human, under stress or fatigue, temporarily shares those conditions.

When we design for them, we discover universals that endure. The physics of motion, the tolerance of sensors, the patience of feedback loops—all are tested most honestly at the margins. The disabled body is not an exception to optimise away but a teacher of resilience.

Consider tremor, the designer's perennial adversary. In 2016, a study by Imperial College London measured average finger-tip oscillation in essential tremor patients at 7–10 Hz. Yet consumer gesture sensors at the time sampled at 30–60 frames per second, treating each frame as intent. The result: noise mistaken for action. Show the behaviour—a user attempting to pause a video mid-air, the system interpreting ten separate commands. Name the failure: *over-responsiveness to involuntary motion*. Explain: motion sensors without temporal filtering cannot distinguish stability from jitter. Implication: once you stabilise for tremor, you stabilise for life. Temporal smoothing, hysteresis, and dwell thresholds designed to accommodate a shaking hand also protect a tired one. The calibration that dignifies disability also prevents error in the able-bodied majority.

A named example grounds this logic. In 2020, Google's Android Accessibility team released *Voice Access 2.0*, integrating gaze tracking and dwell-time gestures for users with motor impairments. The team found that setting a minimum dwell time of 350 milliseconds before selection, initially to reduce tremor-triggered misfires, improved accuracy for all users by over 20%. The principle generalised: the body, given time, reveals clarity. Waiting became a form of respect.

Limited range teaches similar lessons. The biomechanics of restricted motion expose inefficiencies invisible to designers with full reach. At the University of Cambridge's Inclusive Design Group, researchers in 2019 mapped common gesture arcs for users with partial shoulder mobility. The finding was striking: most people, regardless of ability, operate comfortably within a hemisphere extending 40 centimetres from the torso. Beyond that, precision and endurance fall sharply. Designing within this *comfort envelope*—smaller, nearer, slower—makes interaction not only more accessible but more sustainable. Smartphones already exploit this: Apple's "Reachability" mode halves the effective height of the screen so thumbs, not arms, can finish the job. What began as accommodation has become default ergonomics.

Prosthetics sharpen the argument further. The prosthetic hand is a system of sensors, actuators, and prediction—an embodied algorithm. Every movement is a negotiation between residual muscle signals (EMG), mechanical lag, and intent inference. When researchers at the University of Utah's Center for Neural Interfaces (2020) integrated tactile feedback into a bionic hand, they discovered an unexpected consequence: users moved more slowly but with higher confidence, reducing error rates by half. The same principle, applied to gesture recognition, underpins "confirmation haptics"—tiny vibrations or clicks signalling that a command has landed. Prosthetic research proved what interface designers later rediscovered: speed without certainty exhausts trust.

The motif of *constraint as revelation* recurs. Show a designer watching a user with Parkinson's struggle to complete a swipe. Name the insight: *movement as dialogue, not demand.* Explain: tremor is not noise to suppress but a rhythm to match. Algorithms that anticipate rather than interrupt produce interfaces that feel sympathetic, not punitive. Implication: machine empathy begins with mechanical patience.

Counter-examples are instructive. VR systems that demand sustained arm gestures—Meta's early Quest controllers, or HTC's 2017 Vive—privilege bodies that do not tire easily. After ten minutes, even those bodies tremble. The designers had not failed ergonomically; they had failed inclusively. When researchers at Stanford's Virtual Human Interaction Lab (2021) re-engineered a VR selection gesture to operate within a 20-degree arc rather than full extension, task completion rates rose for all users. What accessibility had discovered, performance refined: range limits liberate precision.

Designing for prosthetics also challenges assumptions about what a "hand" must do. A 3D-printed prosthesis may rotate differently or lack tactile feedback altogether. Interaction models that rely solely on fine-grained finger poses collapse. Yet once interfaces begin to accept alternate input—pressure sensors, EMG signals, or head tilts—they evolve from *gesture recognition* to *intent recognition*. The implication is systemic: diversity of input breeds robustness of system. The inclusive interface becomes a fault-tolerant one.

Apple's AssistiveTouch, introduced in 2011 and continually refined, exemplifies this principle of adaptive equivalence. Users who cannot perform multi-finger gestures can map those commands to single taps or dwell actions. The engineering challenge—ensuring that one signal can safely emulate many—produced a framework for gesture abstraction later reused in the Vision Pro's hand tracking. Accessibility work, initially peripheral, became the kernel of the next platform's input logic. The direction of innovation reversed: the margins wrote the core.

The social dimension follows the technical. When interfaces dignify constrained motion, they shift public perception of agency. Show a commuter using a head tilt to answer a call; bystanders no longer see incapacity but discretion. Name the outcome: *normalisation through visibility*. Explain: the more diverse gestures become, the less any single motion codes as "abnormal." Implication: inclusion scales not by hiding difference but by multiplying forms of fluency. The visible diversity of gesture becomes social proof that accessibility is not a retrofit but a foundation.

A quieter motif runs beneath—*fidelity*. Designing for tremor teaches machines to wait; designing for prosthetics teaches them to infer; designing for range teaches them to constrain. Each adjustment refines the dialogue between signal and meaning. Fidelity here is not accuracy alone but understanding. Systems that tolerate deviation without collapsing embody what the social theorist Rosemarie Garland-Thomson called "misfit design"—architecture that expands to meet the body, not the reverse. When gesture interfaces behave like that—flexible, forgiving—they cease to be assistive technology and become humane technology.

Accessibility research has a measurable innovation yield. A 2017 report by the UK Design Council found that inclusive design projects generated returns up to four times higher than conventional ones, owing to their discovery of unanticipated user segments. Microsoft's adaptive hardware line, initially niche, became a model for modular input across devices. The metric is not sentiment but survivability: products that work for constrained bodies tend to endure longer because they fail less often in messy reality. The physics of human variance make them robust.

Still, the temptation persists to separate "accessibility" from "innovation"—as if one were ethics, the other excellence. The record says otherwise. Many of the defining technologies of the last half-century began as disability aids: typewriters from Braille devices, the telephone from Alexander Graham Bell's work with the deaf, voice recognition from speech therapy software. Each moved from necessity to convenience to ubiquity. The lesson is historical, not rhetorical: invention starts where constraint bites hardest.

The counterpoint deserves honesty. Some accessibility features do not generalise neatly. Eye-tracking systems for users with locked-in syndrome, for instance, demand environmental control far beyond mass-market feasibility. Designing for disability first cannot mean designing *only* for disability. The reconciliation lies in *translation*: extracting the principle, not the apparatus. Eye-tracking may not suit everyone, but its underlying insight—intention inferred before motion—has already migrated into predictive typing and attention-based gestures. Innovation moves by abstraction, not replication.

The most advanced accessibility research now blurs categories altogether. In 2022, a team at MIT's Media Lab developed *AlterEgo,* a wearable that detects subvocalised speech through neuromuscular signals along the jawline. Intended for people with limited speech, it also hints at silent, private computing for everyone. The loop closes: accessibility as prototype, universality as consequence. The disabled body again acts as the avant-garde of interface evolution, revealing what all bodies might one day adopt.

The quiet motif returns—constraint as revelation. When we start from limitation, we design systems that forgive, adapt, and endure. The inverse rarely holds: technologies built for the median user crumble at the edges. Accessibility-first design is therefore a strategy of realism, not benevolence. It asks: if the system can survive tremor, occlusion, prosthetics, and fatigue, what remains that could break it?

If it cannot, what must we change—our algorithms, our assumptions, or our patience?

The unresolved tension endures. To design for disability first is to accept slowness, redundancy, and calibration as virtues. Yet markets prize speed, minimalism, and scale. The question every designer must face is this: when the next product brief demands elegance at pace, will we remember that the surest route to universality still begins at the margins?

Chapter 4
Seeing Through and Seeing With (AR/VR)

In February 2023, surgeons at St. Mary's Hospital in London wore headsets during a complex spinal procedure—not for spectacle, but for survival. Through the transparent lenses of a Microsoft HoloLens, digital vertebrae floated above the patient's real spine, glowing in precise alignment with the bone beneath. The operation was quieter than most. No one stared at a flat monitor; everyone looked through it. Yet in that silence lay a profound shift: for the first time, digital information occupied the same physical space as human intention. What began as a 3D toy for architects and gamers had become a tool of clinical precision—and, more subtly, a mirror of human attention itself.

Augmented and virtual reality are often framed as technologies of immersion, but the more revealing question is not *what* they show, but *how* they divide. Every pixel inserted into the visual field competes with the world already there. Attention, once flat, becomes volumetric—a resource with depth, density, and dwell time. The promise of "heads-up" computing has long been sold as freedom from distraction. Yet the paradox remains: seeing more often means noticing less. Each layer we add to perception demands a hierarchy of focus, and those hierarchies can help or harm depending on how they are built.

In an aircraft hangar in Hamburg, Airbus engineers test maintenance procedures through AR overlays that highlight bolts and pressure lines. The results are impressive: inspection time drops by 30%. But fatigue rises too. Workers report visual strain after long sessions, their eyes fighting to reconcile competing depths—the real bolt and its ghostly twin. This is the core problem of AR design: not realism, but registration. Too close, and overlays occlude; too distant, and they detach. The geometry of attention becomes the geometry of ethics: how much digital density can a human safely inhabit before the world itself becomes background noise?

The challenge shifts again when environment dictates risk. In domestic spaces, AR may guide a child through homework or a cook through a recipe; the cost of error is minor. In an industrial yard, a misplaced overlay could hide a hazard. The rules of augmentation must therefore adapt to context. In a ward or a factory, the overlay is not decoration but liability. The best systems now use risk-informed layers: highlight only what saves time *and* prevents harm. The logic is architectural—each environment has its own visual bandwidth, and designers must allocate it with the care of an engineer rationing oxygen.

Presence—so often the measure of immersion—is in truth a physiological negotiation. The body does not care about narrative; it cares about equilibrium. When motion cues from the inner ear disagree with those from the eye, nausea follows. The early years of virtual reality were haunted by this betrayal. Even now, simulator sickness remains the quiet tax on every promise of "embodied computing." At NASA's Ames Research Center, researchers still use flight simulators to study recovery times, setting limits on angular acceleration and frame latency. Their findings echo across design disciplines: comfort is not a by-product of fidelity but a craft of constraint. The trick is not to simulate reality perfectly, but to fail gently.

Yet immersion need not mean enclosure. The future lies in porous realities—systems that can switch between "seeing through" and "seeing with." In the first, information overlays the world; in the second, it collaborates with it. Seeing *through* is instruction. Seeing *with* is partnership. A mechanic who glances at a jet engine through AR glasses sees torque values and safety notes; a field medic using mixed reality in a disaster zone sees vitals hovering over the wounded but can also reach and act without hesitation. The tool does not intrude; it orbits the task, staying just within peripheral readiness.

What distinguishes a demo from a durable workflow is not spectacle but stamina. Many prototypes of the past decade dazzled investors and fatigued users. Sustainability depends on repetition: can a worker, student, or surgeon return to the same AR interface daily without loss of comfort or trust? The transition from novelty to normality demands attention to training time, task rhythm, and recovery intervals. Lockheed Martin's AR-guided assembly of spacecraft panels achieved consistency only after reducing cognitive load—one visual cue at a time, one frame of clarity earned through discipline rather than dazzle.

And here lies the deeper significance of AR and VR: they are less about simulation than calibration—of perception, of patience, of the thresholds between focus and fatigue. They force designers to treat attention as a finite physical medium, to measure presence not by awe but by endurance. The philosophical question is not whether the digital will merge with the real; it already has. The question is whether humans will remain its reference plane, the horizon against which every new overlay must align.

The motif of this chapter—the interplay between *seeing through* and *seeing with*—is ultimately about trust in perception. We will move from the mechanics of spatial attention to the ethics of overlay density; from the bodily limits of comfort to the institutional limits of reliability; from isolated demos to long-term, high-stakes workflows in clinics, factories, and homes. What we will discover is that the success of immersive technology depends less on how convincing the illusion is, and more on how well it lets reality breathe.

Before we look further, one question lingers: as our tools grow capable of painting information directly onto the air, who decides what deserves to be seen, and what must be left invisible? The answer may define not just the design of interfaces, but the texture of reality itself.

Attention as a 3D Resource

In February 2019 at Mobile World Congress in Barcelona, Microsoft unveiled HoloLens 2 alongside partners from Airbus. On the stage, a technician looked through the visor at an aircraft panel while fasteners and torque values hovered in space, seemingly stitched to the metal itself. The demo was quiet, confident, persuasive. Yet the deeper lesson sat just off-screen. For the technician to benefit, the overlay had to *compete* with the real rivets, labels, glare, and human hands already in view. Information had entered the same volume as the task. From that moment, attention stopped being a flat surface and became a three-dimensional budget: depth, density, and dwell.

Show the visor illuminating a bolt head while a real spanner glints in peripheral vision. Name the conflict: spatial overlays versus the world. Explain: the brain must reconcile two depth fields—the rendered layer and the physical scene—while moving, grasping, and avoiding risk. Implication: the designer is no longer arranging panels on a screen; they are allocating scarce visual oxygen in a room. When augmentation crosses from novelty to work, *where* a cue sits is as important as *what* it says.

Treat attention, then, as a 3D resource with three levers. First is *density*: the amount of visual information per unit of space. Second is *depth*: the placement of overlays at distances the eye can fuse without strain. Third is *dwell*: the time a cue remains before it becomes noise. Each lever has thresholds set by physiology, not fashion. Overdraw any of them and the scene becomes fog.

Density declares its cost immediately. In an aircraft hangar or a factory aisle, too many labels at once create what technicians call "snow". Snow hides hazards. The rule of thumb is conservative: one actionable element per foveal fixation, two to three contextual elements in parafovea, and the rest deferred until summoned. This is not minimalism as taste; it is minimalism as safety. The behaviour to monitor is head jitter and re-reads; when density drops within humane limits, both fall, because the eye no longer hunts for signal.

Depth is trickier because it lives in biology. The eye converges on a target and the lens accommodates to bring it into focus. AR breaks this coupling by placing a virtual label at a different focal plane from the object it annotates. The result can be subtle discomfort or outright fatigue. A disciplined approach pins overlays to *task depth*: if you annotate a valve at 60 centimetres, keep the label within that convergence band. Push secondary cues behind or ahead by deliberate steps, not scatterplot. The implication is design craft as choreography: pull the next instruction into the user's depth only when their gaze commits, then send it back when the hand arrives. Make depth earn its keep.

Dwell is where time rescues space. Leave a cue up for too long and it becomes wallpaper. Remove it too fast and it becomes a flicker that chips away at trust. A useful pattern is graded persistence: a cue arrives at full salience, dims gently once acknowledged, and lingers as a hairline outline until completion. The behaviour to watch is "recall taps" or equivalent re-query actions; the right dwell curve lowers them without raising error. In short, let time carry memory so space can breathe.

All three levers converge on a blunt truth: *heads-up is not heads-free*. We have confused the posture of attention with the relief of attention. Lifting information into the line of sight does not remove cognitive load; it repositions it. A pilot can see an artificial horizon in a head-up display and still miss a warning light if the luminance is wrong. A surgeon can read an angle in her visor and still misplace it if the measurement floats at the wrong depth. The head may be up; the mind is still full.

A named case makes the point concrete. In Hamburg, Airbus engineers have trialled AR inspection flows that speed up panel checks. Productivity improved. Yet teams reported greater visual fatigue late in the shift. The cause was not bad content but shallow rules: overlays clung to the same depth and luminance whatever the background. When the system was tuned to push non-critical cues into peripheral space and to fade them dynamically against reflective surfaces, comfort rose and rework fell. The implication is general: *adaptive salience* should be a first-class feature, not a postscript. Let the overlay read the room before it edits it.

Domestic spaces tell a softer version of the same story. Recipe prompts hovering above a chopping board feel delightful—until steam, knives, and children enter the frame. Here density and depth become ethics. A timer that floats too low occludes the blade; a step that lingers too long invites overconfidence. A humane kitchen overlay rides high, retreats to the wall when hands approach the board, and compresses into a single pictogram when motion gets brisk. Measure near-misses—hesitations before cuts, re-glances mid-chop—and treat those metrics as seriously as completion time. Speed without safety is theatre.

Clinical spaces raise the stakes again. In a ward round, vitals pinned above a patient's bed can prevent error. The same overlay can also betray confidentiality if it blooms before consent. Context must govern density. In a multi-bed bay, the default should be *latent cues*: small, private anchors that expand only within the clinician's cone of gaze and within the patient's permission window. The signal to watch is not clicks but glance latency—the time between first look and confident action. If overlays are doing their job, that latency contracts without raising voice-to-voice verification, because comprehension has kept pace with caution.

A credible counter-example reminds us that sometimes theatre is the point. In museums and stadiums, large overlays attract and teach. Density invites play before it retreats for transaction. Reconcile this with restraint by staging: lead with spectacle to recruit attention, then collapse to micro-guides to respect space. The metric is not "engagement minutes" but *clearance*: can people move without collision while still learning? If yes, spectacle has been domesticated.

Why, physiologically, does "heads-up" still demand such care? Because attention has geometry. Humans sample the world through a narrow fovea (~2 degrees), guided by saccades that land two to three times per second. AR that assumes a constant, wide, cinema-like gaze exhausts those mechanics. Good systems place their most critical cues at the next likely landing spot, not wherever looks pretty in a render. The motif to hold onto is modest: *meet the saccade*. Anticipate where the eye will go and seat the overlay there, not an instant sooner.

Motion adds another dimension to the budget: *stability*. Mixed-reality content that lags or swims breaks trust. Even tiny registration errors—centimetres at arm's length—force the brain into compensatory micro-corrections. Temporal smoothing and model-based prediction help, but the interaction rule is plainer: move the cue *less* than the hand would move it. Let the digital world be a touch steadier than the real one. The behaviour to watch is micro-pause before commit; when overlays feel stable, that pause shrinks because the hand believes what the eye is told.

All of which explains why "heads-up" fails when it pretends to be a neutral upgrade. In cars, head-up displays reduce glance down time, which is good, but they also tempt designers to add weather, music, and messages to the windscreen, which is not. The road is already a full overlay. The correct question is not "can we show it?" but "what must now be hidden?" Heads-up is a trade, not a gift. Treat every new annotation as a subtraction elsewhere: a warning admitted means a flourish evicted.

Two further rules sharpen the craft. First, *align modality with risk.* In noisy or high-risk environments, show less but *signal* more clearly with secondary channels. A crisp spatial audio cue can carry urgency without visual clutter; a haptic pulse on the wrist can confirm a selection without reaching for more photons. Second, *bind instruction to action.* Present the next step at the depth of the object it governs and dismiss it as the hand arrives. Do not narrate from the balcony when the scene is on the stage.

A pair of examples shows how these rules travel. In Fort Worth, Lockheed Martin's AR guidance on spacecraft assembly moved from a showpiece to a shop-floor tool only when overlays were sequenced ruthlessly: one fastener, one torque, one confirmation—no galleries of extra data. Training time dropped because cognitive load did. In London theatres experimenting with caption glasses for accessibility, designers learnt to place text just below the stage horizon, not directly over faces; audiences read *with* the performance, not through it. The visible behaviour was fewer head bobs, more steady viewing. Both cases turn on deference: the overlay yields to the work.

A limitation keeps us honest. Current optics often render at a fixed focal distance, so even disciplined placement cannot fully solve accommodation–vergence conflict. The reconciliation is to design *forgiveness* into scenes. Avoid rapid alternation between near and far labels; collapse clusters into a single anchor with a micro-menu; give the eye a place to rest—neutral zones of plain space where nothing changes. In VR, the equivalent is comfort mode locomotion and snap turns; in AR, it is calm breathing room around hands. Give the user somewhere to park their gaze.

The quiet motif returns: attention as oxygen. Every overlay consumes some. Some consumption is vital, some is theft. The ethics of AR and VR begin with this ledger. To be a good custodian of attention is to measure what you take. So track the right signals: mis-selections per task when overlays crowd; glance latency when depth mismatches; re-query rates when dwell curves are off; nausea reports when motion prediction lags. Publish them internally as hard constraints, not soft suggestions. Make density, depth, and dwell as measurable as frame rate.

We are left with a forward test. If you had to justify each pixel in your field of view the way a pilot justifies each item on a checklist, which would remain? Which would you dim, delay, or delete to return oxygen to the room? Heads-up can be liberating—when it remembers that the head is attached to a body that moves through risk. Heads-free is a myth; heads-wise is a choice.

Context Boundaries: Homes, Factories, Wards

In April 2020, clinicians at Imperial College Healthcare NHS Trust in London donned Microsoft HoloLens headsets on COVID-19 wards to keep senior decision-makers "in the room" while reducing exposure. The headsets streamed a clinician's viewpoint to colleagues outside the isolation bay, while key vitals hovered above the patient's bed. It worked. Decisions accelerated and fewer people entered hot zones. Yet an interesting constraint shaped every screen: overlays could not drift across oxygen taps, bed-rails, or monitors. Nothing was allowed to obscure hands, lines, or alarms. In a crisis, mixed reality learnt the oldest rule of the ward: first, do no harm to perception. The headset drew a boundary around reality and stayed behind it. That boundary—variable across homes, factories, and wards—defines whether augmented systems help or hinder. It is a design line as real as tape on a floor. Respect it.

Show a house, a hangar, a hospital. Name the difference: hazard profile. Explain: each environment carries distinct risks—domestic clutter and children in kitchens, heavy plant and moving loads in factories, sterility and confidentiality in wards. Implication: the same overlay cannot behave identically in each place. Information must inherit the room's rules. Treat context like voltage: mismatched overlays shock.

Homes tolerate charm and tolerate delay. Factories tolerate neither. Wards tolerate nothing that smuggles error. These tolerances are not tastes; they are safety budgets. In the kitchen, floating timers and step-by-step prompts may sit high on a wall and shrink politely when hands approach the knife. In a factory aisle, an overlay that annotates a torque sequence must never occlude pinch points or hide a forklift's trajectory. On a ward round, vitals can bloom within the clinician's cone of gaze, but names and diagnoses must stay latent until consent is clear. The motif returns: the tape on the floor. If the overlay crosses it, trust leaves the room.

Begin with the home. Show a parent cooking while a child darts through. Name the design task: graceful retreat. Explain: domestic overlays should give way to bodies, pressure, and heat. When a hand enters the working plane, UI should lift and simplify; when motion accelerates—whisking, chopping—it should compress to icons or step counts at the edge of vision. Implication: domestic AR succeeds when it behaves like a considerate guest. Measure near-miss hesitations before cuts, glance latencies toward the hob, and re-reads of steps; if those shorten without raising errors, density and placement are serving the home's low-stakes, high-ambiguity rhythm.

Now the factory. Show a technician at Airbus in Hamburg aligning fasteners with an AR visor; a crane moves overhead; a colleague crosses behind. Name the pattern: hazard-aware occlusion. Explain: overlays must be repelled by danger zones—drawn off sharp edges, kept out of lift paths, dimmed against glare. Systems should inherit safety signage hierarchy: what's red in paint stays red in pixels. Implication: overlays in industry should read the room before they redraw it. Measure mis-selections near hazards, head jitter indicating visual search, and rework rates after guided steps. When overlays respect exclusion zones and luminance, the numbers calm down. People do too.

The ward is different again. Show a bed space at St Mary's in London: oxygen line, pump, drip, monitor. Name the boundary: sterility and dignity. Explain: the headset cannot demand gestures that break scrub or ask for confirm taps that force a nurse to touch the visor. It cannot display identifiable data until the patient's privacy status is clear to all in the bay. It must support deference to consent rituals and hand hygiene. Implication: clinical overlays must be operable hands-free with voice, glance, and foot-switch fallbacks; patient-sensitive data should appear only within the wearer's narrow gaze cone and collapse when another body enters that cone. Measure glance-to-action latency and staff hand hygiene compliance in MR-assisted workflows; if both remain strong, the overlay has earned its place.

Across environments, one claim holds: spatial computing is an amplifier. It makes good choreography better and bad layout worse. Show a poorly lit factory shelf with overlapping labels; AR superimposes more labels, and chaos deepens. Name the failure: additive clutter. Explain: overlays that annotate flawed physical signage multiply confusion. Implication: fix the room before you flood it. Hazard-aware AR starts with physical housekeeping—contrast, light, clear lines—then adds pixels as the last layer. Improvements here are visible: fewer re-reads, fewer "what now?" mutters, fewer aborted tasks. You are measuring human relief.

Density follows context. Domestic spaces accept lightweight narration; industrial ones demand parsimonious, state-coupled prompts; clinical ones insist on event-driven minimalism. The rules are learnable. In homes, show depth-stable prompts at wall or appliance depth and let them dwell longer; attention is intermittent and interruptions frequent. In factories, pin instructions to the object's working depth and advance by completion detection, not by time; attention is continuous but must pivot to hazard instantly. In wards, use latent anchors that expand on fixation and shrink at motion onset; attention is shared, and dignity is a co-actor. Implication: do not ask users to "choose a profile"; make the system infer the profile from light, sound, proximity, and schedule. The boundary tape ought to lay itself.

Risk informs not just what to show, but what to hide. Show a head-up display in a car that tries to be clever: music, messages, weather on the windscreen. Name the temptation: heads-up inflation. Explain: the road is already an overlay. Anything non-critical is theft of attentional oxygen. Implication: reserve windscreen real estate for road-consequential cues—speed, hazards, arrows—push the rest to a peripheral instrument or drop it entirely. Measure lane-keeping variance and glance durations; if they improve, a subtraction saved a life.

Workflows reveal exposure. In Fort Worth, Lockheed Martin's AR-guided assembly achieved credibility only when each overlay encoded a small commitment: one fastener, one torque, one confirmation. Show the behaviour: a hand arrives, the cue brightens, and vanishes on completion. Name the tactic: micro-staging. Explain: micro-staging limits the amount of mental state a worker must remember at once, shrinking the surface on which errors can land. Implication: hazard-aware overlays are *narrow* and *sequenced*. The metric is not raw speed but rework and deviation per build stage; those curves tell you whether the overlay has learned the shop floor or just visited it.

Privacy is a hazard in its own right. Show a clinician approaching a curtain bay with a visor. Name the rule: consent-first reveal. Explain: overlays containing identifiers should remain placeholders until the wearer performs a consent ritual—a voice phrase or gaze dwell that doubles as an audit mark—and the patient is appropriately covered. Implication: treat dignity as a safety layer. The numbers to watch are patient complaints, data exposure incidents, and time-to-rapport at the bedside. If rapport survives and incidents fall, risk-informed design honoured the ward.

A credible counter-example keeps us cautious. Public museums and stadiums sometimes benefit from theatrical overlays: big beacons draw people in and teach at a distance. The limitation is duration and density. Reconcile it with staging: recruitment uses spectacle; instruction uses restraint. You measure the right things—congestion, pass-through time, collision reports—not only applause. If queues move and bodies do not bump, the show respected the room.

Fallbacks matter where risk is high. In homes, a missed gesture costs time; in factories, it can cause harm; in wards, it can cost a life. Show a sterile radiology suite trialling touchless image manipulation. Name the safeguard: redundant confirmation channels. Explain: pair mid-air pinch with a foot-switch or a sterile elbow tap; pair voice with a dwell; provide a "deadman" hold that halts playback when contact breaks. Implication: hazard-aware overlays commit to multimodal failsafes by default in high-risk zones. Measure abort-and-recover rates; rising recoveries with steady completions signal that the guardrails are catching slips before they cascade.

Then there is the matter of light and sound. Domestic spaces flicker with televisions and sunlight; factories roar; wards hum and beep. Show an overlay that ignores this, flooding every context with the same palette and tones. Name the error: modality deafness. Explain: the environment sets the channel. In kitchens, visual cues may dominate; in factories, spatial audio cuts through; in wards, haptics and dim visuals respect sleep and pain. Implication: choose the signalling modality that least competes with the room's dominant channel. You'll see it in behaviour: fewer repeats, fewer "say again?" moments, fewer night-time awakenings.

The motif returns to the tape on the floor. In every environment, draw a mental line where pixels yield to physics. In a home, it is the countertop and the hob; in a factory, the moving edge and the lift path; in a ward, the bed-rail and the face. Program the line. When hands or hazards cross it, overlays should retreat automatically. This is not flair; it is ethics turning into software. The measure is late-shift steadiness: do users still trust the guide after hours of work? Trust is continuity under fatigue.

Two named contrasts sharpen the frame. First, Airbus's inspection trials show that industrial overlays succeed when they inherit safety colours, obey line-of-sight priorities, and bind instruction to object state. Second, Imperial's COVID-19 pilots show that clinical overlays earn their keep when they reduce exposure without increasing cognitive load—streaming to colleagues, pinning vitals, shrinking at touch. Each case rests on the same principle: adopt the room's risk model, don't impose one. That makes the overlay a guest of the environment, not an invader.

A limitation keeps this honest. Current optics cannot always match focal planes to real depth; devices are heavier than glasses; voice fails in noise; gestures fail in gloves. Reconcile this with *risk-weighted abstention*. If the device cannot behave safely in a context—foggy yard, dim ward, loud floor—it should degrade gracefully or withdraw. Nothing in the field is better than the wrong thing in the face. Record withdrawal events as a virtue, not a defect; they prove the system respects its boundary.

We end with the forward test that matters. Imagine the overlay asked permission from the room before it spoke—from the cooker, from the crane, from the patient. What would each allow? What would each forbid? Homes will admit guidance if it moves when knives move. Factories will admit instruction if it never blocks hazard and never steals luminance from warnings. Wards will admit augmentation if it honours sterility and consent before anything else. Design the overlay to pass those interviews. If a line of tape has to be laid in code, where will you put it, and what will you refuse to cross?

Presence, Nausea, and Cognitive Load

In March 2020, Valve released *Half-Life: Alyx* from Bellevue, Washington. The game arrived with a telling default: teleport or "shift" locomotion, not smooth analogue movement. Reviewers praised the choice as much as the set-pieces. The outcome was concrete—longer first sessions, fewer abandonments—because the studio treated comfort as design, not as a disclaimer. Presence was earned, not forced. Presence should never punish physiology.

Show the player stepping into a narrow virtual corridor while their real body stands still. Name the conflict: cue mismatch. Explain: the vestibular system reports no acceleration while vision announces forward motion; the brain resolves the contradiction as threat. Implication: designers must reconcile, not deny, the dialogue between eyes and inner ears. This is the first law of immersive craft: perception is a negotiated treaty.

The science is old. In 1975, J. J. Reason's sensory conflict theory framed motion sickness as disagreement between visual, vestibular, and proprioceptive cues (Reason & Brand, 1975). In 1993, Kennedy, Lane, Berbaum, and

Lilienthal introduced the Simulator Sickness Questionnaire (SSQ), still the field's standard for symptom tracking. These anchors matter because they turn an aesthetic problem into an instrumented one. If presence is to be more than awe, it needs thresholds and tests.

Begin with *latency*, the invisible tax on trust. Motion-to-photon lag above a few tens of milliseconds erodes stability; saccades land on moving targets; the world swims. Oculus's public best-practice notes have long pushed for high refresh (90 Hz+) and low end-to-end latency with strict frame pacing (Oculus, 2017). Show a user turning their head; now count stutters. Name the metric: dropped-frame rate under head rotation. Explain: a single stutter can increase SSQ disorientation scores; repeated stutters compound nausea. Implication: ship comfort budgets as hard constraints—e.g., *no more than one dropped frame per 10 seconds during 120°/s head yaw on target hardware*. Test it. Fail it, and delay features rather than degrade physiology.

Next, *optic geometry*. Inter-pupillary distance (IPD) miscalibration forces the eyes to converge unnaturally; vergence–accommodation conflict asks them to focus at a fixed plane while converging at virtual depths. Show a user reading a floating panel "at arm's length". Name the stressor: vergence–accommodation split. Explain: repeated depth hops without rest increase oculomotor strain; users report brow ache long before nausea. Implication: keep critical text at the device's optical sweet spot; cluster depth changes; insert neutral "rest planes". The behaviour to watch is blink rate and dwell time before re-reads; stabilise both and comprehension rises as symptoms fall.

Locomotion is the emotional core. Two examples show how comfort scaffolds presence. Valve's *Alyx* (2020) offered three modes—teleport, shift, continuous—with vignette and snap-turn options. Snap-turns (discrete angular steps) reduce vestibular–visual conflict by avoiding smooth yaw without matching ear cues. The metric that moved was completion length of first sitting; players stayed longer. Sony's PlayStation VR ecosystem, launched in 2016, layered "comfort ratings" and default vignettes for smooth locomotion; studios that adopted these conventions reduced refund and abandonment rates. Comfort is measurable. Treat it that way.

But do not over-generalise. Flight simulators and racing rigs present a credible counter-example. Skilled users tolerate continuous motion longer, especially when a fixed frame—a cockpit, a dashboard—grounds vision. Name the exception: stable reference frames. Explain: the virtual cockpit acts as a visual anchor; the brain forgives motion when something "solid" remains. Implication: reconcile by providing diegetic frames for free-move scenarios—helmet rims, vehicle bodies, wrist-anchored HUDs. Measure SSQ nausea subscale differences with and without frames at equal speeds. If the frame stabilises, you may safely expand motion envelopes—*for that cohort*.

The motif through all of this is *recovery by design*. Assume some users will wobble. What then? Recovery is not an apology screen; it is a protocol. Show a user who has just experienced vection-induced nausea. Name the sequence: step-down, reset, return. Explain: first, drop to a static, horizon-present scene with low spatial frequency and minimal parallax; second, restore control via gaze or small hand motions; third, reintroduce complexity in layers when the user signals readiness. Implication: build a one-button "calm scene" directly into the shell and expose it to players and operators. Measure time-to-comfort fall (self-reported) and heart-rate variability as proxies. The goal is not to prevent all symptoms—they vary—but to shorten their half-life.

Comfort also lives in *attention budgets*. AR and VR differ here. In AR, overlays compete with a live world; in VR, overlays are the world. Both can drown a user in density. Show a headset flooding the fovea with tooltips. Name the failure: attentional overdraw. Explain: working memory carries three to four items; every extra label steals stability. Implication: enforce "one step foregrounded, one step pending" rules; demote the rest. Observe glance latency and back-and-forth head jitter; when overlays thin, jitter drops and dwell smooths.

Now craft thresholds. Without numbers, teams drift. Reasonable, defensible ranges exist across the literature and industry practice. *Angular velocity*: keep induced yaw below user-driven head-turn speeds unless a stable frame is present; snap-turn at 30–45° increments with brief blinks or vignettes. *Translational acceleration*: avoid non-user-initiated surges; ramp velocities; begin and end moves with eased curves (LaViola, 2000; Stanney et al., 2020). *Text*: maintain at or near optical focal distance; avoid small fonts at virtual near-depths. *Audio*: couple spatial audio to virtual anchors; sudden off-screen audio with no visual correlate raises startle and load. These are not dogma; they are perimeters. Stay inside them by default; cross them deliberately with justifications and tests.

Speaking of tests, make them bite. The SSQ is the backbone, but pair it with behaviour. Pre- and post-exposure SSQs (total and subscales: nausea, oculomotor, disorientation) plus task metrics yield truth. Add a head-motion stress test—controlled yaw and pitch sequences at set speeds—and a short vection challenge (striped tunnel) to profile sensitivity. Log motion-to-photon latency under instrumented head turns using a photosensor rig; measure dropped frames during worst-case scenes. Run A/Bs on vignette gains and snap-turn step sizes. The laboratory precision pays dividends: when comfort regressions creep in, you will see them in numbers before they show up in refunds or in clinicians cutting sessions short.

Recovery is also social. In clinics and training centres, operators need escalation ladders. Show a trainee pilot at NASA Ames pausing during a motion-base simulator run; the instructor reduces gain, freezes visuals, and preserves audio to keep presence without vection. Name the craft: graded de-immersion. Explain: remove the offending cue first; keep others stable; never pull the floor from under perception all at once. Implication: give coaches sliders—visual gain, vignette strength, locomotion mode—and train them to intervene. Record intervention counts per hour and subsequent SSQ deltas; the right ladder lowers both.

Hardware matters. Higher refresh helps; better lenses reduce smear; lighter headsets lower neck load and fatigue. Yet hardware alone does not absolve software. Valve Index raised comfort ceilings with 120–144 Hz modes; nonetheless, games that ignored locomotion craft still made users ill. Conversely, *Alyx* felt comfortable on lower-spec hardware because it deferred to human tolerances. Presence is partnership. Treat devices as ceilings; design as the floor.

Inter-pupillary distance calibration is a small hinge with a big door. Automatic IPD detection or easy mechanical sliders drop oculomotor complaints dramatically. Show two users sharing a headset in a lab; the one who skipped IPD fitting leaves early. Name the trap: friction that invites misfit. Explain: if fit is optional, discomfort becomes default. Implication: force a quick, accurate fit step; make it delightful; store profiles; remind users to refit on handoff. Track early exits and self-reported eye strain; a proper fit turns both curves.

Design *diegetic rest*. Games did it first: a lift, a safe room, a cockpit. Enterprise can learn. Provide recurring low-motion segments where cognition continues while movement quietens—inventory review, briefing, data entry. Users recover without leaving presence. Watch for SSQ drift over forty-minute sessions with and without these seams. The curve with seams shallows; you have bought stamina.

One more example, from healthcare. In 2018–2021, several UK trusts piloted VR for burn dressing changes and physiotherapy. Programmes that paired high-engagement content with strict comfort guardrails—teleport, slow fades, soft audio—kept sessions within tolerable bands; those that chased spectacle saw high early drop-off. The visible decision was whether the VR experience matched pain's own rhythms: shorter loops, predictable transitions, and immediate exits. Clinical comfort is care.

A limitation keeps us honest: susceptibility varies wildly. Hormonal cycles, migraine history, sleep debt, and even reading disorders can modulate cybersickness risk (Stanney et al., 2020). No universal threshold will suit all bodies. Reconcile this with *adaptive comfort*. Offer per-user comfort profiles that quietly adjust vignette strength, locomotion, and snap-turn sizes based on early micro-signals: micro-sway, blink rate, corrective head motions, frequent pausing. Privacy-respecting, on-device inference can manage this without sending biometric profiles to the cloud. The measure is convergence: do individual SSQ scores stabilise over multiple sessions as the system learns? If so, adaptation is real, not rhetoric.

Finally, language matters. Call comfort settings "comfort", not "advanced". Place them first-run, not buried. Teleport is not lesser; it is wiser. Teams that dignify protective defaults report better reviews and longer play or work times. Words steer pride. Pride steers choices. Choices steer physiology.

We return to the motif: presence as a pact. The pact reads simply—*we will never buy immersion with your equilibrium.* That pledge has consequences. It means delaying flashy movement until the optics can carry it. It means shipping vignettes and snap-turns even if trailers look less cinematic. It means investing in test rigs and SSQ runs rather than polishing particle effects. It means teaching coaches to de-immerse with grace.

The unresolved question is the razor's edge of the medium: how far can we push embodied illusion before we must step back for the body's sake? Put it as a release test for your next AR/VR build: if your delight requires users to ignore their inner ears, what will you change—your locomotion, your optics, your defaults, or your ambition? Comfort is not a constraint on presence. Comfort *is* presence, sustained.

From Demo to Durable Workflow

In May 2019 at Lockheed Martin's plant in Fort Worth, technicians assembling F-35 substructures trialled augmented-reality guidance on the line. Early showpieces gave way to a quiet shift: specific fastener sequences floated at the workface, torque values appeared only when a wrench approached, and on-the-spot verification replaced after-the-fact inspection. The outcome was not applause in a demo hall but an internal decision: expand the system to more stations because rework fell and training time shortened. The lesson was prosaic and profound. AR/VR succeeds when the spectacle recedes and the shift lead nods. Day two matters more than day one. That is the seam to design for.

Show the glossy concept video: perfect lighting, immaculate floors, a task completed in a minute that usually takes twenty. Name the failure: *non-representative conditions*. Explain: demos remove variance—noise, fatigue, interruptions—so they inflate performance and hide fragility. Implication: to cross the seam between pilot and practice, build the mess into your method. Measure performance in the worst hour of the shift, not the first hour of the trial. If the curve holds at 15:00, you have something worth scaling.

Boeing's much-cited wiring trials offer a checkable anchor. Between 2015 and 2017 in South Carolina and Washington state, teams used head-mounted displays to overlay harness routes on 787 fuselage sections, reporting faster completion and fewer errors (Boeing/Upskill, 2017). Show the behaviour that made the difference: annotation bound to the exact depth of the work, one step present, the next step ready, nothing else. Name the principle: *micro-staging*. Explain: large tasks decompose into atomic actions with immediate verification; cognitive load stays within working memory. Implication: durable workflows require sequencing rules expressed in code—no more than one active instruction in fovea, strict dismissal on completion, and automatic pause when hands or hazards enter the frame. The metric is rework per station; when micro-staging is real, rework flattens.

A counter-example is instructive. In 2020, an automotive plant in the Midlands piloted VR for complex gearbox assembly training. Trainees performed brilliantly in the rig and stumbled on the floor. Name the gap: *fidelity illusion*. Explain: VR captured geometry but missed the affordances that matter—tool weight, cable drag, restricted posture, and line noise. Implication: reconcile by blending modes. Use VR for procedural scaffolding, then AR on the line for transfer, with a final supervised live run. Measure *transfer delta*: time-to-first-independent-completion minus time-to-VR-completion. If the delta shrinks cohort-by-cohort, translation is working. If it does not, you have a cinema, not a pipeline.

Training time is the hinge on which ROI turns. Shorten it without degrading judgement and the programme earns its keep. Show the onboarding that scales: first-run fit for IPD and comfort, a three-minute "comfort contract" that sets locomotion and snap-turn defaults, and a one-page runbook glued to the device cart. Name the craft: *friction budgeting*. Explain: every minute spent fighting the tool is a minute stolen from learning. Implication: budget your friction like you budget your frames. Record setup time, first-error time, and first-success time; publish them on the wall. If leaders can glance and see the median new-hire reaching competence in hours rather than days, expansion writes itself.

Reliability is not mean time between failures alone. It is the predictability of get-started, stay-started, and recover-gracefully. Show a hospital educator in Manchester rolling a case of headsets into a teaching ward. One unit refuses to track. Name the invisible killer: *start-of-session attrition.* Explain: when a third of sessions begin with troubleshooting, adoption dies quietly. Implication: engineer *boring starts*. Devices charge in carts, auto-update off-hours, self-test on undock, and expose a single green/red readiness light. Measure *abort-before-content* rate. Drive it down ruthlessly. Reliability begins before pixels render.

Return to Lockheed's seam. The expansion decision did not rest on averages; it rested on *variance*. The stations that struggled did so consistently at the same step transitions—overlay flicker under bright reflection, occlusion when a second pair of hands entered, torque prompts that persisted a beat too long and blocked the next fastener. Name the tactic that fixed it: *line-side telemetry*. Explain: log per-step dwell, mis-selection, undo, and back-step counts; correlate them with light level, time of day, and operator. Implication: ship instrumentation and accept what it reveals. Durable workflows are tuned on the seam, not theorised in the lab.

Healthcare offers a second named example with a different seam. In April 2020, Imperial College Healthcare NHS Trust used HoloLens on COVID-19 wards in London to stream a clinician's viewpoint to colleagues and overlay essentials—oxygen saturation, drug doses—above the bed. The concrete outcomes were reduced exposure and faster consults. What made it durable were *consent-aware overlays* and *hands-free recoveries*. Show the behaviour: identifiers stayed latent until a brief gaze-based unlock; critical values pinned at bed depth; a foot-switch advanced steps when gloves or masks confounded voice. Name the pattern: *risk-informed restraint*. Explain: the overlay inherited the ward's rules—sterility, dignity, deference to alarms. Implication: in clinical rollouts, ROI is not time alone; it is fewer breaks in sterile field and fewer staff exposures. Log both. The seam respects bodies as well as budgets.

ROI slips if support is centralised. A single expert becomes a bottleneck and, eventually, a saboteur by absence. Show the anti-pattern: a Slack channel full of "Who knows how to..." posts. Name the need: *local ownership*. Explain: create a cadre of line champions—operators, not evangelists—who own day-two reality: battery swaps, fit checks, content bug reports, and runbook updates. Implication: measure mean time to recovery for common failures and the proportion of issues resolved without central engineering. If local resolution approaches 80%, you are scaling process, not just devices.

We should speak plainly about content. Hype promises AI that "just understands the task". Day two finds a subject-matter expert uploading seven PDFs and a spreadsheet. Show the content author peering at a tool called "Studio." Name the threat: *authoring debt*. Explain: if content creation requires engineers, the pipeline clogs and updates lag behind reality. Implication: build a two-speed stack: stable primitives maintained by specialists (tracking, registration, audit), and domain content editable by SMEs under guardrails. Track content update lead time from change request to live; when it drops under a week for routine edits, you have a living system rather than a fossil.

Reliability in AR/VR is also infrastructure: light, space, network, power. In a factory, reflective surfaces blind sensors; in a hospital, Wi-Fi handoff kills streams; in a home, sunlight washes displays. Show the plant adding a matte finish to a jig, the ward adding a dedicated SSID and QoS for video, the kitchen adding a small hood over a stove-mounted camera. Name the habit: *field hardening*. Explain: small physical interventions often buy more reliability than software cleverness. Implication: budget for paint and brackets as seriously as for licences. The visible metric is failure cause distribution; when "environmental" shrinks, your system is moving from demo to daily.

Now to procurement, the quiet saboteur. Many projects die at the purchase order because the business case counts licences but omits rework avoided, training shortened, or incidents prevented. Show the simple ledger that convinces a CFO: time-to-competence curves, rework curves, incident curves, and device uptime. Name the instrument: *operational ROI*. Explain: tie every curve to money: labour hours saved, scrap reduced, penalties avoided, patient harm averted. Implication: state assumptions and publish ranges; update them quarterly with real data. Confidence grows when your estimates get more accurate as deployments spread.

A credible limitation keeps us honest. Beyond a certain density of overlays or session length, gains reverse. Visual strain and cognitive fatigue rise. The reconciliation is to schedule *rest seams* into the workflow. Show a spacecraft assembly flow that inserts a thirty-second still frame after each major stage for documentation and eye rest—no parallax, no prompts, a clear horizon. Name the move: *built-in recovery*. Explain: presence without pause is extraction; presence with pause is endurance. Implication: measure SSQ oculomotor sub-scores and late-shift error clustering; if both settle, your pipeline respects bodies.

Trust is not a feeling alone; it is a set of reversible mechanics. Durable workflows carry *undo* into the field. Show a torque applied in error; the overlay offers an immediate "mark and reverse" pathway that summons a supervisor if thresholds are crossed. Name the ethic: *reversibility at speed*. Explain: people explore and adopt when errors are survivable. Implication: track undo frequency, time-to-recovery, and the proportion of undos that avert rework. Where those metrics exist, usage grows; where they don't, tools sit in cupboards.

The motif returns—*day two*. On day two, batteries will fail, staff will rotate, fixtures will move, and someone will attempt a task the content never anticipated. Systems that survive share three traits. First, *legible state*: every user can see what the system thinks—tracking good, registration confidence, network health—without guessing. Second, *local editability*: the right person can fix a typo, swap a part number, or change a tolerance within minutes, with audit. Third, *graceful abstention*: when confidence drops or risk rises, the system steps back and tells you why. This is humility converted into reliability.

Education and maintenance are the long tail of scaling. A programme that cannot afford refreshers rusts. Show a quarterly ten-minute micro-module pushed to devices—new gestures, revised prompts, a reminder on IPD fit. Name the practice: *maintenance of competence*. Explain: skill decays; clamp the decay with regular, light lifts. Implication: monitor performance drift across cohorts; if week-twelve looks like week-four, your refreshers work. If not, add a seam, not a sermon.

There is also the politics of adoption. AR/VR threatens some roles and flatters others. Ignore this and you'll meet polite resistance. Show the tact that works: invite the best sceptic to co-own the pilot, attach the safety officer's checklist to every overlay, and treat champions as partners, not mascots. Name the outcome: *distributed legitimacy*. Explain: legitimacy moves along the path of respect. Implication: track voluntary usage on unsupervised shifts; when usage holds on nights and weekends, the culture has moved.

Two final examples bring the seam into focus. In Barcelona in 2019, BMW previewed Natural Interaction—gaze, voice, and small hand cues bound to in-car targets. The show was smooth; the scale-out succeeded where per-seat mis-

triggers were driven down by binding gestures to seat-local cones and by short, on-device tutorials at start-up. The metric that mattered was not applause but *mis-trigger rate by seat*. In London theatres from 2018, caption glasses for deaf and hard-of-hearing audiences matured from novelty to necessity when text placement settled just below the stage horizon and devices self-checked on pickup. The behaviour that told the truth was *early returns to the kiosk*: they fell.

We return to the seam. From pilot to practice is a change of question, not only a change of scale. Demos ask, *Can this be done?* Durable workflows ask, *Can this be done again tomorrow by someone tired, under pressure, in the worst corner of the room?* That question has a cost and a yield. It demands discipline—instrumentation, runbooks, rest seams, reversible paths, local ownership. It pays in curves that hold and in devices that leave their carts. The unresolved test is simple and sharp: if the cameras were off and the executive left the building, would the shift lead still set the headsets out at dawn? If not, what must you change—your sequencing, your ownership model, your comfort budgets, or your business case—to make day two as inevitable as day one?

Chapter 5
The Thin Line to the Brain

In December 2022, a man named Noland Arbaugh sat in a Texas lab with a small array of electrodes pressed against the surface of his brain. Quadriplegic after a diving accident, he lifted a cursor across a computer screen with nothing but intention. The moment—filmed by Neuralink and watched by millions—was presented as a triumph of will made visible. Yet what the system actually "heard" from his cortex was not thought, nor language, nor emotion, but voltage patterns correlated with specific motor imagery. A mathematical model guessed, refined, and displayed a signal close enough to feel miraculous. The distance between thought and cursor was just a few millimetres of cortex—and an ocean of interpretation. That ocean is the territory this chapter crosses: the thin line between reading the brain and believing we can.

The promise of neural interfaces has always danced on the edge of metaphor. For decades, headlines have promised "mind control" and "thought-to-text", flattening the science into sorcery. But beneath the theatre lies a field of extraordinary rigour. Brain–computer interfaces (BCIs) do not decode ideas; they detect correlations between electrical activity and movement, focus, or speech attempts. The signal is faint, the noise immense, and the risk—ethical and biological—real. Every millivolt must earn its claim. The work of the coming decade will not be to make BCIs *more magical*, but more truthful: to clarify what they actually know, and to build social contracts strong enough to hold them.

Clinical pioneers already know the stakes. In 2004, researchers at Brown University implanted a microelectrode array—the BrainGate system—into the motor cortex of a man with spinal cord injury. By 2012, participants could control robotic arms to grasp cups or steer cursors with measurable accuracy (Hochberg et al., *Nature*, 2012). These were not consumer gadgets but hospital devices, surrounded by ethicists, clinicians, and engineers. Every movement was rehearsed, consented, and reversible. The beauty of those studies lay not in spectacle but in restraint: the understanding that a signal may enable motion, but it must never compel it.

That principle—*command through consent*—is what separates assistive technology from intrusion. When we translate it beyond the clinic, it becomes design philosophy. Imagine a future in which a lightweight headset infers your level of attention to adjust notifications, or an office device predicts fatigue from EEG patterns. Who owns that data? Who decides when the system should act, or pause, or forget? Neural design without consent protocols is surveillance by physiology. Command must always remain reversible; input must always come with an *undo*.

Yet consent alone cannot defend dignity if the system's origin forgets its roots. BCIs were born in rehabilitation medicine—born to give agency back, not to extract it. Turning clinical instruments into consumer conveniences demands humility. Every electrode, every algorithm, carries the moral lineage of its first use: to restore voice to those who could not speak, movement to those who could not move. To trivialise that heritage by selling "neural wellness" or "mind optimisation" apps without validation is to erode the credibility of an entire field. Lessons from assistive BCIs must travel intact into the marketplace: transparency, testing, reversibility, and a presumption of care.

The engineering challenge ahead is not merely precision but interpretation. Signals are easy to collect and perilous to misread. The difference between intention and attention, between recognition and recollection, is not just semantic—it is ethical. A sensor might capture changes in alpha rhythm when a user views an image, but whether that equates to *liking* or *agreeing* is a leap of faith disguised as inference. Neural correlates are *correlates,* not confessions. The discipline that will define neural computing is therefore not data science but epistemology: the study of what we can claim to know from signals that whisper.

This is why the next generation of BCIs must embed *reversibility* in every layer. A neural command, once sent, should decay in time unless renewed; permissions should lapse automatically. The concept of *time-locked consent*—borrowed from medical ethics—will soon become interface design. You will authorise an action not indefinitely, but for the next hour, the next session, the next gesture. Neural data, like medication, expires. In that expiry lies safety.

The dignity test sits as the chapter's quiet motif: a checklist that asks of every brain-connected system, *does this expand agency for the least powerful?* The measure is simple but ruthless. If a neural interface enhances convenience for the able but excludes or exploits the vulnerable, it fails the test. If it gives employers access to worker fatigue but not workers access to rest, it fails. If it trades introspection for extraction, it fails utterly. Dignity must be the unit of progress as surely as bandwidth is the unit of data.

History reminds us how easily enthusiasm can outrun ethics. In the 1970s, deep-brain stimulation trials promised cures for everything from depression to aggression, sometimes with disastrous results. In the 2010s, commercial EEG headbands promised cognitive enhancement with little validation. Each wave follows the same arc: discovery, exaggeration, correction. The maturity of neural technology will be measured by how swiftly it learns the rhythm of that arc—and how deliberately it resists repeating it.

As the line between assistive and augmentative use blurs, the social contract must strengthen. What we are building is not a single interface but a new sensory channel between person and machine, one that collapses distance faster than language can moderate it. The risk is not dystopia—it is drift: the quiet normalisation of systems that act before we ask. A neural interface should be a mirror that waits for permission, not a gate that swings by habit.

This chapter follows that tension from lab bench to living room. It will trace how signals become stories, how consent becomes design, and how dignity becomes the boundary condition for progress. Along the way, it will show that the hardest engineering problems are not electrical but ethical: not how to reach the brain, but how gently to leave it.

The frontier ahead is not a question of hardware miniaturisation or algorithmic accuracy alone. It is a question of trust, built millisecond by millisecond between voltage and meaning. The next revolution in human–machine interaction will not come from reading minds but from respecting them. The thin line to the brain is also the line of responsibility—and it runs both ways.

Signals, Noise, and What BCIs Can Actually Infer

In April 2019, at the University of California, San Francisco, neurosurgeon Edward Chang and his team published a study that stunned the scientific community. Using a set of electrodes resting directly on the cortical surface, they reconstructed intelligible sentences from neural activity as participants spoke aloud. The precision was remarkable: 97 per cent word accuracy when limited to a small vocabulary, dropping steeply once the sentences turned novel (*Nature*, Chang et al., 2019). The story was reported as "mind reading". It was not. The electrodes detected electrical patterns in the motor cortex that control lips, tongue, and larynx—movement, not meaning. The algorithm predicted phonemes, not thoughts. The gap between articulation and intention, between movement and mind, is the central fact of brain–computer interface (BCI) research. The closer we get to decoding neural activity, the more urgently we must resist the fantasy of omniscience.

BCIs translate physical correlates of thought, not thought itself. Every electrode—whether implanted in cortex, pressed against the scalp, or worn as a headband—listens for electrical potential differences caused by populations of neurons firing together. These signals fade quickly and are submerged in noise: muscular artefacts, heartbeat, blinking, environmental interference. The earliest electroencephalography (EEG), captured by Hans Berger in Jena in 1924, required stillness and shielding to record the first alpha rhythm. A century later, even the best non-invasive sensors face the same physical limits: skull, skin, and motion blur distort the signal-to-noise ratio. The noise is not a technical nuisance. It is a boundary of inference—a reminder that neurons whisper, and silicon shouts.

Every BCI must choose between intimacy and longevity. Implanted arrays such as Utah microelectrodes, used in the BrainGate trials from 2004 onwards, achieve millisecond precision and can isolate activity from tens to hundreds of individual neurons. They allow direct motor control, as when a participant guided a robotic arm to drink coffee unaided. Yet those same electrodes provoke scar tissue that degrades signal quality within years. The visible behaviour is signal drift; the biological cause is the body's immune rejection. Implanted systems are powerful but impermanent. At the opposite end, consumer EEG headsets promise accessibility but sacrifice granularity. Their dry electrodes read averages from millions of neurons at a distance, more akin to weather forecasts than to words. Between these extremes, electrocorticography (ECoG) balances fidelity with clinical viability—used during surgery, tolerated for weeks, but unsuitable for daily use. Each modality carries a physics of truth. What a device *can* read determines what it *should* claim.

The motif that threads through this field is translation—and every translator must face ambiguity. Show the difference between "signal detected" and "signal understood". Name the temptation: *magical thinking*. Explain: marketing, media, and wishful inference inflate correlation into comprehension. Implication: a new literacy is required, one that treats neural data as a *hint* rather than a confession. When a user wearing a headband scores higher on an "attention" scale, the metric often reflects eye-blink suppression or frontal muscle tension, not focus in any cognitive sense. The visible behaviour—less blinking—produces a cleaner waveform, and the algorithm mistakes cleanliness for concentration. The ethical outcome is confusion weaponised as optimism.

One example clarifies the boundary. In 2021, researchers at Stanford University used implanted arrays to enable a man with paralysis to "type" by imagining handwriting. The system achieved 90 characters per minute (Willett et al., *Nature*, 2021). Yet the decoder worked only because the user rehearsed letter shapes, each with its own unique neural signature in the motor cortex. The model learned pattern–

motion pairs, not language or intent. The difference is not pedantic; it defines consent. If a system can only infer rehearsed patterns, its actions are predictable and reversible. If it claims to read spontaneous thought, reversibility vanishes. Evidence must remain the anchor of inference.

There is a counter-example worth studying. In 2013, a flurry of consumer EEG products emerged—NeuroSky, Emotiv, Muse—promising mood detection, focus tracking, even emotion regulation. Their devices used four to fourteen scalp sensors and proprietary "engagement" metrics. Independent studies later found weak or inconsistent correlations between device readings and cognitive states, especially in uncontrolled environments. The gap between marketing claim and measurable reliability exposed the field's credibility risk. Once hype enters the bloodstream, correction becomes harder than discovery. Reconcile the paradox: public imagination funds progress, but exaggeration poisons trust. The solution is radical transparency—publish accuracy rates, error margins, and environmental dependencies as visibly as battery life.

The question, then, is what BCIs can *actually* infer with reliability today. Implanted systems can reconstruct intended hand trajectories with mean angular errors below ten degrees; ECoG systems can decode speech elements at accuracies approaching 80 per cent when vocabularies are constrained to a few hundred words. Non-invasive EEG can detect broad states—wakefulness versus drowsiness, engagement versus relaxation—with confidence only under controlled conditions. Beyond that, claims dissolve into noise. No system can yet discern belief, emotion, or abstract reasoning directly from brain activity. The metrics that look persuasive on conference slides—correlation coefficients, confusion matrices—collapse under real-world variance: sweat, movement, caffeine, daydreaming. The brain is not a keyboard.

Show the temptation to cross that line. Name the danger: *over-interpretation*. Explain: once a correlation exists, the urge to extrapolate to causation follows. Implication: ethical governance must regulate inference, not just collection. A company may not store "belief data" because such data do not exist in any measurable form; yet if its algorithms label EEG patterns as "attention level 0–100", the label itself becomes a fiction with consequences. Teachers may grade focus, employers may rank engagement, insurers may judge risk. The harm arises not from the signal but from the story told about it.

Ethical limits must therefore be anchored not in speculation but in *instrument truth*. Medical devices are bound by clinical validation, informed consent, and post-market surveillance. Consumer BCIs need the same evidentiary spine. The *Council of Europe's Convention on Human Rights and Biomedicine* (Oviedo, 1997) already enshrines autonomy and consent for interventions "affecting the human brain." That principle now extends to algorithms interpreting neural data. Command without consent is coercion;

inference without evidence is fraud. A brain signal interpreted beyond its accuracy range is not innovation—it is superstition with a dashboard.

Reproducibility defines maturity. A BCI that works only in one lab, with one participant, under one set of conditions, is a *demo*. A technology that maintains performance across environments, operators, and users begins to earn the name *tool*. The transition from demo to durable instrument mirrors earlier scientific revolutions: the move from single microscopes to standard optics, from idiosyncratic AI models to benchmarked datasets. Standardisation is not bureaucracy; it is the price of credibility. Benchmarks for neural decoding—shared datasets, open metrics, declared error bounds—will be the scaffolding on which public trust stands.

Noise remains the great teacher. Engineers filter it, ethicists interpret it, philosophers embrace it. In noise lies humility—the acknowledgment that meaning is context-dependent and that no electrode, however fine, escapes the probabilistic nature of biology. To measure the brain is to eavesdrop on a conversation among billions of neurons speaking in dialects we barely know. The implication is profound: *uncertainty is not a flaw but a feature*. It preserves privacy by physics, guarding the sanctum of thought with entropy. Where the signal fades, personhood begins.

This motif—the whisper amid static—defines the proper posture for the field. The goal is not omniscience but *fidelity within limits*. Fidelity requires restraint. To design BCIs responsibly is to decide which inferences *not* to make, which data *not* to store, and which correlations *not* to monetise. Ethical strength will be measured not by what we decode but by what we decline to decode.

There is a practical corollary. Every BCI pipeline—from electrode to interface—should include *uncertainty display* as a core feature. Users must see confidence intervals for neural predictions just as radiologists see probability scores on scans. A cursor moving under brain control should visibly "breathe" with uncertainty, signalling to both user and system when doubt exceeds threshold. Such feedback loops protect autonomy; they remind us that partnership with machines is probabilistic, not prophetic.

We might imagine, in years ahead, lightweight BCIs aiding communication for those who cannot speak, augmenting attention for those who must focus, and restoring function after injury. Each success will depend on a chain of evidence that never exceeds its link strength. The real danger is not technological failure but conceptual inflation—the slow drift from inference to assumption, from signal to story. The corrective is constant calibration: scientific, ethical, and linguistic. We must learn to describe neural data without myth.

The unresolved question, and the one that will thread through every advance, is this: how much uncertainty are we willing to live with before acting on what a machine believes about our minds? Between voltage and intention lies translation. Between translation and truth lies restraint.

BCIs will change what we can *do*—but the greater test is whether they change what we believe we *know*.

Command, Consent, and Reversibility

In May 2017, a patient at the University of Pittsburgh Medical Center, identified only as Nathan, used a brain–computer interface to control a robotic arm with remarkable dexterity. Through an implanted array in his motor cortex, he could reach, grasp, and even shake hands. During one trial, engineers observed something subtle but unsettling. After a software update, the system misfired, translating resting neural activity into movement—Nathan's robotic arm twitched when he was thinking of nothing in particular. Control returned only when the array was recalibrated, but the episode prompted a crucial redesign: an *emergency pause* gesture—an intentional signal to halt all output. That pause became an ethic encoded in code. Consent in neural systems is not a contract signed once; it is a continuous, embodied conversation.

When machines interface with the body, permission must exist at the speed of thought. A keyboard or touchscreen requires deliberate motion; a brain interface operates closer to impulse. That proximity magnifies responsibility. A click is explicit; a cortical pattern is not. The dilemma is architectural: how to allow command without coercion, and how to make withdrawal of consent as simple as granting it. The future of brain–machine communication depends not on faster decoding but on *reversible design*—systems that can forget as easily as they act.

Consent in neural technology must be active, ongoing, and revocable. In medicine, these principles are routine. A participant in a clinical BCI trial, for instance, can withdraw from the study at any moment, triggering device deactivation and data deletion. But when neural interfaces migrate beyond hospitals—into rehabilitation clinics, workplaces, or homes—consent becomes diffuse. The legal paper gives way to gesture, routine, and interface flow. What was once a sterile protocol must become a daily ritual. The design question is therefore behavioural as much as technical: *how does a user know, moment to moment, that they are still in charge?*

Consider the approach taken by the BrainGate research consortium (Brown University, Massachusetts General Hospital, and Stanford University). Their 2021 protocol introduced "neural session boundaries": the interface required conscious initiation of recording, followed by an automatic timeout after periods of inactivity. This time-locked structure reduced the risk of inadvertent capture and gave users clear cognitive markers—start, act, disengage. The mechanism mirrored a surgeon's count before incision or a pilot's checklist before flight. Command was bounded by ceremony. The visible behaviour was calm confidence; the deeper ethic was *structured consent.*

Contrast this with commercial EEG systems designed for convenience. Consumer headsets, from meditation trackers to "focus assistants," often stream raw neural data continuously once paired with a smartphone. Few offer granular control over what is recorded, when it is stored, or how long it persists. The asymmetry is stark: laboratory-grade BCIs treat consent as a design axis, while consumer-grade devices treat it as a checkbox. This inversion of rigour—stronger safeguards where risk is smaller, weaker where scale is larger—reveals a moral blind spot. The implications extend beyond privacy. Continuous, irreversible neural capture erodes autonomy by design.

The principle of *reversibility* offers an antidote. Reversibility means that every neural command—every inferred intention or decoded pattern—can be undone, expired, or voided by the user. In practice, this requires *state memory* and *decay logic*. Commands must carry timestamps, contexts, and lifespans. A prosthetic hand that closes on command must open again on a timed release unless the signal renews; a cursor that moves under thought control must pause when confidence drops below threshold. Neural intent should always degrade toward neutrality. The brain drifts; the system must forgive.

A vivid example came from the work of the Wyss Center in Geneva (2020), where researchers connected a man with late-stage motor neuron disease to a spelling interface using implanted electrodes. Over months, as neural signals fluctuated with fatigue and metabolic changes, the system adapted through continuous calibration. When drift exceeded tolerance, output froze automatically. The principle was simple: silence is safer than guesswork. That humility—refusing to act without clear consent—protected both patient and integrity. The system's restraint became its greatest reliability.

The motif of *undo* recurs across ethical design. Undo is not an afterthought; it is the proof of freedom. In the early days of graphical computing, the "undo" command revolutionised creativity by transforming error into exploration. In neural systems, the stakes are higher: without undo, the boundary between control and compulsion dissolves. Imagine a neural assistant that launches a financial transaction when detecting "purchase intent" or a prosthesis that grips too hard because it misreads tension. Without fast, embodied reversal—an eye flick, a subvocal cue, a predefined "stop" pattern—mistakes become invasions. Undo must be physical, not philosophical.

The most robust consent mechanisms will blend temporal logic and bodily feedback. The notion of *time-locked permissions* borrows from cybersecurity but fits the neuroethical frame. Permissions to act—whether moving a robotic arm or sharing neural data—should expire automatically after defined intervals or context changes. For instance, a headset authorised for cognitive training could default to "no transmit" after ten minutes of inactivity or upon removal. Such automatic expiry embodies a form of *forgetting by default*, an engineering expression of restraint. Consent becomes a renewable act, not a permanent grant.

This philosophy is already influencing medical device regulation. In 2022, the U.S. Food and Drug

Administration's guidance on brain–computer interface devices required "explicit user control over initiation and cessation of data transmission." The phrasing matters: control must be perceptible, not abstract. The European Union's Artificial Intelligence Act (draft 2024) extends similar principles to "biometric and neurodata systems," demanding demonstrable reversibility and transparency. Ethical design is migrating from declaration to enforcement. The result is a slow but real alignment between law and interface.

A counterpoint must be acknowledged. Critics argue that excessive safety layers could compromise usability, especially for users with severe motor impairment who rely on continuous connection. A paralyzed user might find repetitive authorisation fatiguing or disruptive. This is a valid tension. The reconciliation lies in *adaptive autonomy*: systems that infer when the user's intention persists and maintain operation within short, renewable windows. Consent rituals can be streamlined without being erased. The rhythm should follow the user's energy, not the engineer's comfort.

The notion of ritual is worth lingering on. Anthropologists describe ritual as a means of framing power—making transitions visible, manageable, and shared. In neural interfaces, rituals mark the boundary between self and system. The act of donning a headset, initiating a session, confirming a signal—all become gestures of consent. Properly designed, these gestures reinforce agency rather than friction. Improperly designed, they dissolve awareness into automation. The difference between empowerment and exploitation is often one click—or one thought—apart.

In clinical contexts, consent rituals already carry gravity. Before every recording session in invasive trials, a coordinator asks the participant to confirm understanding, even if procedures are identical to the day before. This repetition is not bureaucracy; it is pedagogy. It reminds both parties that neural data is personal data of the highest order. Extending such rituals into everyday use will require cultural translation. Consumer interfaces must find lightweight equivalents—a visual cue, a haptic handshake, a sound—signalling that connection is live and under control. Silence should mean disengagement.

The quiet motif here is *control felt as confidence*. A user should not wonder whether they are being recorded, just as a driver should not wonder whether brakes will respond. Confidence emerges when reversibility is visible. This is the design opportunity of the next decade: to make permission tangible. Every successful system will show its state at a glance—active, paused, forgetting. Every trustworthy system will allow return to baseline faster than it can act.

The ethical implications extend beyond human comfort. Reversible design constrains corporate behaviour. If permissions expire, so does indefinite data collection. If sessions time out, so does continuous monetisation. By embedding reversibility in protocol, engineers enforce restraint upstream, turning ethics into architecture. The absence of friction for the user must never mean absence of friction for the extractor. The question is not only *can users withdraw?* but *can companies truly let go?*

Historical analogies illuminate the pattern. The "Are you sure?" prompt of nuclear command systems, first formalised in the 1960s, institutionalised hesitation as safety. Each key turn required confirmation from a second actor. Neural command demands a similar structure—not duplication but reflection. A brief pause, a tactile cue, or an intentional gesture before activation embeds dignity into the loop. The millisecond may seem costly; the trust it buys is priceless.

There is, inevitably, a future test. As consumer BCIs mature, pressure will mount to streamline the experience: instant pairing, seamless control, "frictionless thought input." The marketing will favour convenience; the danger lies in invisibility. The thinner the line between thinking and doing, the thicker the ethical boundary must become. Systems that act on the subtlest cues must prove they can *not act* with equal reliability. That symmetry—action and retraction in balance—will define maturity.

Command, consent, and reversibility are not abstractions of law but mechanics of trust. A neural interface that can only act, not retract, is unfit for human use. The ultimate test may come from outside the lab, in the messy, habitual spaces where convenience dulls caution. When a neural input feels as ordinary as a swipe, will users still perceive the weight of permission? The unresolved question is sharp: as control moves inward—from hand to cortex—can our systems preserve the right to *change one's mind* at the speed of thought?

Clinical Roots, Consumer Futures

In April 2012 at Massachusetts General Hospital in Boston, a participant in the BrainGate trial reached for a coffee with a robotic arm and, after months of training, managed a careful sip. The array—a Utah microelectrode grid implanted in motor cortex—converted motor intent into cursor and arm trajectories (Hochberg et al., *Nature,* 2012). The outcome was not showmanship but function: controlled grasp-and-release with measurable accuracy. A decade later, in May 2021 at Stanford, another participant "typed" by imagining handwriting, achieving roughly ninety characters per minute with implanted sensors (Willett et al., *Nature,* 2021). Two rooms, two years, two continents of work between them. One lesson endures. Clinical brain–computer interfaces were built to return agency under clinical scrutiny. They are not demos. They are vows.

The temptation now is to sprint from ward to wearables, from lab to lifestyle, as if the distance were a single packaging step. It isn't. What began as assistive technology under ethics committees and surgical oversight must cross into everyday use without trivialising its origins. The right transfer borrows discipline, not just headlines. It treats *care* as a specification.

Start with what the clinic teaches best: define outcomes that matter. Show the coffee cup in Boston, then name the measure—successful, repeatable grasps per session; minutes under control before fatigue; error rate under drift. Explain: in assistive contexts, benefit is not a vague uplift; it is a quantified restoration—letters per minute spelled by a locked-in patient, degrees of wrist rotation regained by a stroke survivor, phone calls completed without a carer. Implication: any consumer adaptation that cannot specify its *functional* win has likely built spectacle. Translate or don't ship.

Second, keep promises small and verifiable. When Edward Chang's group at UCSF in 2019 reconstructed spoken sentences from electrocorticography, they reported accuracy bounded by vocabularies and conditions; the paper's restraint anchored public sense (Chang et al., *Nature,* 2019). In 2022, Synchron placed an endovascular "Stentrode" through a jugular vein at Mount Sinai in New York, enabling a man with paralysis to text with eye and thought—no open craniotomy, incremental independence, audited outcomes. Show → name → explain → implication: *incrementalism wins*. Clinical BCIs progress by constrained claims and aggressive measurement; consumer BCIs should inherit that rhythm.

Now, the counter-example. In 2013, a wave of consumer EEG headbands—NeuroSky, Emotiv, later Muse—promised "focus" and "calm" with four to fourteen scalp sensors and proprietary engagement scores. Independent tests found that much of the variance tracked blink rate, jaw tension, or posture rather than cognitive state in the wild. Reconcile the tension honestly. Non-invasive devices can coach breathing, support habit loops, or gate simple interactions; they cannot read belief or intent. The implication is design, not denunciation: scope features to physics, and annotate uncertainty in the interface itself. Confidence bars are not a nicety; they are a moral boundary.

Transferring from clinic to consumer requires more than efficacy. It requires *ritual*. In the ICU, data capture begins only after a coordinator confirms consent each session; ECoG grids record during surgery, then stop; implants time out. This choreography reduces risk and centres the person. Consumer-grade systems must translate that choreography into lightweight rituals: an obvious session start, a visible "recording" state, a default timeout, a one-gesture "all stop". Show the behaviour: a runner dons a neuroband for cadence training; LEDs indicate armed, recording, forgetting. Name the pattern: *time-locked permission*. Explain: the system assumes amnesia unless renewed; the user never wonders if something still listens. Implication: ritual preserves dignity at scale.

The clinic also teaches humility about noise. Every signal drifts. In Geneva in 2020, the Wyss Center's spelling interface for a man with advanced motor neuron disease included automatic freeze when decoder confidence fell; nurses could resume only after recalibration. Drift-proofing by *abstention* is counter-intuitive to consumer makers raised on "always on". It must become normal. If the signal is shaky, the honest product is quiet. Loyalty grows from restraint.

A quiet motif threads through all of this: *carry the clinic*. Carry its metrics. Carry its reversibility. Carry its consent. When carried well, assistive lessons unlock consumer clarity rather than caution theatre. Consider cochlear implants, the most widespread neural prosthesis. Their transfer was not a leap from operating theatre to "neuro-audio" fashion; it was a decades-long path of indications, candidacy criteria, mapping protocols, and device hygiene, now informing consumer hearables with transparency about processing delays, battery life, and environmental limits. The assistive spine—expectations set by evidence—made broader adoption sturdy.

What about comfort and fatigue—consumer determinants often glossed? Clinical programmes measure time-on-task before nausea, headache, or cognitive overload. That language belongs in consumer briefs. Show the Stanford handwriting work's speed (≈90 cpm) and error rates. Name the dependency: titration of training sessions and adaptive decoders. Explain: users' bodies are not constants; medication, sleep, hydration, and stress alter signal quality. Implication: consumer BCIs that adapt to circadian and metabolic drift—quietly lowering sensitivity at 22:00, prompting breaks, decaying permissions—will feel eerily right. Those that pretend to constancy will feel extractive.

Translating assistive robustness into daily life also means designing for *hands-busy, eyes-busy* realities. A lab lets you sit still; a kitchen or bus does not. Borrow from clinical redundancy—multiple channels for the same action. A consumer neuro-cursor that pauses on low confidence should accept a tongue tap, a blink code, or a wrist haptic as a confirm. The clinic calls these *fallbacks;* the home calls them *grace.* Measure the metric that matters—abort-and-recover time. A system that recovers quickly will be trusted; one that stumbles gracefully will be used.

Trust itself must be demystified. In the ward, trust accrues through meeting thresholds: infection rates, adverse events, device uptime. In consumer land, trust is too often a vibe. Replace it with audits. Publish false positive and false negative rates for core inferences; disclose the training populations; state the contexts in which performance fails. The clinic survives scrutiny; the product should ask for the same. A privacy white paper without error bars is marketing, not medicine.

Clinical roots place a boundary around *who benefits first.* Assistive BCIs prioritise those for whom alternatives are few: locked-in patients, high-cervical injuries, progressive neuromuscular disease. Consumer futures should keep that priority in sight: features that scale from disability to convenience, not the reverse. Eye-gaze and dwell interaction, built for ALS and brainstem stroke, now enrich AR headsets for everyone in glare or gloves. Tactile confirmation, refined for prosthetics, quiets mid-air interfaces. The flow of benefit should remain outward, not upward.

There is a commercial temptation to invert that flow: chase wellness markets with "cognitive enhancement," then backfill into care. It rarely works. Clinical trust is cumulative; it does not borrow from lifestyle branding. The right sequence is different. Prove durable benefit in constrained, high-stakes contexts; harden protocols; open APIs for assistive ecosystems; *then* explore mass channels with the same guardrails. If that sounds slow, remember the prize: a category that does not collapse under its own myth.

Two named transitions show the right posture. First, Synchron's endovascular BCI—implanted through blood vessels rather than open brain—moved from Melbourne first-in-human operations in 2019 to the first U.S. implant at Mount Sinai in July 2022. The company published capabilities modestly—text, messaging, web use—while designing follow-up care and home-use routines. Second, Meta's sponsored research in 2021–2022 shifted from invasive speech decoding towards wrist-based electromyography (EMG), conceding that many "neural" wins lie outside the skull. Both choices reflect an ethic: find the smallest intervention that yields meaningful control.

The counter-pressure is design theatre. Consumer devices sell ease; clinical devices sell honesty. Reconciling the two requires *legible state*. Users must see what the system thinks: signal quality, whether data are local or transmitting, when permissions expire. A tiny icon will not do. Make state a first-class citizen: a live ledger of what the device just did, why, and for whom (which app, which service), with a one-gesture erase. The clinic logs everything because accountability is survival; the home will need that memory if BCIs are to avoid the fate of other opaque wearables—novelty, then a drawer.

Cost and training time determine whether consumer futures are not just possible but equitable. The clinic already optimises both—nurses trained to fit devices; rehab teams tuned to attention spans; families taught to maintain hygiene. Consumer BCIs must copy the playbook: fifteen-minute fit sessions, templated onboarding that sets comfort and consent, quarterly micro-modules pushed to the device, and community champions who are not engineers. Measure the curve: hours to first independent use; weeks to stable habit. Publish it. Markets grow where learning shrinks.

All this prudence should not dull the imagination. Assistive innovations often become everyone's infrastructure. Predictive decoders built for shaky signals will stabilise smart glasses in bright kitchens. Session boundaries meant to protect trial participants will tame data glut in schools. Reversible design invented for prosthetic mishaps will become the reason a consumer device avoids a scandal. The clinic gives us not only ethics but *techniques*—noise models, calibration rituals, drift detectors—that will make everyday systems civil.

A final caution belongs here. There is a risk of sanctifying the clinic so completely that it paralyses consumer invention. Some ideas can be tested ethically outside hospitals: EMG bands for silent input; on-device inference for attention gating; consensual shared control in games. The test is not provenance alone but posture. Do you carry the clinic's habits into the wild—measurement, reversibility, humility? If yes, create. If no, wait.

The motif returns—*carry the clinic.* Carry it across price points, across rooms, across roles. Let it travel not as constraint but as craft. Then ask the forward question that will govern this field for a decade: when a neural feature leaves the ward and enters a wrist, what proof, what ritual, and what restraint must walk with it so that the power that once restored a sip of coffee does not, in new clothes, take choice away?

The Dignity Test

In 2014, at a rehabilitation centre in Lausanne, a 29-year-old man who had been paralysed from the chest down since a cycling accident took his first hesitant steps using a neuroprosthetic system. Electrodes implanted in his spinal cord relayed signals from sensors in his brain, translating motor intention into muscle activation. The technology, developed by the École Polytechnique Fédérale de Lausanne (EPFL), restored motion, but what moved the room was not gait—it was expression. When asked what the moment meant, the participant replied, "I can stand when I choose." The phrase became an unplanned manifesto for neural design: *to choose* is the essence of dignity.

Every neural interface—from implant to headband—claims to extend human capability. The deeper question is: for whom, and under what conditions? The dignity test is not a sentiment; it is a method. It asks one hard thing of designers, investors, and ethicists alike—does this interface expand agency for the least powerful person who might use it? If not, it is not ready.

The clinic, once again, supplies the baseline. In assistive BCIs, progress is measured not in novelty but in independence: how many words can a locked-in patient spell per minute; how many daily actions can a prosthesis complete without assistance. Each metric is an index of restored choice. Dignity, in this frame, is the measurable distance between dependence and participation. Yet as neural interfaces drift into consumer markets, that clarity evaporates. The promise shifts from restoration to enhancement, from necessity to curiosity. The ethical compass spins unless recalibrated by the same measure: *agency gained, not agency flaunted.*

Show the contrast. Name the cases. Explain the gap. Implication: the dignity test must travel. In 2022, Synchron's "Stentrode" implant enabled patients with severe paralysis to communicate via text, using an endovascular route that reduced surgical risk. The trial reported both technical reliability and psychological relief: participants described the joy of messaging loved ones unassisted. Contrast this with a 2023 consumer EEG headset that claimed to detect "emotional engagement" during work tasks, streaming neural metrics to employers. Both products read brain signals. Only one passed the dignity test. The other quietly inverted it—turning private cognition into managerial data.

What distinguishes restoration from surveillance is consent coupled with control. The least powerful user—the patient, the worker, the child—must be able to revoke access faster than a system can infer. The clinic encodes this principle by design: session-based recording, human oversight, and mandatory reconsent. In consumer BCIs, those guardrails too often vanish under convenience. The interface's grace lies not in seamlessness but in visible boundaries. When everything is frictionless, so too is exploitation.

The test is subtle because indignity rarely announces itself. It creeps through defaults—auto-start sessions, opaque cloud storage, algorithms that classify users by neural pattern clusters. Dignity erodes in the gap between what a user believes is happening and what the system actually does. The fix is engineering transparency, not rhetorical assurance. A system that shows when it is listening, what it has learned, and how to delete that memory gives users the factual basis for trust. Visibility is not decoration; it is power shared.

History offers an instructive precedent. When cochlear implants emerged in the late twentieth century, they were hailed as miracles. Yet within the Deaf community, they sparked fierce debate about autonomy and identity. Some saw them as tools of access; others as instruments of assimilation. The tension endures because both sides defend dignity—the dignity of hearing regained versus the dignity of Deaf culture preserved. Neural design cannot flatten such tensions; it must hold them open. A responsible interface invites choice, not conformity.

The motif of *standing when one chooses* extends beyond mobility. It marks any system where initiation and cessation remain under personal command. The BrainGate consortium's 2021 trials required participants to actively start each session; signals were ignored until users confirmed readiness. This ritual, inherited from clinical ethics, is what many consumer platforms now lack. The implication is simple: any interface that acts without explicit initiation—be it a headset, wearable, or implant—risks converting people from users into subjects. The measure of dignity is the capacity to say *not now*.

Dignity also demands inclusivity by design. Neural devices developed solely on homogeneous datasets—young, affluent, neurotypical—exacerbate exclusion under the guise of precision. If a BCI fails to decode signals from an older user, or misclassifies neural patterns from individuals with atypical rhythms, it is not neutral; it is structurally biased. Bias in a system that acts on the body becomes bodily inequality. The dignity test, applied here, is practical: *who did we test on, and who did we forget?*

There is a counter-example worth grappling with. In 2019, a start-up released a consumer EEG sleep tracker claiming to enhance rest through neurofeedback. Early users reported improvements, but follow-up studies revealed that nearly 30 per cent of the sample experienced increased anxiety due to over-attention to brain metrics. The product amplified self-surveillance rather than self-knowledge. Its failure was not technical; it was ethical misalignment. It made users more aware but less free. The dignity test would have caught it early: does the system foster agency, or dependence on its readings?

Dignity is not sentimentality about fragility. It is structure for strength. Assistive BCIs show that careful constraint—limits on inference, explicit handover, reversibility—builds confidence. Consumer BCIs must mirror that discipline. Each neural action should carry the logic of consent embedded within its timing and scope. A cursor that moves when thought commands it must stop when certainty fades. A system that cannot stop cannot respect.

Thread the motif again: standing when one chooses. A user who can start, stop, and override maintains dignity even in dependence. The same principle applies socially. BCIs in educational or workplace settings should empower the least powerful party—the student, the worker—to opt out without consequence. The question is diagnostic: *can the person with least leverage refuse participation and still belong?* If not, the system has failed the dignity test.

One might ask whether dignity can be quantified. Perhaps not directly, but its absence leaves measurable traces: dropout rates in clinical trials, user fatigue, adoption skewed toward elites. When systems respect autonomy, retention rises and trust compounds. When they erode it, participation withers. The correlation is not poetic; it is behavioural evidence.

Policy is beginning to echo these lessons. Chile's 2021 constitutional amendment recognised *neurorights*—mental privacy, identity, and agency—as protected categories. The move was symbolic yet significant: it framed dignity not as benevolence but as law. Europe's AI Act (draft 2024) echoes the principle, classifying neurodata as sensitive and requiring clear consent. Regulation, in this sense, is the dignity test writ in statute.

Still, ethics cannot rest solely in compliance. Checklists become excuses when detached from conscience. The true dignity test operates upstream, at the level of design intention. A team that asks, "Would we give this to someone whose only defence is trust?" builds differently. Interfaces born of care behave as care, even in error. Interfaces born of extraction behave as extraction, even when accurate. Dignity is not a feature; it is a foundation.

Yet no test resolves the deepest tension: power asymmetry evolves faster than empathy. As BCIs mature, the entities capable of building them—corporations, states, research consortia—will outsize any single user's capacity to contest misuse. This is why the dignity test must stay simple and blunt enough to survive scale. *Does it expand agency for the least powerful?* The question fits on a whiteboard. It also fits in a courtroom.

Perhaps the truest measure of readiness for any neural interface is whether it makes the smallest, quietest user more visible, more able to say *yes* and *no* with equal force. If the answer is uncertain, the work is not finished. The dignity test is not a gate at the end of development; it is the pulse at the centre of the design. And its rhythm, constant and inconvenient, keeps the field human.

Chapter 6
Anticipation with Accountability

In January 2020, a commuter in Tokyo opened her phone to find a push notification suggesting she leave ten minutes early for work. The alert cited an accident on the Chūō Line. She followed the advice, arrived on time, and silently thanked the app's foresight. Later, she learned the crash report had been algorithmically inferred, not confirmed—drawn from abnormal sensor readings and user motion data. The prediction was lucky, not factual. It had guessed right for the wrong reason. The commuter's gratitude masked a deeper trade: her daily movements had become inputs in a system that could nudge behaviour before truth caught up. The prediction was efficient. It was also opaque.

Anticipation has always been a mark of intelligence. To sense what comes next—to pre-empt a fall, refill a glass, or adjust tone mid-sentence—is a human art. Yet in digital systems, anticipation crosses into automation, and automation into governance. When an interface predicts what we need, it begins to shape what we want. The line between service and soft coercion narrows with every suggestion that feels natural. The question no longer asks *how well does it guess?* but *who benefits when it does?*

Prediction, when embedded in daily tools, becomes power exercised quietly. Spotify's "Discover Weekly," launched in 2015, trained listeners to trust machine taste. Netflix's auto-preview feature shapes attention by withholding friction.

Amazon's anticipatory shipping patents imagine goods dispatched before purchase. Each is efficient by design, persuasive by effect. Show, name, explain: they all work by closing the temporal gap between thought and action. Implication: as anticipation accelerates, accountability must keep pace—or the machinery that claims to help us begins to decide for us.

Accountability, however, cannot be retrofitted by policy alone. The challenge is architectural. A system that predicts must also remember *why* it predicted. Each decision should carry a traceable ledger of triggers, data sources, and confidence levels. The "anticipation ledger" is not a metaphor but a technical discipline—a running diary of the model's reasoning that users can inspect, contest, or reset. It transforms guessing from mystique to dialogue. Transparency becomes not a marketing claim but a structural guarantee: you can see what moved the machine, and you can unmake it.

That clarity is rare. What most people encounter is legal wallpaper—thousands of words of privacy policy drafted to immunise rather than inform. The result is paradoxical: we are surrounded by disclosures yet starved of understanding. True transparency must shrink, localise, and activate. A notice should appear *where* and *when* it matters—before the camera guesses your mood, before the recommendation narrows your horizon—not buried on page twelve. Short, situated, actionable: this is what transparency that users actually read must look like. The ethical interface will display explanation as fluently as it renders animation.

But transparency without renewal is theatre. Feedback loops, once established, tend to tighten. Predictive systems feed on their own success—serving what was clicked, rewarding what was familiar, curating outlier behaviour into extinction. Netflix, Facebook, TikTok, and their peers all suffer the same pathology: success breeds sameness. To anticipate too well is to entomb curiosity. The antidote is intentional surprise. Systems must be designed to *inject novelty*: scheduled profile resets, exploration spaces, randomised exposure. The goal is not chaos but room to breathe. An interface that occasionally mispredicts can preserve freedom better than one that never errs.

There is precedent for this balance. In 2018, the BBC's Research & Development team experimented with "serendipity layers" in personalised news—algorithms tuned to surface stories from outside a user's habitual geography or topic. Engagement dropped marginally; satisfaction rose markedly. People liked being surprised, provided they understood *why*. It was a proof of dignity through design: to be anticipated without being confined. That insight should guide all predictive systems that claim ethical intent.

Yet accountability demands more than comfort. It demands instrumentation for what usually goes unmeasured: error, hesitation, reversal, and trust. Companies obsess over clicks, but clicks are reflexes, not votes. A more serious metric asks what happens *after* the action: did the user undo, dwell, regret, or repeat? Trust can be modelled not by frequency but by forgiveness—how much error a person tolerates before they disengage. A trustworthy system allows missteps without penalty; it signals awareness of its own fallibility. The truest predictor of ethical design may be how gracefully an interface admits it was wrong.

The motif of *the ledger* returns here—not as bureaucracy but as memory. A digital ledger that records both decisions and reversals becomes a map of mutual learning. The user sees how often they have accepted or rejected the system's suggestions; the system learns where its confidence outstripped consent. Over time, this co-evolution humanises prediction. The interface becomes accountable not only for outcomes but for process.

Still, prediction will always carry risk of asymmetry. The entity that anticipates first gains advantage—be it advertiser, insurer, or state. The defensive frontier is dignity itself. If a system anticipates to constrain, it violates personhood; if it anticipates to enable, it extends agency. The distinction is behavioural, not rhetorical. A navigation app that reroutes around traffic saves time; a credit model that pre-emptively lowers one's score for "risky" search terms steals opportunity. The ethics of anticipation must be judged by who keeps the choice.

The next decade will make these distinctions unavoidable. Brain–computer interfaces, biometric analytics, and affective AI will guess not only what we might buy but what we might feel. Prediction will enter the nervous system. That is why accountability must harden now—through design audits, open ledgers, and user sovereignty baked into every inference. The goal is not to halt anticipation but to domesticate it, to make foresight serve without surveillance.

If earlier chapters examined the intimacy of interfaces with mind and motion, this one confronts their ambition: systems that think ahead. Anticipation without accountability is a mirror that edits its reflection until we no longer recognise ourselves. But anticipation with accountability could be the highest form of empathy—a design practice that listens forward while standing still.

The unresolved question—our chapter's through-line—is simple but consequential: how far should an interface go to know us before it starts to own us? Between guessing and guiding lies the thin, negotiable space of ethics. To navigate it requires a new literacy—one that treats prediction not as prophecy but as promise, measurable, retractable, and shared. The work ahead is to ensure that every machine capable of anticipating our needs remains equally capable of apologising for its assumptions.

Prediction as Power

In February 2012, the *New York Times* reported that Target—headquartered in Minneapolis—had inferred a teenager's pregnancy from purchasing patterns and mailed coupons to her home before her family knew. The analytics worked as designed; the fallout revealed a different truth. Prediction changes behaviour. Quietly. What looked like service became shock. The company's model collapsed the boundary between "might need" and "must know", converting a household into a hypothesis. When guessing crosses that line, power is no longer neutral; it directs the room.

The tension is not new. Every concierge, librarian, or maître d' trades in anticipation. But when software anticipates at industrial scale, the asymmetry grows teeth. It observes at resolution no person can match, acts at speed no person can question, and learns from feedback loops that tighten with every click. Service and soft coercion begin to rhyme. The ethical hinge, then, is not whether we predict, but how we govern the act of prediction so that convenience does not disguise control.

Show the good faith case. Name it. Explain it. Implication: when a system's guesses are transparent, consentful, and reversible, prediction feels like care. When they are opaque, sticky, and unaccountable, prediction becomes pressure. Spotify's "Discover Weekly" (launched July 2015 by the Stockholm-based company) offered a weekly set of thirty songs based on listening history. The behaviour to measure was not total play time but *adoption without lock-in*: users could ignore a week, unfollow, or reset taste without penalty. The product's power lay in proportion. It suggested. It didn't trap. The model earned permission by staying smaller than the listener's choice.

Now show the speculative case. In December 2013, Amazon was granted U.S. Patent 8,615,473 for "anticipatory shipping"—pre-positioning goods in a region based on predicted demand, dispatching before a purchase is final. The prediction moved upstream, from interface to logistics. No harm is inherent in that optimisation; packages can await confirmation and return if unused. But the design lesson is stark. As anticipation shifts closer to action, accountability must move closer too. If the warehouse bets on your appetite, the app must show its working. If not, the bet can become a nudge disguised as fate.

Prediction, in short, is power because it edits context. It decides what arrives in your field of view and, just as importantly, what is quietly withheld. That editing is not neutral. We should therefore instrument the editor. Enter the *anticipation ledger*—a running account attached to every consequential guess. It records five things in plain language and machine form: (1) the trigger ("we noticed three late commutes this week"), (2) the data used ("calendar titles and live traffic within 5 km"), (3) the model's confidence ("0.72 on a 0–1 scale"), (4) the action proposed or taken ("leave 10 minutes early"), and (5) the opt-out or reset path ("mute for a week; delete traffic features"). The ledger's purpose is epistemic hygiene. It turns *because the model says so* into *because of these observable reasons*. It also makes refusal practical.

Without a ledger, small frictions—hesitation, undo, rebound to prior state—remain invisible. Systems then misread compliance as satisfaction. You tapped. You must have liked it. Yet clicks are not votes; they are often escapes. A legible ledger, exposed at the moment of influence, changes the arithmetic. It gives the person enough context to accept, amend, or refuse, and it gives the system enough feedback to learn when to back off. Put differently: a ledger redistributes power by turning guesses into offers rather than faits accomplis.

Consider a navigation app that shows a "leave now" prompt as rain begins. With a ledger, the prompt would declare the trigger ("storm cell approaching per Met Office radar"), the data scope ("location on device; no historical routes uploaded"), and an expiry ("this prompt will vanish in 20 minutes"). The behavioural metric to watch is *reversal rate*: how often users cancel the suggestion within thirty seconds. High reversals tell you that the model is overreaching. Without that visibility, engineering teams will chase click-through and ship a worse nudge next quarter.

The motif of the ledger matters because prediction corrupts quietly. Feeds narrow as they succeed. A recommendation gains traction, similar items flood the surface, novelty thins, and a life gets edged into grooves. Eli Pariser's "filter bubble" argument (2011) was not a mathematical proof; it was a civic warning. Prediction shortens the distance between curiosity and habit. A ledger, paired with design that periodically injects dissimilar items, keeps the horizon open. It makes space for *what you didn't know to ask for* and shows that space on purpose.

Service turns coercive through four design moves: *opacity*, *stickiness*, *silencing*, and *shame*. Opacity hides the trigger and the model; stickiness buries opt-outs; silencing ignores correction; shame frames refusal as error. Reverse each move. Light the trigger. Allow one-tap opt-outs that persist. Instrument dissent—hesitation, undo, backtracks—and treat them as first-class signals. And when people choose "no", thank them; they just taught you a boundary. You will see the change in behaviour: lower rage-quit, shorter dwell on prompts, steadier long-term usage, and higher post-task satisfaction even when immediate clicks dip.

Two more named, checkable examples clarify the spectrum. First, Apple's App Tracking Transparency (iOS 14.5, April 2021) forced apps to seek permission to track across other companies' apps and websites. It did not ban prediction; it constrained unconsented data jumps. The visible effect for users was a short, situated prompt at the moment of risk. The implied ledger lived in policy more than interface, but the principle holds: anticipate, then ask. Second, the BBC's experiments with personalisation have repeatedly surfaced a public-service tension: maximise engagement or maximise exposure to diverse content. When prototypes introduced "editor's picks beyond your profile" flags, some users clicked less, but reported higher satisfaction with their *mix*. The metric that matters here is not a session spike; it is retention without narrowing—*people still here next month who still see difference.*

A credible counter-example keeps us honest. In 2014, Facebook's "Year in Review" auto-assembled a celebratory montage from users' photos. For Eric Meyer, whose daughter had died that year, the algorithmic festivity was cruelty. This was not predictive targeting; it was automated context blindness. The fix is not to abolish year summaries but to add an *anticipation pause*. Before pushing an emotionally loaded montage, present a gentle ledger: "We found these moments. Would you like to review or skip?" Prediction without discretion becomes harm. Prediction with discretion becomes care.

Power also concentrates at the edges of time. The closer a prediction sits to an irreversible action—placing an order, making a diagnosis, dispatching help—the more stringent the ledger must be. A calendar prompt that moves a meeting autonomously based on "likely conflicts" is not a convenience; it is a social act that affects others. Here the ledger should expand to show *who else is impacted,* and default to *dry-run mode*: simulate first, then ask. Watch *downstream correction load*—how many follow-up messages and fixes a "helpful" automation creates. If that load rises, your prediction is exporting labour.

The legal layer helps but cannot substitute for craft. GDPR's "right to explanation" and access/erasure rights formalise power for individuals; they do not make explanations readable or refusals easy at the moment of influence. The ledger must live where the guess lives. It must be as glanceable as a notification, as simple as a light switch, and as durable as an audit trail. Engineers will bristle—latency, layout, clutter. Ship it anyway. A ledger that costs milliseconds can save reputations measured in years.

Metrics decide culture. If teams are rewarded for click-through, they will ship coercion with a smile. If they are rewarded for *trust*, they will instrument *reversals*, *hesitations*, and *regret*. You can measure regret. Ask one question after high-stakes predictions: "Was this helpful, harmful, or neutral?" Correlate with undo and follow-on actions. Trust is not a mood; it is tolerance for error while staying. Design your dashboards to show that staying.

Anticipation also intersects with equity. The least powerful—children, precarious workers, those navigating care systems—are most easily nudged and least able to contest. The ledger therefore doubles as dignity device. It must show not only *what* and *why*, but *how to exit* without penalty. In schools, for instance, a learning platform that "suggests" remedial content based on quiz performance should display confidence, alternatives, and a "try something different" door that does not brand the pupil with a deficit. The behavioural readout you want is *profile recovery*: how quickly a user can escape a mistaken model path. If recovery is slow, your prediction is a trap.

Architecturally, the ledger needs three layers: *local*, *personal*, and *public*. Local is the pop-up next to the prompt—short, situated, actionable. Personal is the per-user log—

searchable, erasable, portable. Public is the model card—what kinds of data and labels the system relies on, with known failure cases and bias audits. Together, these layers align momentary choice with institutional accountability. They also shift the balance of expertise: people can bring their ledger to complaints, regulators, or advocates. "This is what your system did to me, and here is the record."

Designers will worry about "breaking the spell". Good. Spells should break. A humane interface is not a magician; it is a partner that can show its hands. Anticipation is most impressive when it can be argued with. The conversation—small, fast, legible—turns power from a directed edge into a shared loop. Paradoxically, explaining the trick makes the audience stay. They feel seen without being steered.

There is no perfect boundary between service and coercion. Context will always move it. But the forward test is crisp enough to steer builds this quarter. For any predictive feature you plan to ship, ask: *If this guess is wrong, how easily can the person tell, tell us, and turn it off?* Then ask the harder one: *If this guess is right, who else benefits besides the person—us, our partners, an advertiser—and have we made that benefit visible and optional?* If the ledger cannot answer those questions in under ten seconds of attention, the feature is not ready.

Prediction will continue to creep closer to the bone: sensors in rooms, wearables on wrists, models trained on speech rhythm and gaze. The industry's reflex will be to reduce friction until behaviour flows. Our obligation is to preserve a thin seam where intent can catch breath. A ledger lives in that seam. It keeps the guess on a leash. It makes anticipation answerable to the one who must live with its consequences. The unresolved question sits there, sharp as a dial: how much of your future should a system be allowed to write before you have read the draft?

Transparency the User Will Actually Read

In January 2021, WhatsApp announced a privacy-policy update that would allow limited data sharing with its parent company, Facebook, for business messaging. The notice landed globally and, within days, millions of users—especially in India—downloaded Signal and Telegram. The company postponed enforcement by three months and reworded the notice, but the concrete outcome remained: a single push notification had triggered a mass migration. The paradox was stark. A message designed to inform had functioned as a warning. It asked for assent and received exit. Five words explain the failure: the notice was not *for* users.

Show the card on the screen: dense text, low contrast, no next-step clarity. Name the problem: *legal wallpaper*. Explain: disclosures drafted to minimise liability cannot maximise comprehension. Implication: transparency that nobody reads is a form of opacity. If we want informed consent, we must write for the human who stands between law and machine. The unit of design is not the policy. It is the small card at the moment of decision. That card must be short, situated, and actionable. It must be honest about stakes. It must carry exits that work.

The WhatsApp incident underscores a broader truth. Users rarely read policies because policy appears when their attention is elsewhere. They are in the middle of a task. They have goals. So the notice must bind itself to intention. It should appear where the choice matters, not where legal teams prefer. It should map to the next behaviour, not to the next paragraph. When transparency follows task, it becomes part of the interface, not a prelude to risk.

The psychology here is not mysterious. Working memory is small. People parse by scanning. We therefore design disclosures as micro-interfaces, not paragraphs. Show, name, explain, imply: show the salient risk or benefit; name the data and purpose; explain retention and sharing in one line; imply control by offering a first-class alternative now. The motif we will return to is *the small card*. A good system lives or dies by that card.

Two checkable examples show the range. In April 2021, Apple rolled out App Tracking Transparency (ATT) in iOS 14.5. Apps requesting cross-app tracking had to present a brief, native prompt: "Allow X to track your activity across other companies' apps and websites?" Two buttons. No scroll. The card appeared at the precise moment tracking would begin. Adoption of tracking fell. Users decided. The disclosure worked because *it was a decision*, not a document. Contrast that with the labyrinthine cookie banners that followed GDPR's enforcement in Europe (from May 2018), many designed to dark-pattern an "Accept All". The same legal mandate, two design philosophies. One respected agency. The other negotiated against it.

Short is not shallow if it is *situated*. Consider the NHS COVID-19 app launched for England and Wales in September 2020. It presented concise, contextual notices: Bluetooth contact tracing, area risk levels, and venue check-ins using QR codes. Crucially, the app explained *on the spot* how anonymous tokens worked and when data left the device. The notice changed as context changed. The metric to watch was adoption with retention: did people keep the app despite mixed headlines? They did. The card met the moment.

Now the engine: what does "actionable" mean when applied to transparency? It means the card offers a meaningful fork. *Proceed, but with limits. Proceed later. Don't proceed yet.* In other words, legible alternatives. If the only "choice" is *Accept* or abandon the product, we are not asking. We are forcing. The visible behaviour that distinguishes actionability is *calm engagement*: shorter dwell before decision, fewer rage-quits, stable long-term usage. Teams that instrument these signals see an effect: clarity depresses immediate click-through but raises satisfaction and retention. Short-term drop, long-term gain. Design leaders should commit to the trade.

Transparency that works is layered with intent. First layer: the small card—what's happening now, why, and how to control it. Second: a local ledger screen that aggregates recent decisions ("Tracking disabled for X; Location used for Y yesterday; Data set to delete in 7 days"). Third: a human-readable policy with an index that matches the interface, not the lawyer's table of contents. Each layer points to the others. The motif remains the same: cards, not walls.

Skeptics worry that short, situated cards cannot capture nuance. That is a limitation worth naming. Complex models, multi-party data flows, and regulatory obligations do not compress cleanly. But compression is not erasure if we anchor to *verbs*. Instead of "We may process your information for service improvement", write "We use crash logs to fix bugs; we keep them 30 days; you can delete them now." Verbs force specificity. They compel commitments: keep, share, delete, learn, forget. Every abstract noun we remove—*experience, personalisation, engagement*—reduces plausible deniability and increases legibility.

There is a common counter-example. Some firms relocate complexity into a "Learn more" link that opens a thousand words. The card looks simple. The truth is elsewhere. This fails for two reasons. First, the "elsewhere" is not where the decision lives. Secondly, more words rarely add more clarity; they add more surface for ambiguity. Reconcile this by *promoting the constraint,* not burying it. If a decision has a hard edge, the card should say so: "This feature requires background location; without it, arrivals can't be predicted. You can turn it on just for today." The user can then choose *intentionally bounded consent*—powerful because it models restraint.

Situating the card is craft. Place it where hands, eyes, and intention already are. If camera access is needed for a deposit cheque, ask within the camera view, not at app start. If microphone access enables voice notes, ask after the first long-press, not on install. If contact upload powers friend suggestions, ask at the moment of *Find friends*, not as part of an onboarding bundle. You will see the effect in *decision-to-action latency*: how quickly users move from consent to task. Lower latency indicates the card matched intention; high latency hints at suspicion or confusion.

A second, named example sharpens the point. In late 2020, Apple introduced privacy nutrition labels on the App Store. Whatever their imperfections, the labels moved disclosure from PDF to product shelf. Before download, a shopper could see categories of data collected—contact info, location, identifiers—and whether they were linked to you. The card sat in the right aisle. It shortened the distance between knowledge and choice. That is the metric to honour: knowledge-to-choice distance.

Short does not excuse euphemism. The card must acknowledge stakes, including harm. When the stakes are emotional—as with memorial slideshows, pregnancy tracking, or mental health prompts—the card should slow the interface and expand its tone. The BBC's trials with "serendipity layers" in personalised news demonstrated that people can embrace friction if they understand why it exists. "We're showing a story from outside your usual topics to broaden your view." It is a sentence that treats the reader as a citizen, not a metric.

The card must also carry *reversibility*. A notice without an undo is a trap with a tooltip. Good transparency pairs choice with memory: "You allowed X last week. Undo?" Time is part of truth. Consent decays. Systems that assume permanence invite regret; systems that offer periodic reminders and resets convert regret into learning. The behaviour to monitor is *silent churn*: users stop using features without telling you why. Well-timed reminders reduce silent churn by giving people a social way out: no shame, no maze, just a quick backtrack.

Design language matters because it sends social signals. "Allow" versus "Share". "Track" versus "Help keep free". Words steer. A rule of thumb: choose the word you would use if you were asking a friend for the same thing. "May we use your location to show nearby clinics?" reads like a favour, not a right. "We collect your location to improve services" reads like a fait accompli. The first elicits consent; the second elicits resignation or resistance.

Sometimes, transparency must announce uncertainty. A recommendation system may be experimenting; a fraud model may be flagging a transaction with low confidence. The card should say so. "We're not sure. We could be wrong." This is not weakness; it is legitimacy. It invites the user to correct, to teach, to partner. Systems that admit error early see fewer escalations later because the relationship starts from candour, not from theatre.

Regulation can nudge, but design carries. GDPR's right of access and erasure codifies recourse; the California Consumer Privacy Act and its successor strengthen similar rights; Chile's neurorights amendment gestures at neural data's sanctity. Yet rights without readable prompts at the point of capture are rights unused. The card is where statute becomes practice. If your interface can ask for consent in five seconds, it can show a *real-time* path to delete in the same five. Anything less suggests that transparency is selective: fast for intake, slow for relief.

Equity enters here. The burden of reading legal wallpaper falls heaviest on those with the least time, patience, or language fluency. Short, situated, actionable cards are therefore instruments of fairness. They reduce the literacy tax of participating in digital life. To claim inclusivity while hiding choices in dense screens is to talk equity and practise extraction. You can measure this. Run comprehension tests with non-specialist users across age and language groups. Track time-to-understanding and the accuracy of recalled terms. If comprehension rises while complaints and support tickets fall, the small card is doing large work.

A credible limitation: too many cards can paralyse. Consent fatigue is real. Reconcile by *batching decisions to moments of meaning* and by respecting prior answers. If a user has declined ad tracking three times, your system should remember across products and devices when lawful to do so. The card's purpose is not to win a click. It is to calibrate a relationship. Over-asking erodes that purpose.

Return to the motif: the small card. Imagine the interface as a city. Policies are building codes; cards are street signs. No one reads the code at a crossing. They read "Give way." The sign must be clear, placed before the turn, and backed by rules that make the road safe even for those who never glance up. That is the standard: transparency you can live by without studying it.

We end on a forward test. Before shipping a notice, read it aloud to someone who is busy, sceptical, and tired. Ask them one question: *could you act on this in ten seconds with confidence and a way back?* If the answer is no, the card is not ready. If the answer is yes, you have replaced wallpaper with a door. And beyond that door is the only transparency that counts: understanding that changes what a person can choose.

Feedback Loops That Do Not Trap

In July 2015, Spotify in Stockholm launched Discover Weekly: thirty songs, refreshed each Monday, stitched from a listener's habits and the tastes of similar users. It felt like magic. For many, it still does. Yet the team made a quiet decision that mattered more than the playlist itself: they placed it alongside, not instead of, existing libraries and radio-style stations. Discover Weekly was an invitation, not a corridor. The lesson is durable. Closed loops shrink human choice. When a system's predictions become the path rather than a path, horizons narrow. The work of design is to resist that narrowing with structures that keep curiosity alive.

The trap is mechanical as much as cultural. Recommender systems learn from behaviour; behaviour follows the menu; the menu is shaped by the model. A circle forms. Left unchecked, the circle tightens. The remedy is not to abandon feedback loops but to ventilate them: inject novelty purposefully, create exploration spaces with different rules, and build profile resets that are genuine, fast, and reversible. The motif to hold in mind is the *open window*. A healthy loop breathes.

Show the dynamic in action. Name it. Explain it. Implication: optimisation seeks local maxima—peaks that look tall from up close but sit in a valley from afar. Without oxygen, a system will keep you in the valley because it performs well there. The visible behaviours: repeated artists, repeated topics, repeated political angles; a "for you" feed that becomes a filing cabinet. Users scroll further but feel less. Your metrics may look golden—time on site up, sessions per day up—until retention and satisfaction flatten because the system trained people to tolerate more of the same.

Two named examples clarify the range of remedies. In April 2018, the BBC's Research & Development group in London prototyped "serendipity layers" in personalised news products. The interface flagged a subset of stories as *beyond your usual topics* and surfaced them at bounded intervals.

Engagement dipped slightly; self-reported satisfaction rose; perceived breadth improved. The result taught two things. First, that novelty can be scheduled without feeling random. Second, that disclosure—telling people *why* they are seeing something different—matters as much as the content itself. In May 2018, Google introduced *Full Coverage* in Google News, a mode that shows diverse angles and timelines on a story regardless of a user's profile. Here the exploration space is explicit: a sealed room where personalisation is suspended and plurality is the rule. Users clicked less in the moment but returned to the feature for complex stories. Short-term dips bought long-term trust.

The counter-example is equally instructive. When platforms have attempted "surprise for surprise's sake", novelty became noise. Several media apps tried random injections without signalling purpose; users felt the system was broken rather than expansive. Reconcile the tension by tying novelty to *meaningful cadence and context*. The right dose and timing of difference protects attention rather than scattering it. Exploration must feel like a guided walk, not a shove into the street.

How, then, to prevent narrowing horizons in the fabric of a system? Begin by measuring the right things. Measure *catalogue breadth per active user* over time; if the number of unique artists, sources, or categories decays, you are shrinking the window. Measure *diversity exposure index* at the session level: the proportion of items outside a user's top decile of historical preferences. Measure *profile entropy*: the variability of a user's consumption over weeks, not hours. These are not vanity metrics; they are guardrails. They reveal when loops tighten beyond comfort.

Injecting novelty works best when it respects two rules: declare itself and be defeasible. Declare itself: "We've added three unfamiliar sources to broaden your view." People accept difference when treated as citizens, not targets. Be defeasible: let users snooze novelty or refine its scope ("more abroad, less sport"). The visible behaviour to watch is *acceptance after explanation*: does the same user keep the feature on after seeing the label for a week? If yes, novelty has turned into norm.

Exploration spaces should operate as alternate physics. Think of them as laboratories inside the product where a user can wander without consequence. Google's *Full Coverage* is one; Wikipedia's "Random article" button is another; Apple Music's genre stations, when detached from the main profile, can be a third. In each case, the key property is *non-contamination*. What you do there should not back-propagate into your core model unless you explicitly permit it. The model learns less; the person learns more. The benefit is cognitive relief. People can explore without fear that a one-off curiosity—searching for a children's song, reading about a niche conspiracy, sampling a novelty track—will stain their feed for weeks. You will see the effect in *exploration dwell without churn*: time spent in the space rises without increasing the rate at which people mute or abandon core recommendations.

Profile resets must be real. Not performative toggles buried in settings. Real resets do three things. They clear history; they clear *derived* features (clusters, embeddings, lookalike segments); and they show the user what will remain—purchases, follows, or legal records you cannot erase—and why. A good reset prints a receipt: *we deleted your watch history; we kept the purchase invoice required by law; we removed your account from categories A, B, and C*. The behavioural metric here is *post-reset regret*: how often do users attempt to reverse the reset within a week? Low regret indicates the reset matched intent; high regret suggests the reset was either too blunt or too opaque. Provide a *sandbox profile* as well: a temporary, non-committal taste that users can try for a weekend. If it suits them, they can merge or replace. If it doesn't, their original horizon returns untouched.

There is a second route out of traps: *purposeful randomness*. Not chaos, but controlled stochasticity during selection. Injecting a small probability of selecting from the long tail, conditioned on freshness and basic relevance, keeps the model honest. It also hardens it against adversarial optimisation—content engineered to exploit ranking quirks. The motif returns: windows must open. A model that always takes the highest predicted click starves new ideas; a model that sometimes samples from the unexplored learns faster and keeps cultures alive. You will see this in *new-to-user adoption rate*: the proportion of "first-time" categories that turn into follow-on consumption within a fortnight. When purposeful randomness is tuned well, that number rises without depressing satisfaction.

The social dimension matters too. Filtering is not only individual; it is communal. In 2016–2020, major platforms struggled with political recommendation loops that amplified outrage. Some introduced "community notes" or context panels; others raised credible sources in public-health crises. These are not perfect. They are, however, early forms of *plurality rebalancing*. The trick for non-news systems is to borrow the form without the politics: provide sidebars or overlays that situate a recommendation within a broader map. "People who watched this tended to split between A and B next." Maps discourage tunnels. They also create a sense of *agency through awareness*: the person sees the fork rather than just the path.

What about users who explicitly signal a desire for deep focus—bingeing a genre, mastering a skill, living inside a mood? Respect the intention, then protect against brittleness. Offer "Focus modes" with clear entry and exit. During entry, declare the consequence: "We'll show mostly jazz for two weeks." During exit, invite a palate cleanser: "Ready for a wider mix?" The behavioural outcome to measure is *recovery to baseline breadth*: how quickly and completely people return to varied consumption after a deep dive. If recovery is slow, the focus mode became a rut. Adjust its decay curve.

A credible limitation persists. Injecting novelty and creating exploration spaces can suppress short-term click-through and revenue. Teams will feel the pressure. The reconciliation is to shift the time horizon of success. Track *monthly breadth retention*: the proportion of users whose category diversity remains within their healthy range over a month, alongside *net promoter score by perceived variety*. These are leading indicators of resilience. Organisations that adopt them see fewer "model winters"—moments when the feed feels stale and the growth curve sours. Patient breadth pays compounding dividends.

Interfaces should invite users to steer the loop explicitly. Small, durable controls—*more like this, less like this, show me something different*—work when they are respected. The graveyard of ignored buttons suggests a cultural issue, not a UI issue. Honour the click. Show its effect. "We'll show fewer videos from X and similar channels." Log it in a per-user ledger so people can revisit choices. You are training a relationship. The felt behaviour is *earned trust*: people try the knobs again because they felt heard last time.

Design for children and other vulnerable users demands stronger boundaries. For young accounts, make exploration spaces the default; keep resets prominent; suppress features that exploit stickiness. A child's profile should forget faster than an adult's, not slower. The metric to report to guardians is *variety health*: a simple monthly summary—five categories explored; no single category exceeded 40 per cent. That is not paternalism; it is stewardship.

The physicality of exploration matters in spatial interfaces. In AR/VR, narrowing can become motion sickness of the mind: the scene repeats, the path repeats, curiosity wanes. Here "exploration rooms" can be literal: hubs where the laws change—no autoplay, slower transitions, thicker explanations. The rule holds: change the physics to change the loop. Observe *pause-to-leave ratio*: in healthy rooms, pauses lead to considered choices, not to exit.

Language is a lever. Labelling novelty as "outside your usual orbit" or "a fresh route" primes curiosity; labelling it "random" primes scepticism. The words should tell the truth without belittling preference. The aim is to normalise difference as a feature of the system and of the self. People are plural. Let the interface say so.

None of this works without governance. Product teams must be able to prove to auditors—and to themselves—that their loops do not trap. That is where the *anticipation ledger* from the previous section returns in a new role. Extend the ledger to include *exploration incidents*: when and how the system deliberately showed something outside profile, what the response was, and how it will pace future injections. Publish aggregate, anonymised statistics: average breadth, reset usage, recovery curves. Accountability is not a memo; it is a dataset.

Finally, remember that model choice expresses values. Collaborative filtering rewards popularity; content-based models reward similarity; knowledge graphs reward structure; stochastic bandits reward learning under uncertainty. Blend them consciously. If your blend chases only immediate likelihood, it will entrench the past. Add a term for *public good*—exposure to verified civic information, or to underrepresented creators—and declare it. Align your objective with the society you claim to serve. The interface will show your priorities whether you name them or not. Better to name them.

The window must stay open. That is the motif, and the measure. Before you ship the next iteration of your feed, ask three questions that a tired engineer and a sceptical user could both answer in ten seconds. How does the system keep space for firsts? How can I reset without penalty? Where can I explore without consequence? If those answers are obvious in the interface itself, your loop is likely to breathe. If they are not, a valley awaits. The forward test is sharp: when the model is very sure, can you still make it consider the unknown—and will the person see that choice, take it, and come back grateful that the window never closed?

Metrics That Matter: Error, Trust, Dignity

In March 2018, a self-driving Uber test vehicle struck and killed pedestrian Elaine Herzberg in Tempe, Arizona. The system had detected her six seconds before impact but alternated between classifications—"vehicle", "bicycle", "unknown object"—and, crucially, failed to trigger a braking response because its code suppressed "false positives" to avoid unnecessary stops. The car's designers optimised for efficiency, not reversibility. Their metric of success—miles per disengagement—measured steadiness, not safety. It was a lesson paid in blood: what we choose to measure decides what we learn, and what we ignore defines what we destroy.

The paradox is brutal. Modern systems are rich in data but poor in meaning. They track clicks, taps, dwell times, and completions—behaviours measurable in milliseconds—while trust, doubt, and regret, which unfold in heartbeats and hindsight, remain invisible. Yet those invisible states determine whether people stay, believe, or forgive. The craft of humane metrics begins there: measuring hesitation, reversal, and post-task satisfaction not as noise but as signal. It means treating error as information and dignity as data.

Show the problem, name it, explain it, draw implication. The name is *metric myopia*: the narrowing of goals until what matters most becomes immeasurable. Organisations love simple numbers—conversion rates, engagement minutes, net promoter scores—because they travel well in slides. But metrics shape culture. When they ignore hesitation, systems learn arrogance; when they ignore reversals, they confuse friction with failure; when they ignore post-task sentiment, they optimise for obedience, not confidence. The implication is systemic: every click that conceals regret erodes trust, and every regression that celebrates efficiency without empathy compounds it.

Two named examples show what different choices look like. In 2017, Google's Search Quality team introduced a measure called *long click*—how often users clicked a result and did not immediately return to the results page. It replaced raw click-through as a proxy for satisfaction. The behavioural difference was subtle but profound: a long click captured *post-task success,* not mere curiosity. Search improved because the metric respected outcome, not just interaction. Meanwhile, in 2019, Twitter's researchers developed an internal index of *conversation health*—tracking not volume but civility and response diversity. It was messy to compute, hard to automate, and politically charged, yet it shifted the discourse from *engagement* to *environment*. The question became not "how much talk?" but "what kind of talk?" When metrics point towards meaning, products behave differently.

Now, the motif: hesitation as mirror. Watch the pauses. A person hovers before clicking *confirm,* edits a message twice, or moves the pointer toward *cancel* before committing. These micro-delays, measured at scale, reveal uncertainty—the moral emotion of the interface. Yet few systems record them. The metric to build is *hesitation duration before irreversible action*. In medical software, it can signal unclear prompts; in e-commerce, manipulative layouts; in social media, ethical unease. In every case, hesitation is not inefficiency—it is care trying to find words. When a team learns from hesitation, it builds better confidence cues.

Reversals, too, speak truth. A reversal is an undo, a backtrack, a manual override. The user's way of saying, *I didn't mean that.* In interface design, the *reversal rate per 100 actions* is a diagnostic of coercion. High reversal rates mark systems that push too far, too fast; low rates with high dropouts suggest systems that deny the chance to reverse.

The balanced state is *forgiveness elasticity*: easy reversibility within a sensible window. The NHS e-Referral Service (launched 2015) monitors cancellation and rescheduling patterns not as operational noise but as proxies for comprehension and trust. Where reversal spikes, communication failed. Measurement turned reflection into feedback.

Post-task satisfaction closes the triad. Asking "Was this helpful?" is not trivial if the data are treated seriously. Netflix, since 2017, has used binary thumbs instead of five-star ratings because the signal is clearer and faster to interpret. But thumbs alone are not truth. The deeper measure is *retained enjoyment*: whether users who finish a series continue to explore its genre a week later. Retention curves are behavioural diaries of trust. If satisfaction decays rapidly after bingeing, the interface may have delivered compulsion, not contentment.

The counter-example is Amazon's early obsession with *conversion rate*. It was a triumph of logistics but a poverty of feeling. People clicked because they had to; the metric never asked whether they would return gladly. Over time, Amazon added *customer lifetime value, repeat purchase frequency,* and *negative review ratio*—metrics that acknowledge long memory. Yet even those remain economic. The humane leap lies beyond economics: instrumenting for dignity, the right not to be reduced to performance.

How does one measure dignity without trivialising it? Through *asymmetry audits*: who benefits most from errors, and who bears their cost? If a navigation app's "optimised route" saves minutes for drivers but doubles risk for pedestrians, the metric is unjust. If a recruitment algorithm reduces screening time but filters neurodivergent applicants disproportionately, the metric is dishonest. In 2022, the UK's Centre for Data Ethics and Innovation proposed *disparity impact tracking*: recording error rates across demographic subgroups before deployment. It is a simple extension of quality assurance; it is also an act of moral clarity. Dignity enters the spreadsheet.

The motif returns: the mirror. Systems should see their own blind spots. One technique is to create *regret surveys*—brief prompts after high-stakes interactions asking, "Do you wish you'd chosen differently?" Not star ratings, not satisfaction scores, but counterfactual reflection. When linked with behavioural traces, regret data expose where designs coerce subtly—checkout flows, location permissions, or autoplay sequences. The value lies in *correlation with silence*: if people do not complain but still stop returning, regret existed unspoken. Measuring it gives silence shape.

We can name a success case. In 2020, the fintech firm Monzo in London introduced a "retry" option after payment decline notifications, replacing the old abrupt failure screen. They also tracked *stress keywords* in support chats following declines. Within six months, measured stress mentions fell by 18 per cent; call times shortened; trust scores rose. The lesson: error instrumentation that humanises failure improves efficiency indirectly. When systems apologise well, users forgive faster.

Ethical metrics often resist automation. *Trust latency*—how long after a problem users resume normal behaviour—is one such measure. After a data breach, for instance, watch *restored engagement curves* instead of media sentiment. When Equifax's breach (September 2017) exposed 147 million records, their sign-up rates for credit monitoring lagged far longer than share prices suggested. The human half-life of trust is slower than the market's. Systems that acknowledge that lag—through openness, restitution, and clear timelines—rebuild credibility sooner. Trust has kinetics. Measure them.

A credible limitation exists: human signals are noisy, cultural, and manipulable. Platforms that gamify feedback often distort it. Yelp's "Elite" reviews, for example, skew toward hyper-engaged users, underrepresenting casual satisfaction. Amazon's "Was this review helpful?" metric can be brigaded. The reconciliation is triangulation: no single metric stands alone. Combine quantitative traces (clicks, hesitations, reversals) with qualitative moments (comments, free-text feedback) and periodic ethnographic sampling. The goal is not precision; it is proportion. Better to be roughly right about trust than exactly wrong about clicks.

For all their sophistication, AI systems remain dependent on human labels of success. When DeepMind trained

AlphaGo in 2016, the score was simple—win or lose. But for systems that govern people, the score must be plural. We must teach machines not just to perform but to *defer*. That demands metrics of uncertainty and humility. For instance, flag decisions that exceed a model's confidence threshold, log when humans override them, and calculate the *deference rate*: the percentage of cases where machine certainty yielded to human judgment. A high deference rate may slow throughput but signal maturity. The system knows when not to act.

Dignity, ultimately, is a metric of proportion between machine confidence and human consequence. The stronger the impact on a person's life, the higher the standard of explanation and reversibility required. This should not be abstract. A banking algorithm that declines a mortgage should surface the top three features influencing that outcome, offer appeal pathways, and record how often reversals occur after review. The metric is *appeal success ratio*. If that number climbs, the model is learning humility.

Teams need dashboards that show not only what went right but what went *wrong and forgiven*. Include *reversal recovery rate, hesitation decay, trust latency, appeal success, disparity impact*. Watch them together. Their interplay tells the story of moral resilience. A dip in reversals with stable satisfaction may mean clarity improved. A drop in hesitation with rising error may mean recklessness. Patterns become ethics.

There is also the quiet power of invisible metrics—the ones you do not display to users but feel in the culture. Track the ratio of *user-to-employee reversals*: how often internal dashboards override or reinterpret user intent to meet quarterly goals. If that ratio rises, your company trusts metrics more than people. The dignity test fails in-house before it fails in public.

The frontier challenge is building *trust instrumentation* at planetary scale without intrusion. Privacy-preserving telemetry can sample aggregate signals of friction—latency before accept, undo frequency, dwell after cancel—without recording content or identity. The European Data Protection Board in 2023 outlined frameworks for *human oversight indicators*: evidence that users remain active decision-makers rather than passive endpoints. Embedding such measures aligns design with law and decency.

We return to the motif one last time: the mirror must see movement, not pose. Metrics that matter are kinetic; they trace change in relationship, not snapshots of compliance. They measure whether systems learn to listen, and whether people feel heard.

Before shipping the next update, run the forward test: if every metric you track improved by 10 per cent, would the user's dignity necessarily rise? If you cannot say yes, your dashboard is lying to you. Measure what you'd want measured against yourself—error, trust, and the grace to reverse. Anything less is engineering without conscience.

Chapter 7
Interfaces for Many, Not the Median

In February 2020, a young software engineer named Anirudh Sharma sat in a café in Bengaluru, watching his mother struggle to order through a touch-screen kiosk. The screen was slick, the icons small, and the instructions only in English. When she finally managed to select her meal, the system rejected her bank card—its chip slightly worn from years of use. Behind her, a queue of younger, tech-savvy customers waited with polite impatience. The design had worked perfectly for everyone except the person who most needed it to. Sharma later wrote in his notebook a line that has since circled design conferences worldwide: *"Edge cases are the product."*

That phrase encapsulates both a technical truth and a moral provocation. Every interface is an argument about who counts. When designers optimise for the average—speech without accent, eyes without tremor, bandwidth without limits—they flatten humanity into statistical convenience. The median user is a fiction, and yet this fiction quietly governs much of our technology. To design for the median is to build a world that fits nobody quite right, a world where effort flows upwards to the privileged and friction trickles down to the rest. The chapter that follows begins from the opposite premise: that the margins are where quality begins.

The story of accessible design has often been told as a tale of accommodation—an act of benevolence towards those "less typical" users. But look closer and you see a different pattern. Voice recognition's great leaps forward did not come from the perfect pronunciation of American broadcasters; they came from the messy brilliance of accented speech and environmental noise. Predictive text learned resilience through dyslexic typists. Contrast modes in visual interfaces, originally for the partially sighted, became lifelines for everyone in sunlight. Accessibility is not a charitable feature—it is a stress test of universality. Each time a product broadens its range of motion, it becomes more human, not less efficient.

Designers know this intuitively, yet markets often resist the insight. Efficiency worship has a seductive simplicity: one persona, one workflow, one target demographic. But as global reach has grown, the definition of "normal" has collapsed. Interfaces travel faster than culture. A hand gesture polite in one region reads as obscene in another. Colour palettes carry meanings that flip across borders. Even the act of gaze—where and how long one looks—obeys cultural rules. When Microsoft introduced its adaptive controller in 2018, designed for players with limited mobility, it did more than expand access to gaming. It reframed design itself as cultural translation: to make something universal, you must begin with the particular.

The motif running through this chapter is the *mirror that widens*. It invites us to ask: who is reflected, who is cropped out, and how might the frame grow without distortion? Inclusivity is not an aesthetic flourish but a structural discipline—a way of constructing systems that can absorb difference without collapsing. That discipline begins not with technology, but with humility: acknowledging that no single cultural, linguistic, or physical baseline should dictate the contours of interaction.

Consider language. A British user muttering into a voice assistant from a noisy kitchen, a Nigerian trader dictating in pidgin over 3G, and a Tokyo commuter whispering into a headset all inhabit different sonic worlds. The median microphone algorithm cannot serve them equally. Yet the alternative is not chaos. It is *layered design*: systems that listen to context as much as to content, that learn local speech patterns without exporting bias across borders. Companies that have taken this path—Google's inclusion of Indian English and Nigerian English variants in 2022, Apple's addition of regional dialect understanding in 2023—prove that accuracy improves when diversity trains the model. Edge cases make the average smarter.

The argument extends beyond language into the physical. Interfaces increasingly assume stillness, precision, and visual focus, yet millions of users live with tremor, fatigue, or low vision. The irony is profound: as devices grow more adaptive in code, they grow less forgiving in touch. Accessibility specialists at the University of Dundee's Centre for Inclusive Design (2019) demonstrated that minor adjustments—larger tap targets, reduced motion jitter tolerance—lowered error rates across all age groups. It wasn't just better for those with tremor; it was better design, full stop.

Bias cascades begin where data ends. When training sets exclude variance, systems misinterpret reality at scale. A photo classifier that mistakes darker skin for shadow is not malfunctioning—it is performing as trained. A health app that predicts fertility only for women with Western hormonal profiles is not broken—it is incomplete. Preventing these cascades demands more than "de-biasing" after the fact; it requires new data strategies that see underrepresentation as a technical flaw. The measure of fairness is not parity of output but equity of effort: how much extra labour a person must perform just to be seen.

This chapter also steps into the terrain of *cultural ergonomics*—the subtle grammar of movement and meaning. When Facebook first launched its "thumbs-up" icon globally, some regions recoiled; the gesture reads as rude in parts of the Middle East and West Africa. Designers scrambled to localise without fracturing the brand. The lesson was simple but overlooked: politeness itself is embodied. A nod, a tap, a swipe—all carry social weight. The future of interface design will hinge on such anthropological sensitivity, turning localisation from a marketing afterthought into an ethical phase of creation.

But inclusion is not only cultural; it is infrastructural. Billions interact with technology in conditions far from Silicon Valley's assumptions: patchy networks, low-end devices, high sunlight, shared phones. In 2023, the Indian government's Digital Public Infrastructure initiative required all major service apps to support offline or low-bandwidth modes. This wasn't merely policy—it was philosophy. Offline-first design treats connectivity not as default but as privilege, and designs accordingly. The result: systems that fail gracefully, store locally, and sync when possible. The same architecture that empowers rural users makes cities more resilient under strain. Resilience scales both ways.

Low-resource design is moral engineering as much as technical optimisation. When WhatsApp introduced its "data saver" mode and voice-message caching for areas with unreliable coverage, adoption surged in sub-Saharan Africa. What began as an inclusion feature became a growth engine. Ethics, it turns out, can be profitable—but only when dignity is priced in. Which leads to the hardest frontier of all: business models.

Pricing and access are not peripheral to user experience; they are part of it. The decision to gate features behind subscriptions, to segment markets by device, or to monetise through surveillance shapes dignity more deeply than any pixel or icon. The empathy gap between those who build and those who buy—or cannot buy—is the quiet axis of inequality in technology. A phone that assumes constant data is not just expensive; it is exclusionary. A service that withholds basic functions unless a user consents to tracking has converted consent into currency. The challenge for designers and executives alike is to see pricing as interface: the first and most consequential dialogue between a system and its user.

The scope of this chapter is deliberately wide because inclusion touches everything—architecture, data, gesture, business, and belief. Yet its ambition is focused: to show that designing for many, not the median, is not a matter of empathy alone but of excellence. Systems built for variance survive volatility. Products designed for difference endure change. The median, by contrast, is brittle; it breaks when the world tilts.

The closing question, therefore, is not rhetorical but diagnostic: what if every edge case became a design brief, every outlier a teacher, every constraint a source of creativity? To design for many is to rehearse the future—a future where no one has to fight to fit. The mirror that widens reflects us all, not as anomalies or averages, but as the full measure of what it means to belong in a world built by human hands and guided, at last, by human regard.

Edge Cases Are the Product

In May 2022, Google's AI ethics team published an internal memo following a field test of voice recognition in Lagos. The system, trained predominantly on American and British English, failed to interpret more than 30 per cent of utterances from Nigerian speakers using the same commands—"call Mum," "set alarm," "send message." The error was not linguistic; it was systemic. The model had learned to hear power. It was fluent in dominance but deaf to variation. Engineers called it an *accent gap*. Sociolinguists called it an *audibility hierarchy*. Either way, it exposed a truth that haunts every technological interface: when diversity is treated as an edge case, exclusion becomes a feature.

That single field test cost Google millions in retraining and localisation, but the price of bias cannot be measured only in currency. Each misrecognised syllable erodes trust, each flicker of inaccessibility whispers who the system is truly for. Design, like democracy, is judged not by how it treats the median but by how it treats the margins. The quiet motif here is *the hinge*: edge cases are not exceptions to design but its pivots. When we strengthen the hinge, the whole door holds.

Edge cases—accents, low vision, tremor, disability, linguistic nuance—have long been treated as post-hoc fixes or compliance requirements. Yet history shows they are the birthplace of progress. The first telephone amplification devices, developed in the 1920s for the hearing-impaired, laid the foundations for modern audio engineering. Captioning, pioneered for accessibility in the 1970s, evolved into subtitles that now serve the majority of streaming users. Every feature once labelled "assistive" has a habit of becoming essential. The difference lies not in need but in perspective: inclusion accelerates quality.

Consider the voice interface again. In 2011, when Apple launched Siri, the system's training corpus was overwhelmingly composed of male American voices recorded in quiet studios. It failed dramatically in homes where background noise—children, kettles, or traffic—blurred its inputs. Only after Apple's team expanded its data to include noisy, accented speech, and women's higher-pitched tones did reliability climb above 85 per cent. The fix for the so-called "edge" became the defining driver of robustness. A model tuned for diversity withstands entropy.

A parallel story unfolded in the design of visual interfaces. In 2015, Microsoft's Seeing AI project began as a research tool to assist users with visual impairments by describing scenes aloud. Its object-recognition algorithms, designed to narrate the world to blind users, uncovered biases in existing computer-vision datasets. For instance, facial recognition accuracy for light-skinned men hovered around 99 per cent, while for dark-skinned women it dropped below 70 per cent (Buolamwini and Gebru, 2018, MIT Media Lab). Confronted by this inequity, Microsoft refactored its dataset, introducing parity benchmarks across ethnicity, gender, and lighting conditions. The outcome was not just fairness—it was fidelity. Low-vision testing improved visual perception for *everyone*. By seeing more kinds of faces, the system learned to see better.

Show, name, explain, imply. The pattern repeats across domains. Edge conditions expose systemic weaknesses because they stress-test assumptions. A tremor that destabilises a cursor reveals poor tolerance for movement jitter. A regional accent exposes narrow phonetic modelling.

A low-bandwidth environment exposes bloated code. Each so-called anomaly is a diagnostic, not a distraction. Designing for it builds flexibility into the core. The metric of excellence is not perfection under ideal conditions but resilience under variation.

The motif of the hinge returns. When one fixes the hinge—the point of maximum strain—the door serves everyone more reliably. In human–computer interaction, that hinge often lies where biological diversity meets mechanical uniformity. The people who speak differently, see differently, or move differently are not the edges of usability; they are its architects. The challenge is to turn this principle into method.

A mature data strategy begins by assuming that bias is not an error in code but a property of collection. Datasets are mirrors of attention. What is absent is often more revealing than what is present. When speech-recognition models rely on public podcasts, they inherit the demographics of those who get published. When gesture-recognition systems are trained in laboratories staffed by men, they overfit to masculine motion. The technical solution is deceptively simple: diversify data sources intentionally and weight them contextually. The cultural solution is harder: accept that neutrality is an illusion.

In 2020, Mozilla launched Common Voice, a global open dataset for speech technology. It invited volunteers worldwide to record phrases in their own dialects, from Basque to Kiswahili. By 2023, over 130,000 contributors had uploaded 29,000 hours of speech across 90 languages. The project's strength was not its scale but its messiness—real-world noise, hesitation, and imperfection. Machine-learning models trained on Common Voice performed better in variable conditions than those trained on studio audio. Bias reduction, it turned out, required embracing chaos.

Contrast this with facial recognition systems deployed in public safety. Several police contracts across Europe were suspended between 2019 and 2022 after independent audits revealed disproportionate false positives for minorities. The technology's defenders argued for better calibration; its critics argued for moratoria. The reconciliation lies in governance. Systems that shape access to rights or justice must meet stricter thresholds than those that recommend songs or books. *Bias cascades*—the compounding of minor data asymmetries into large-scale exclusion—demand proportional accountability. The higher the human consequence, the higher the evidentiary bar.

There is a temptation to believe that larger datasets naturally yield fairness. Yet size amplifies bias if composition remains skewed. The solution is not infinite data but *structured diversity*: a deliberate architecture of sampling, annotation, and weighting. Netflix's 2019 content-personalisation overhaul demonstrated this principle in practice. After analysing global recommendation patterns, engineers found that users in Brazil and South Korea received fewer local-language suggestions than users in English-speaking countries, despite equivalent engagement. The cause was simple: metadata coverage favoured Anglophone titles. By expanding annotation to regional languages and genres, Netflix not only corrected bias but discovered latent demand. Diversity uncovered revenue.

Bias cascades also occur in physical design. Smartphones, for example, standardised around dimensions comfortable for men's hands. Research by the University of Cambridge (2019) found that 90 per cent of female participants reported thumb strain during one-handed use. That oversight was not malicious; it was methodological. Prototypes tested among engineers replicated their own ergonomics. Companies now run *anthropometric audits* to map the range of human hand sizes, grip strengths, and reach. The technical term is "inclusive anthropometry"; the moral term is respect.

Even the tempo of interaction holds bias. Voice assistants that cut users off after fixed pauses penalise stammerers and non-native speakers. Cursor dwell times optimised for steady hands exclude those with Parkinsonian tremor. Inclusive design must therefore measure *temporal variance* as a first-class input, not as latency to eliminate. The user's rhythm is the system's duty.

A credible counter-example tempers the optimism. Some designers argue that over-accommodating edge cases bloats complexity and confuses the majority. Indeed, there are costs. Over-tuning interfaces can fragment user experience or slow performance. But the reconciliation lies in modular design: systems that detect context and adapt gracefully. Android's accessibility suite, for instance, activates high-contrast text or simplified gestures dynamically, based on sensor input and prior user preferences. Inclusion becomes conditional intelligence, not static compromise.

The economic argument follows naturally. Accessibility budgets are often justified as compliance with regulation—the Web Content Accessibility Guidelines (WCAG) or local disability acts. Yet firms that embed accessibility early report measurable returns. Microsoft's Inclusive Design research (2021) linked improved error recovery rates in its Office suite to features originally built for users with motor impairments. The data point is clear: inclusivity is quality assurance. Edge users expose fragility that mainstream testing misses. The broader the test pool, the stronger the product.

The hinge holds another secret: empathy scales through iteration, not slogans. Every company now claims to "design for all," yet few instrument their systems to verify it. The missing metric is *equity delta*—how performance varies across demographic or physical subgroups. If your product performs 20 per cent worse for those with tremor, that gap is not a footnote; it is an engineering defect. Measuring such deltas requires humility, but the reward is precision.

Ethically, the stakes are profound. Technology has moved from serving needs to shaping norms. When voice assistants mishear accented names, when cameras misread darker faces, when biometric gates reject trembling hands, the harm is cumulative. These small abrasions teach people to lower expectations, to self-censor, to adapt to machines that will not adapt to them. This is the moral cost of treating edge cases as afterthoughts. Inclusion, by contrast, restores dignity as a metric of quality.

The motif closes where it began: the hinge as design philosophy. To build systems that last, engineers must treat variation not as entropy but as essence. The world will always speak with accents, see in gradients, move with tremors. The task is not to normalise those differences away but to make technology fluent in them.

Before the next dataset is approved or the next interface launched, one diagnostic question remains: if your system performs flawlessly for the median user but falters for those at the margins, is that efficiency or fragility? The answer decides not only what kind of product you build—but what kind of world it builds you back into.

Cultural Ergonomics: Gestures, Gaze, and Politeness Vary

In 2013, when Samsung launched its Galaxy S4 with gesture control in Seoul, the feature made global headlines. Users could answer calls or scroll through photos with a simple wave of the hand—no touch required. Yet, in early rollouts across India and the Middle East, the same system triggered errors at astonishing rates. Field engineers discovered that everyday conversational gestures—hand waves, head tilts, nods—were being misread as commands. The interface mistook social nuance for intent. A single wave meant "no, thank you" in Delhi but "next slide" to the phone. It was a perfect demonstration of cultural ergonomics in failure: technology that understood physics but not context.

That story still circulates among interface designers as a cautionary tale. It reminds us that gestures and gaze—those micro-languages of daily life—are never universal. Each society trains its body differently. A raised eyebrow that signals challenge in London might mean curiosity in Tokyo. The same hand gesture can summon or insult, depending on which side of a border it's performed. Yet most design pipelines still assume universality. They treat localisation as a late-phase translation problem rather than a foundational act of cultural engineering. The result is a stream of subtle misfires that accumulate into mistrust.

The motif running through this chapter is *the invisible script*: the unspoken choreography of interaction that every interface either respects or breaks. Cultural ergonomics is the study—and increasingly the practice—of designing systems that fit this invisible script rather than overwrite it. The stakes are high. As technology embeds itself into the rituals of greeting, payment, learning, and care, misunderstanding the body becomes not merely awkward but exclusionary.

To show what this means in practice, consider gaze. In Western design conventions, eye contact signifies attention and trust; camera-centred interactions—from video calls to biometric scans—presume direct gaze. Yet in East Asian cultures, prolonged eye contact can signal aggression or disrespect. When Japanese researchers at ATR Laboratories in Kyoto tested telepresence robots in 2018, they found that users preferred avatars with "softer" eye-tracking behaviour—less constant gaze, more subtle glances. Measured satisfaction rose 23 per cent when the robots mimicked culturally appropriate gaze aversion. A tiny shift in gaze dynamics reshaped comfort, proving that politeness is measurable.

Politeness itself, anthropologists have long observed, is embodied. Edward T. Hall's *The Hidden Dimension* (1966) mapped cultural norms of proxemics—how distance encodes intimacy or respect. Yet digital interfaces have largely ignored this insight. A voice assistant that interrupts too quickly violates conversational turn-taking in cultures where pauses signal deference. A chatbot that uses first names without context can feel uncomfortably forward in collectivist societies. In each case, the system is grammatically correct but socially tone-deaf. The future of interface design must reckon with these gradients of grace.

Nowhere is this clearer than in gesture recognition. Microsoft's Kinect, launched in 2010, was a marvel of hardware precision but a lesson in cultural blindness. Early iterations were optimised for tall users performing Western-style motions—broad, shoulder-based gestures. In smaller living spaces or among populations with subtler expressive habits, accuracy plunged. Engineers in Tokyo reported misreads during bowing motions; users in Lagos found the sensor ignored smaller hand signals. By 2015, Microsoft had revised Kinect's skeletal tracking model using datasets that included a wider range of body types and movement patterns. The system's fidelity improved by over 30 per cent across non-Western markets. Diversity of motion became diversity of meaning.

But gestures are only one axis. Politeness theory, developed by sociolinguists Penelope Brown and Stephen Levinson in the 1970s, describes how communication navigates "face"—the social need to maintain dignity and harmony. Interfaces that ignore face perform rudeness at scale. The digital equivalents of interruption, condescension, or over-familiarity—too many notifications, false urgency, informal tone—erode trust precisely because they breach this subtle etiquette. When WhatsApp adjusted its read-receipt system in 2014 to include optional "blue ticks," backlash was strongest in regions where social relationships depend on strategic ambiguity. People wanted plausible deniability, not omniscient transparency. The adjustment—adding a toggle to disable read receipts—was an act of digital politeness.

Localisation, then, is not an accessory but a discipline: the act of re-rooting a product in the soil of lived culture. Yet many organisations still treat it as translation—a task for linguists at the tail end of development. Proper localisation begins in research and ends in empathy. Airbnb learned this the hard way when its early Chinese-language interface translated "host" literally as *zhǔrén*—a term connoting servitude rather than hospitality. Bookings lagged until the company restructured its entire localisation process to involve cultural consultants at design phase, not post-production. The same redesign yielded interface metaphors drawn from Chinese symbolism—doorways, homecomings, mutual respect—rather than Western "sharing economy" tropes. Adoption soared. The metric of localisation success was not just linguistic accuracy but emotional fluency.

A counter-example exposes the boundary. In 2016, Facebook introduced its "Reactions" feature—five emoji icons meant to express nuanced emotion beyond the "Like." The set included a thumbs-up, heart, laugh, surprise, sadness, and anger. Globally rolled out, it was widely used but occasionally misread. The thumbs-up, already controversial in certain Middle Eastern and Mediterranean cultures, resurfaced as a cultural flashpoint. Yet removing or altering it regionally risked fragmenting the platform's brand identity. The compromise was data-driven adaptation: local algorithms subtly adjusted the prominence and predictive order of reactions based on region. It was an elegant, statistical form of cultural ergonomics—reconfiguring the invisible script without redrawing the interface.

Behind these examples lies a deeper methodological shift. Traditional human–computer interaction (HCI) assumed universality: once a button works for one person, it works for all. Cultural ergonomics inverts that premise. It treats universality as something *earned* through plural testing. A 2019 study at the University of Trento measured usability scores for mobile apps across Italy, India, and Kenya. Interfaces rated "intuitive" in Italy dropped by 40 per cent in perceived clarity elsewhere. The same gestures—pinch, swipe, tap—carried different temporal rhythms and expectations of feedback. Local usability is not deviation; it is truth in detail.

Designers who internalise this begin to see patterns in difference. A respectful interface in Saudi Arabia might default to neutral avatars or gender-sensitive colour palettes. In Nordic regions, minimalism conveys sophistication; in parts of Latin America, it reads as emptiness. Even sound cues hold moral weight. The chime that signals transaction success in Japan—the soft *pon*—would sound trivial to American ears but embodies *omotenashi,* the Japanese ethic of considerate service. Each detail reinforces the same lesson: etiquette is architecture.

The motif of the invisible script returns here with force. To design culturally ergonomic systems, teams must first surface what is normally implicit. Ethnographic research—observing how people actually use technology in context—remains the most powerful tool. When M-Pesa mobile banking spread through Kenya after its 2007 launch, it succeeded not because of technological novelty but because its interface mimicked local social practices of debt and trust. The system's confirmation messages mirrored verbal affirmations used in informal lending. That cultural alignment made it feel natural, not foreign. Attempts to replicate M-Pesa in other markets without these nuances failed repeatedly. Cultural ergonomics does not travel by export; it must be re-grown each time.

The counter-argument is efficiency. Some executives claim that deep localisation fragments ecosystems and dilutes economies of scale. They point to Apple's globally standardised interface—identical gestures from California to Cairo—as proof of universality's advantage. Yet Apple's uniformity conceals careful adaptation. The company's product manuals, Siri voice models, and even emoji keyboards are deeply localised. Its design language may appear monolithic, but its semantics bend subtly to context. The art is to maintain coherence without sameness—a balance that demands investment early, not patching late.

Cultural ergonomics also forces difficult questions about power. Whose comfort defines the default? Whose gestures teach the machine? When global corporations export interfaces rooted in Western habits of expression, they perform cultural imperialism through convenience. The antidote is representation—not tokenism but redistribution of authorship. When local designers, translators, and ethnographers co-own product decisions, cultural variance ceases to be an obstacle. It becomes design intelligence.

Metrics can capture this intelligence. Instead of counting localisation "languages supported," measure *misfire frequency*—how often gestures or phrases are misinterpreted by region. Track *interaction hesitation time* across cultures; a long pause may indicate discomfort, not confusion. Quantify *adaptation success* by user retention after regional release. Such metrics, when integrated into design review, turn empathy from aspiration into discipline.

As interfaces mediate more of public and private life—from healthcare kiosks to border control gates—the moral dimension of cultural ergonomics grows unavoidable. To misread a smile is awkward; to misread a consent gesture can be catastrophic. AI systems that interpret body language or gaze for behavioural predictions already risk codifying cultural stereotypes as "insights." The responsibility, therefore, extends beyond localisation: it demands *interpretive humility*. Designers must learn to say, "We do not know what this gesture means here," and then go find out.

The hinge of this argument—the invisible script—closes on a forward test. Before releasing any gesture, phrase, or behavioural model, ask: does this system presume a universal body, or does it listen to the one in front of it? If design continues to chase uniformity, it will automate misunderstanding at scale. But if it treats cultural ergonomics as its baseline, not its burden, technology may yet learn the oldest human art of all: to mean well, and to be understood as it meant.

Low-Resource Environments: Offline-First, Low-Light, and Noisy Settings

On 25 April 2015, after the Gorkha earthquake struck Kathmandu, volunteer mappers using OpenStreetMap and responders carrying phones with cached maps from MAPS.ME began navigating blocked streets while cell towers flickered on and off. Hospitals overflowed. Power was rationed. Yet ambulances still found viable routes because the interface did not insist on a signal. The design had anticipated scarcity. It worked without asking permission from the network. The network will fail. Plan.

Low-resource contexts are not edge cases. They are a daily reality for billions and an occasional reality for everyone. Trains dive into tunnels. Storms cut power. Crowds saturate cells at stadiums. The paradox is blunt: the more our tools depend on connectivity, the more dignity depends on design that is ready to be alone. Offline-first is not nostalgia for dial-up; it is an ethic of care. It keeps people capable when infrastructure stutters.

Show the principle in action. Name it. Explain it. Implication: *offline-first* means the core task runs locally and degrades gracefully, then syncs when it can. In September 2016, Google piloted YouTube Go in India with a simple premise—preload videos over Wi-Fi, share them peer-to-peer, and expose actual file sizes before download. The visible behaviours were trust behaviours: users saw costs up front and could plan. When the product expanded to Nigeria and Indonesia in 2017, it proved that attention respects frugality. People watched more because the app respected limits. The lesson survives the product's retirement: prefetch and price plainly, or lose the room.

Noise and glare are siblings of low bandwidth. The kitchen at dinner. The bus at rush hour. A clinic corridor with strip lighting. Speech interfaces fail when microphones drown in reverberation; vision models stumble when ISO noise blooms or contrast collapses. Designing for such environments is not an audio-visual afterthought. It is the work. Treat light, sound, and signal as hostile until proven otherwise. Then measure.

Consider low-light first. Camera UIs that display live histogram overlays, exposure warnings, and a "hold still" haptic rhythm reduce blur across all users, but they are vital where illumination drops below 50 lux—domestic night-time. When Google's Night Sight arrived on Pixel devices (2018), the technical breakthrough was computational; the design breakthrough was conversational feedback—explicit prompts to keep steady and a progress indicator during multi-frame capture. Visible guidance turned a lab trick into a public feature. The implication is portable: any system that needs more time or context must *say so* and *show so*, especially when conditions degrade.

Now, noisy settings. A voice assistant that thrives at 60–65 dB SPL (normal conversation) may collapse at 80–85 dB (busy street). The fix is twofold: beamformers and backup. Directional audio arrays help, but the inclusive pattern is a *fallback modality*: quick text dictation with large targets, "press-to-talk" to gate capture, and on-device wake-word detection that sleeps aggressively. In 2020, the NHS app teams trialled "tap-to-confirm" for medication reminders on wards rather than voice confirmations, raising completion rates where alarms already saturated the air. The lesson travels: noise demands touch, not insistence.

Our motif throughout is *the second path*. The second path is the alternate route the product always keeps open—local first, simple first, tactile first. It is the lantern you carry when the lights dim. When bandwidth dips, images load as text cards; when glare spikes, a high-contrast theme asserts itself; when microphones fail, an on-screen keypad appears with fewer, larger choices. The second path is not a permission slip to ship fewer features. It is the discipline that forces clarity about the one thing the interface must let you do *now*.

The strongest historical proof that the second path expands both markets and ethics is M-Pesa. Launched by Safaricom in Kenya in March 2007, it built a financial interface on USSD and SIM-toolkit menus—text, not apps. It worked on low-end handsets, tolerated spotty coverage, and mirrored local cash practices. By 2011, millions transacted daily without data plans or smartphones. The visible behaviour to track was *interruption safety*: you could drop mid-transfer and resume without losing funds. Robustness was dignity. Dignity became growth.

A complementary case: Facebook Lite (launched June 2015). It shipped with a 1 MB installer, reduced memory footprint, and an image-loading policy that postponed high-resolution fetches. By 2020 it had hundreds of millions of users, many on 2G/3G connections. The product's success is often told as a market story. It is also a moral one. When design stops assuming affluence—fast data, bright screens, top-tier chips—more people belong.

Show the risk, too. Name it. Explain it. Implication: a *Lite* strategy can drift into second-class citizenship if features and updates lag or if privacy defaults are weaker. A number of "lite" apps launched between 2015 and 2018 quietly omitted advanced encryption modes and consent flows to save space or complexity. That is not optimisation; that is offloading risk onto poorer users. The reconciliation is design parity: reduce weight, not rights. Ship the same protections in fewer bytes. If you cannot, the feature is not ready to shrink.

Low-resource design is, at heart, systems thinking. Caching strategies, conflict resolution, and sync etiquette matter as much as pixels. Instrument what matters. Track *offline task completion rate* (the share of core tasks possible without network), *sync conflict frequency* (per 1,000 sessions), *cold-start latency* on low-RAM devices, and *glare-mode dwell* (time spent in high-contrast or large-type modes). These are not vanity dials. They are levers that decide who gets served and who is left waiting.

Data architectures need the same humility. Store state locally. Queue writes. Design idempotent operations so repeated submissions do no harm. When re-connecting, prefer diff-based sync; show the merge. In 2019, during Cyclone Idai, NGOs coordinating relief in Mozambique relied on field apps that cached household assessments and later reconciled duplicates on return to base. The UI exposed conflicts as human-readable deltas; caseworkers chose which to keep. Slow truth beat fast loss.

Hardware awareness is equally non-negotiable. Many devices in low-income regions are memory-constrained and thermally fragile. Treat 1 GB RAM as a target, not a tale from the past. Measure *background crash rate on low-RAM tiers;* trim services that swap excessively. Where silicon struggles, move compute to times of plenty: schedule heavy models for charging overnight; run on-device inference in smaller bursts with approximate answers and a "refine on network" pathway later. The second path again.

Lighting and legibility push us into typography and colour. Standard contrast ratios (WCAG 2.1's 4.5:1 baseline) are basement settings, not ceilings. In low-resource contexts, assume scratched screens, cheap panels, glossy covers, and sun. Offer a one-tap *Glare Mode*: bolder weight, increased letter spacing, reduced motion, and monochrome affordances. Measure *error rate per 100 taps* before and after activation. If it does not drop, your style guide is fashionable, not functional.

Noise steers us back to haptics. Where sound cannot carry, vibration can. But haptics must speak a language. Design a small, distinct haptic vocabulary—confirm, warn, wait—and keep it consistent. In 2018 field tests across Mumbai local trains, a ticketing app that added a tight confirmation buzz and a longer "processing" pulse cut double-purchases caused by platform noise and lag spikes. The behaviour changed because the body learned the code.

Language itself becomes a resource. Verbosity burns attention. The interface must compress meaning. Replace "We are experiencing connectivity issues" with "Offline. Saved locally." Replace "Your payment is being processed" with "Paid. Receipt queued." Short verbs, clear state, next step. In scarce contexts, grammar is an affordance.

A credible limitation deserves airing: offline-first raises security concerns. Storing more data locally increases exposure if a device is lost, shared, or seized. The reconciliation is *graduated sensitivity*. Cache references, not content, for the most delicate data; encrypt at rest with keys derived from per-session secrets; expire caches aggressively. Pair with social patterns, too: in shared-phone households, provide *Guest View* modes that reveal no history by default. The measurable outcome is *zero-knowledge failure*: a lost device divulges nothing meaningful. If that cannot be assured, the offline feature is a risk, not a service.

Low-resource design also has a procurement face. Business models shape who gets served. Data-hungry ad-funded models punish the poor twice—first with cost, then with surveillance. Pricing plans that privilege downloads over streams, days over months, or local repair over replacement expand both markets and ethics. When Spotify launched

"Data Saver" and low-bitrate modes, it was a growth tactic. It was also a fairness tactic. The line is thin because the outcomes align: frugality serves both scale and dignity when intent is honest.

The quiet power of *offline by default* emerges in public services. Estonia's X-Road and India's DigiLocker take distinct paths to the same promise: citizens control documents and can present them without live server pings. Where infrastructure buckles under load or politics, that control is resilience. In healthcare, offline-capable vaccination records spared families in rural clinics repeat journeys when networks failed; sync later fulfilled reporting duties. Ethics travelled as convenience.

Our motif returns for synthesis. The second path—local, legible, low-assumption—does not only keep a product useful; it keeps a person sovereign. When the first path is blocked by cost, light, noise, or policy, the second path prevents the quietly brutal message: *come back when you can afford us*. That message has built more churn than any competitor.

Before shipping, set the forward test. Can a person complete the core task with no data, one hand, and a scratched screen, while standing on a noisy bus at dusk? If not, you have built for a showroom, not a street. Then ask the market question that is also the moral one: will the next million users arrive because your interface assumes plenty—or because it works when plenty is rare?

Pricing, Access, and the Empathy Gap

On 16 March 2020 in Nairobi, as the first wave of COVID-19 reached Kenya, Safaricom announced that person-to-person fees on M-Pesa would be waived for low-value transfers, following guidance from the Central Bank of Kenya. Within days, fruit sellers were tap-typing tiny payments in markets that had never taken cards; matatu conductors were accepting fares without coins; clinics were settling bills without queues. The product had not changed its buttons. The business model had changed its ethics. Price is a prompt.

That decision did more than nudge adoption. It altered dignity. People could pay without shame about small amounts. They could choose hygiene over cash without choosing between fees and food. A tariff table had become part of the interface. It always was. We just forget. And when we forget, we export the costs of our forgetting to those with the thinnest margins.

Business models are not neutral plumbing behind the glass. They script what the glass can mean. They decide who waits, who opts out, who leaks data, and who quietly pays more for the same outcome. We talk a great deal about pixels and patterns, less about price and power. This subchapter argues a simple, testable claim: affordability is an interface decision. Change the economics and you change the interaction. Keep the economics misaligned and the most elegant flow charts will still humiliate their users.

Show the hinge. Name it. Explain it. Implication: the "empathy gap" in technology is often a pricing gap wearing a friendly UI. When the default model is subscriptions on high-end devices, the poor pay in friction instead of cash: more taps, more ads, more data burned to reach the same page. When the default is surveillance-funded "free", the poor pay with privacy. Either way, dignity falls through the cracks between design and tariff.

Two named examples frame the spectrum. First, Safaricom and the Central Bank's 2020 fee waivers in Kenya, with a concrete behavioural outcome: low-value digital payments became ordinary in settings where coins once ruled. It was not only cheaper. It felt permissible. Second, a counter-example from New Delhi: in February 2016, India's telecom regulator (TRAI) barred Facebook's Free Basics programme on net-neutrality grounds. Free Basics had offered "free" access to a curated slice of the web. The economics were generous; the design was paternal. The system, not the citizen, chose what the internet was. The outcome was clear: the service halted; public debate clarified that affordability must not narrow horizons. Together, these cases show a rule: price relief that enlarges choice expands dignity; price relief that edits choice undermines it.

What follows is the paragraph-by-paragraph engine for making that rule practical. We begin with the smallest, most measurable unit of experience: the cost of one task. The metric is *effective cost per task*: data, time, and attention spent to do the core thing—book a visit, submit a form, send a message. Teams that budget in this unit design differently. They expose file sizes; they prefetch on Wi-Fi; they cache receipts locally; they let people complete the task offline with a queue that syncs later. These are not niceties. They are price features. You can watch the effect in *drop-off at paywalls* and *rage-quits on metered connections*. They fall when cost is legible and controllable.

Affordability has a rhythm. It lives in peaks and valleys: the end of the month when data is low, the dead zone on a commute, the surprise job loss that turns subscriptions into threats. When designers instrument *affordability moments*—times when the product should soften—they can respond with modes that fit the reality. A reading app that switches to a low-data font and a grayscale mode at 5 per cent battery is not fashionable. It is humane. A video product that shows "download at night over Wi-Fi; expected size 123 MB; available by 07:00" is not clever. It is honest. You can measure the change in *completion under constraint*: tasks that still finish when power, data, and time are scarce.

Affordability also speaks in the grammar of failure. Declined payments and expired trials are not only finance events; they are interface events. Monzo's "retry" after card declines in the UK (2020) paired with clear copy reduced support load and shortened call times because it acknowledged embarrassment and offered a path back without scolding. The behaviour moved because tone moved. The same principle travels to government services. If an application fee fails, show a temporary waiver, a pay-later token, or a cash alternative at a kiosk. The measure to track is *shame exits*: sessions that end on a failure screen without a follow-up within seven days. Make that number fall.

A second named example shows affordability as growth strategy rather than compliance. In September 2016, Reliance Jio's launch in Mumbai collapsed data prices in India and normalised 4G access for millions who had never streamed a video. The technical story is spectrum and towers; the design story is *what became viable*. Interfaces that once had to tiptoe around megabytes could afford to show richer state, prefetch routes, and embed translation models. Markets widened because cost curves bent. The implication is practical: design teams must maintain two mental models—*thrift* and *plenty*—and ship both. When cost falls, features expand; when cost rises again (as it does, unpredictably), dignity persists because the thrift path still works.

Risk hides in the "lite" reflex. Product teams often respond to affordability by shipping cut-down versions that remove features, delays updates, or relax privacy defaults. That is the empathy gap in code. A smaller binary should not carry weaker rights. When Facebook Lite (2015) succeeded with a 1 MB installer and a reduced memory footprint, it was because it kept the social contract intact: same protections, fewer bytes. Where "lite" products have failed, the failure is moral before technical—second-class experiences for second-class citizens. The fix is parity as policy: identical consent flows, identical encryption, identical audit trails. If parity cannot be met, the feature is not ready to shrink.

Affordability is also a posture towards uncertainty. Pre-authorising a sum, renewing silently, or billing in bundles are not just revenue mechanics; they are acts that can corner people. An empathetic interface treats recurring charges as *renewable consent*. It asks before it renews. It gives notice in the place where the person acts, not just by email at 02:00. It offers "pause for 30 days" without penalty. The metric worth watching is *regret refunds per thousand renewals*. If that number is high, your model is harvesting confusion. If it falls after redesign, dignity rose.

The empathy gap widens when "free" means "you pay with yourself". Many advertising-funded interfaces are careful about copy and reckless about capture. They burn data to fetch surveillance scripts; they disguise tracking behind usefulness. The most honest interventions here are structural: on-device inference for personalisation where possible; explicit controls for outbound data; a *data saver* that also saves privacy by default. Apple's App Tracking Transparency (iOS 14.5, April 2021) made the trade visible and defeasible with a small, situated card. The adoption of tracking fell; people chose. If your product claims to respect users, instrument the same choice. When users decline, performance should degrade gracefully rather than retaliate with friction.

We should name the counter-argument. Some leaders claim that deep concessions to affordability kill innovation, because margins fund risk. There is truth. But there is also a false economy. Products that ignore costs merely push them onto help desks, social workers, and families who must bridge the gap with time and patience. The reconciliation is a portfolio view: premium tiers can subsidise public goods while *baseline dignity* remains non-negotiable—comprehension, reversibility, security, and an offline path for the core task. A business finishes the sentence it starts: if it says "for everyone," the price architecture must prove it.

Pricing is rhetoric. It speaks in defaults, whether teams admit it or not. Free trials that require card numbers are not "free"; they are bets against memory. Interfaces that auto-select annual plans are not "helpful"; they are traps set against liquidity. If a model depends on this theatre, the UI will learn to perform it. Replace the theatre with truth. Put the cheapest plan first when you detect pre-pay SIMs. Offer day passes for tools needed once. Display lifetime cost for subscriptions at checkout. The behaviour to monitor is *plan regret after first month*: downgrades plus cancellations tied to misunderstanding. Make it drop through honest layout.

The motif in this section is *the receipt you can live with*. A humane product leaves a trace the user would show a friend without shame. That receipt is not only a PDF. It is the memory of whether the price matched the promise and whether the user felt respected while paying. This is where dignity—so often treated as poetic—becomes operational. Ask, after high-stakes transactions, "Was this affordable for you today?" Then link that answer to concrete offers: a pause, a switch to pay-as-you-go, a referral to an offline channel. Trust is not a mood; it is the felt availability of the second path when money is tight.

Affordability can be expressed as *latency of access* as well as cash. Transport for London's daily fare capping on contactless (2014) turned the city's price system into an ambient assurance: ride until the cap, then stop paying automatically. The design success was invisibility paired with fairness; the user never had to do sums at a gate. Interface and business model blurred into one caring behaviour. That is the aspiration in digital services too: caps that prevent runaway spend, *safety rails* that catch people before debt spirals, and meters that reveal themselves in simple language ahead of commitment.

Data ethics intersects here. If affordability choices push vulnerable users into data-heavy "free" tiers, the model is regression in disguise. The rule to write on the wall: *do not tie dignity to income*. Keep core privacy controls invariant across price points. Do not sell "privacy" as a feature. Sell service, sell speed, sell storage; keep agency a right.

Affordability also shapes inclusion on the supply side. Gig platforms that charge workers to see job offers or that withhold tips to balance guarantees practise extractive pricing that then shows up as hostile UX—mysterious queues, disappearing options, jittery maps. Fix the pay model and the UI can become simple again. You will see the change as a drop in *support contacts per active worker* and a rise in *shift completion without escalation*. Business model changes are measurable in pixels.

Two practical design commitments draw this together. First, *price preview everywhere*. Before a click commits bandwidth or money, show the cost. Name the unit. Offer alternatives: "Download later over Wi-Fi," "Use text-only mode now," "Pay cash at partner shop." Second, *failure with grace*. When money fails to flow, the product should carry the situation lightly—save progress, mark the point, hold state locally, and return the user to a place of control, not a cul-de-sac. These are not merely ethical. They grow markets. People return to products that do not punish them for being poor.

The receipt motif returns for closure. Ask what your product prints in the user's life, not just their inbox. Is it a sense that the system waited for them when they needed time? That it explained, before it charged, in language they could afford to read? That it gave them a way back when something broke? If the answers are yes, your business model is part of your interface in the only sense that matters: it keeps agency intact.

The forward test is crisp and uncomfortable. Would you ship the same defaults if you had to sit beside a user on a pay-as-you-go plan and watch them try to cancel, renew, or pause while their data ticked down? If not, you know where the empathy gap sits. Close it. Price like you design: for many, not the median.

Chapter 8
Patterns of Humane Control

In March 2018, a self-driving Uber test vehicle struck and killed pedestrian Elaine Herzberg in Tempe, Arizona. The car's sensors had detected her six seconds before impact. The algorithms had classified her first as an object, then as a bicycle, then as something unknown. Each shift reset its prediction. The system saw, but it did not *know* what it saw. Worse, its safety driver, lulled by long stretches of automation, did not notice the handover gap until it was too late. There was no clear state, no visible stakes, and no graceful way back to human control. The car was not out of control—it was unaccountable.

This tragedy sits at the uneasy heart of our automated century. As systems decide more on our behalf—routing our commutes, sorting our candidates, even drafting our emotions—the central design question is no longer just *what* technology can do, but *how it gives control back*. Humane control does not mean manual control; it means *legible, reversible, inspectable, and interruptible control*. These are the four anchors of this chapter: legibility, reversibility, provenance, and escalation. Together they form a pattern language for systems that remain intelligible to the people who depend on them.

The motif here is *the visible hand*. When a system acts on your behalf, you should be able to see its hand on the lever, feel its grip ease when you intervene, and trace its fingerprints when something goes wrong. Legibility shows the hand; reversibility lets you move it; provenance records its touch; escalation ensures there is still a human at the other end. Each of these patterns serves the same moral premise: that power without visibility is manipulation, and visibility without remedy is theatre.

The need for legibility first arose not in software, but in the design of early industrial machinery. In 1854, the Great Exhibition in London displayed George Stephenson's safety valve for steam engines—a device that let workers see and release pressure before catastrophe. The idea that "state should be visible before stakes become fatal" has echoed through every domain since. In digital systems, legibility means something equally concrete: banners that reveal what the system is doing, dry-run previews that show predicted outcomes, and shadow actions that simulate risk without consequence. These are not aesthetic details. They are moral prosthetics.

Reversibility, by contrast, concerns time. Once, control systems were built for certainty: commit meant commit. But certainty has become a dangerous luxury in contexts governed by data, where predictions are probabilistic and contexts fluid. Safe exploration must become the default mode. The principle is simple: allow for change, delay finality, and normalise undo. Time delays, soft locks, and consequence previews should not be developer conveniences but civic rights. The nuclear launch protocol's "two-key" system, the delayed-send option in email clients, or the 10-minute hold before deleting a user account—all belong to the same lineage. They make hesitation a design feature, not a flaw.

Provenance is the memory of action. As our decisions intertwine with those of algorithms, we require audit trails that belong to users, not only administrators. In healthcare, aviation, and finance, black boxes preserve facts for investigators; in consumer technology, we have their opposite—opaque logs that serve only the corporation. A humane system reverses that flow. It gives users a view into the sequence of triggers and data that shaped an outcome. When the UK's HMRC introduced auditability into its "Real Time Information" tax system in 2013, disputes about misreported earnings dropped significantly because employees could *see* the timeline of each submission. Transparency without ownership is voyeurism; transparency with provenance is education.

Escalation completes the pattern. Even the most legible, reversible, and auditable systems will fail users if they trap them in loops of automation without recourse. A humane system must provide a single beat—a visible, dignified exit—to a human who can act with discretion. When Google redesigned its account recovery process in 2019, introducing a one-tap "talk to human" fallback that preserved chat context, resolution rates rose and anger fell. People do not expect machines to be perfect. They expect a path back to care. Escalation is not a support feature; it is an accountability valve.

These four principles—legibility, reversibility, provenance, escalation—are not abstract ethics. They are patterns of engineering discipline that express respect. Each restores friction where automation erases it. Each makes power visible again. Together, they sketch a future in which systems do not infantilise users by guessing too much or abandon them by concealing too well.

The challenge is cultural as much as technical. Most product roadmaps still equate control with convenience: fewer clicks, fewer warnings, fewer questions. But convenience, when stretched past comprehension, becomes coercion. The dashboards that make trading frictionless also make ruin instant. The one-click checkout that feels effortless in retail can feel reckless in healthcare or consent. As automation intensifies, designers must rediscover the art of staging—making a system's state and stakes visible at every step, without overwhelming the user or trivialising the risk.

To build such systems demands humility. It means accepting that no algorithm is omniscient, that no data is self-explanatory, and that no prediction is final. It means designing for the moment after the mistake—not to hide it, but to recover from it. And it means training users to see control not as a static possession but as a dialogue: a living conversation between intention and outcome.

The payoff is not only safety but trust. When users can see what a system is doing, undo what it has done, trace how it learned, and reach a human when it falters, they begin to trust automation not because it is invisible, but because it is *understandable*. That is the difference between obedience and confidence.

This chapter traces these patterns in action: from the staging of legibility that reveals intent, to the architectures of reversibility that honour uncertainty, to the audit trails that restore provenance, and the escalation paths that preserve humanity in the loop. Each section asks a single, enduring question: *how much power can a system hold before it owes an explanation?*

The answer, inevitably, will be negotiated in design decisions that feel small: a label, a timer, a button that says "undo". But small details carry large ethics. Humane control is built not from grand gestures but from quiet guarantees—visible state, recoverable time, traceable memory, reachable help. The reader who follows will not only see how these patterns protect users from systems, but how they protect systems from themselves.

Legibility: Show State, Show Stakes

On 3 January 2008, a Boeing 777 operated by British Airways struck the grass short of Heathrow's runway 27L. Both engines had lost thrust during final approach. The flight crew, led by Captain Peter Burkill, had seconds to act. They managed to glide the aircraft to the runway, saving every life on board. Later investigation by the UK Air Accidents Investigation Branch found the cause: ice crystals in the fuel system, undetected by sensors. The pilots had not been warned because the system's indicators showed *normal* conditions until thrust collapsed. The cockpit was bright with data, but blind to consequence. The interface failed its duty of legibility—it showed state, but not stakes.

This story endures in engineering circles because it exposes a universal truth: data alone is not visibility. Systems can overflow with signals and still conceal intent. In aviation, medicine, finance, or software, the danger is identical—a surface that looks transparent but hides what matters. The task of legibility is not to make systems verbose, but *comprehensible*: to reveal what they are doing, why, and what could happen next.

Legibility is not an aesthetic choice; it is an ethical one. Every opaque automation carries moral risk. When a system acts, its intent must be staged in a way the user can interpret and interrupt. This is the principle behind banners that declare *what is changing now,* previews that simulate outcomes, and shadow actions that let users explore without consequence. Each offers a glimpse of intent before commitment. Each earns trust through structure, not charm. The quiet motif of this section is *the rehearsal*: every legible system rehearses its next move in front of the person it affects.

Consider Google's staged "Privacy Sandbox" rollout for Chrome (London, August 2023). The project aimed to replace third-party cookies with new APIs for interest-based advertising. But instead of silently switching millions of browsers, Google presented clear banners: "You're included in Privacy Sandbox trials; here's what changes;

here's how to opt out." The legibility wasn't perfect—many found the copy opaque—but the gesture mattered. It recognised the transition as an *event,* not a background process. Legibility reframes automation from *happening to users* to *happening with them.*

The same pattern shaped another case five years earlier, in September 2018, when Slack launched its "Do Not Disturb" scheduling tool. The company added a visible state banner to every message sent to someone offline: "This person has notifications paused." It was a small intervention—a line of text—but it transformed workplace etiquette. People stopped expecting instant replies; they learned to read presence as a shared social contract. The measurable impact was a 25% drop in after-hours message opens in large enterprises within six months (Slack, 2019). The banner did not just convey information; it enforced empathy.

These examples share a choreography: systems that show state in context reduce friction before conflict. This choreography is ancient. In 1936, British railway engineer Henry Fowler introduced the "driver's eye view" indicator in steam locomotives—colour-coded dials showing boiler pressure and brake state. The goal was not to simplify the machine but to *externalise its rhythm.* By aligning what the engine knew with what the driver could see, Fowler's design reduced overpressure accidents by nearly a third within a year (British Transport Archives). Legibility, when done well, turns machinery into dialogue.

Digital systems often mistake legibility for verbosity. Pop-up alerts, modal dialogues, and terms of service walls attempt to *say* rather than *show*. The result is visual noise that teaches users to ignore warnings altogether—a phenomenon confirmed by the 2016 Carnegie Mellon study "The Cost of Annoying Warnings," which found that 74% of participants dismissed pop-ups within two seconds of appearing. The failure was not attention; it was context. Banners should not interrupt cognition; they should frame it. The design challenge is to stage *just enough foresight*—a momentary preview of consequence that feels like a courtesy, not a compliance exercise.

That principle guided the development of GitHub's "pull request preview" (2012). Before merging code, contributors can view the diff, see conflicts, and simulate the merge in a sandbox environment. It is a dry-run preview—a rehearsal before commitment. The visible behaviour is not warning but confidence: the interface shows both what will change and what will stay untouched. Engineers report a 40% reduction in post-merge defects when using preview-based reviews (GitHub Engineering Report, 2019). Legibility, in other words, is a design strategy for calm.

But legibility must not become a performance. When every click spawns a confirmation screen, the interface shifts from clarity to condescension. Amazon's checkout flow offers an illustrative counterpoint. Its "Buy Now with One Click" feature, patented in 1999, became a symbol of convenience. Yet it removed the stage entirely—no preview, no subtotal banner, no visible step between desire and transaction. The act of buying collapsed into a gesture. The measurable result: higher conversion, but also higher rates of regret and return. In 2017, when the patent expired and rivals copied the pattern, several—including Apple and Shopify—quietly added confirmation banners and visual receipts back into the flow. The paradox resolved itself: restraint can accelerate trust.

A more extreme version of opacity emerged in the algorithmic trading flash crash of 6 May 2010, when the Dow Jones Industrial Average plunged nearly 1,000 points in minutes before rebounding. Post-event analysis by the U.S. Securities and Exchange Commission revealed that automated systems executed trades without visible coordination or oversight. There was no legible state—a trader could not see which algorithms were active or what thresholds triggered them. The consequence was systemic panic, not individual error. Legibility at scale is safety; its absence is contagion.

Modern design has begun to rediscover this truth. When Apple introduced "Sign in with Apple" (June 2019, San Jose), it included a *preview pane* showing which personal data would be shared with the requesting app, plus an option to hide one's real email address. This dry-run transparency was not decoration. It turned an opaque authentication step into an informed choice. The company's research team later reported that uptake of the "hide my email" option stabilised around 35%—a sign not of paranoia, but of *understood control*. A user who knows the stakes is not resisting the system; they are participating in it.

In less privileged contexts, legibility is often the difference between autonomy and dependency. Consider Kenya's Huduma digital ID project (launched 2015). Early prototypes used opaque biometric matching, with little explanation of how data was used. Following public criticism, the programme's later iterations added visible consent banners, session summaries, and printed audit slips for each transaction. Citizens could see when their data was accessed and why. Complaints of "vanishing records" dropped sharply. Legibility rebalanced power. The person became more than a data point.

Yet there is a tension. Full transparency can overwhelm, and partial transparency can deceive. The challenge is *graduated legibility*—revealing system intent at the right granularity, in the right moment, to the right user. Think of Tesla's Autopilot interface: a live road visualisation that shades cars, lanes, and cones in real time. When it works, it builds trust by showing perception. When it misclassifies or flickers, it erodes that trust faster than any crash report. The pattern is fragile: legibility must not promise omniscience. It should display uncertainty alongside confidence.

In this sense, the most honest interfaces might be those that admit what they do *not* know. The "shadow action" concept emerging in safety-critical software borrows from aviation simulators: systems that model possible outcomes without committing to them. A medical AI might display its top three diagnoses, not just its chosen one; a navigation app might preview alternate routes if signal degrades. The action remains hypothetical but visible. The value lies not in prediction accuracy but in interpretability—the user sees how the system reasons. Legibility becomes mutual education.

Revisiting our motif of the *rehearsal,* every transparent system stages a small performance for its human counterpart. It explains its role, shows its props, and lets the human decide when to proceed. The rehearsal, not the act, is where confidence grows. But rehearsals take time, and time is costly. In fast-moving consumer design, that cost is often deemed unacceptable. "People just want it to work," say the optimisers. They are half right. People want it to work *and* to know why. They want the option to watch before they trust.

So the forward test for designers, engineers, and policy-makers is straightforward, though rarely applied: could a first-time user predict what your system will do next, and what it will *not* do, based solely on what is visible? If the answer is no, the interface is not finished.

Legibility's endgame is not perfection but foresight—the humane ability to anticipate without anxiety. It asks technology to speak in complete sentences: here is what I see; here is what I am about to do; here is how you can stop me. When systems reach that level of candour, trust ceases to be a slogan. It becomes a property of the interface itself.

The next question—one this chapter leaves open deliberately—is how far to take this visibility. At what point does showing intent become exposing complexity, and when does exposure itself become a liability? A legible system protects the user from surprise; an overexposed one burdens them with responsibility. The difference is not technical but moral. Who bears the weight of understanding—the human, or the machine pretending to be humble? The future of humane automation may depend on how we answer that question, one banner, one preview, one shadow action at a time.

Reversibility: Safe Exploration by Default

On 22 June 2015, in Mountain View, Google promoted a small experimental feature to Gmail's default settings. "Undo Send" gave people up to 30 seconds to retract an email after hitting send. It did not change the content of any message. It changed time. The feature created a tiny margin for second thoughts—a pause that caught accidental replies-all, late-night misfires, and fingers faster than minds. Within weeks, anecdotes from teams and journalists piled up: projects salvaged, apologies avoided, reputations spared. A button had turned haste into hesitation. The interface had discovered mercy.

Reversibility is the craft of building second chances into systems. Not as a bailout for incompetence, but as recognition that action under uncertainty deserves a safety net. In probabilistic, automated environments, confidence is never absolute; therefore commitment should rarely be instantaneous. Time delays, soft locks, and consequence previews are design's answer to human fallibility. They institutionalise doubt. They make *try-before-commit* the norm. The motif to hold throughout this piece is *the second chance*. We will return to it again and again, because it is the moral geometry of humane control.

Show the pattern; name it; explain; draw implication. The pattern is the *deliberate delay*: a bounded interval between intent and consequence. Gmail's buffer is one version. Apple's Photos app, launched with iOS 8 in Cupertino in September 2014, offers another. "Recently Deleted" keeps removed images for 30 days before permanent erasure. Similar grace periods now exist across cloud drives and messaging platforms. These are soft locks: state changes that feel immediate to users, but which the system treats as provisional. The explanation is simple—the cost of false finality is higher than the cost of a reversible hold. The implication is deeper—when people sense reversibility, they explore more and panic less. Curiosity becomes safer than fear.

Designers often underestimate how much anxiety a hard commit produces. Consider the queue of irreversible actions that litter modern life: cryptocurrency transfers, one-click purchases, and privacy settings that broadcast without preview. "Frictionless" flows trumpet efficiency but convert mistakes into penalties. By contrast, systems that frame consequences in advance build trust without slowing experts. GitHub's code review model is instructive.

Since 2012, "pull request" previews simulate the effect of a change before merge. In 2019, GitHub expanded draft pull requests, making the "not ready" state explicit. Teams reported fewer post-merge reversions and calmer release cycles. The visible behaviour changed because the time horizon changed. People could circulate work without committing it. The second chance invited collaboration rather than daring.

Let's make the idea concrete with two checkable cases and one strict limitation. First, a financial example that blends delay and preview. In 2014, the UK's Faster Payments scheme began supporting *delayed confirmation messaging* in consumer banking apps. Banks including Monzo and Barclays showed a pending screen with the recipient's name and a risk cue ("new payee", "out-of-pattern amount") for a heartbeat before final transfer. The interstitial was short, but it created space for "does this look right?" cancellations. Fraud departments later reported fewer misdirected payments where the name-check surfaced. Efficiency barely dipped; confidence rose. Second, a civic example. Wikipedia's "Show preview" has existed for years, but in 2017 the platform began nudging editors—especially newcomers—towards preview-before-save on mobile. Vandalism fell; fix-up edits fell too. The soft lock reduced churn by catching errors before they polluted history. Reversibility saved both labour and face.

Now the limitation. Some domains resist reversal. Blockchain transactions cannot be clawed back without complicated, social-layer remedies. The irreversibility is not a bug; it's a property. But systems built on such substrates can still surround invariance with reversibility. Exchanges can stage *pre-commit previews* showing fees, routes, and addresses with human-readable handles; wallets can enforce *delayed sends* by default for first-time recipients; networks can add *cancellable mempool holds* at the protocol edge. The substrate stays immutable; the interface becomes forgiving. The second chance moves to the edge.

Time delays shape more than error rates; they shape courage. In health and welfare services, forms that erase on timeout teach helplessness; forms that auto-save drafts teach that progress is safe. The visible behaviour to monitor is *abandonment after error*. When reversibility is present, abandonment drops because recovery is cheap. In workplace tools, a simple "hold-to-send" mic in noisy environments turns accidental commands into intentional ones. A press, a pause, a release. Here the delay is embodied. It communicates respect for context.

Reversibility is often conflated with confirmation spam. It is not the same thing. "Are you sure?" boxes that stop the flow without staging consequences train users to click blindly. That is theatre, not safety. The better pattern is *consequence preview*. Show the delta the action will produce: "You are about to remove 3 teammates; their access will end in 24 hours; files remain shared with the group." When Slack added graceful deactivation previews for admins, confusion tickets fell. When e-commerce flows show tax, shipping, and subscription terms before the final button, regret and chargebacks fall. The shared mechanism is comprehension before consequence. People act wisely when shown the shape of the future.

We can measure these effects. Three metrics matter in practice: *reversal rate per 100 high-stakes actions* (does the system allow and register safe undo?), *post-commit regret signals* (refunds, chargebacks, deletes within a cooling-off period), and *exploration breadth* (how widely users sample features when undo exists). Healthy systems show a counterintuitive pattern: slightly higher early reversal rates, meaning people test and undo, paired with lower long-term regret and higher adoption of advanced features. Safety seeds mastery.

Soft locks—those provisional states—work because they separate user experience from system finality. The Recycle Bin, the "Recently Deleted" album, the "trash" folder in email: all place an object in a reversible limbo. But soft locks fail when hidden. If users do not know how to reverse, they do not act. Therefore, legibility is a prerequisite to reversibility. The bin must be visible; the timer must be labelled; the "undo" must be first-class, not buried. This is why Gmail's *post-send banner* mattered. The system surfaced a promise: you have ten seconds; we will honour it. A promise kept becomes culture.

There is a risk to the other extreme. Over-generous holds can stall organisations. If everything can be reversed indefinitely, nothing can be decided. Reconciliation lies in *graduated irreversibility*. Small acts get long windows; critical acts get short windows plus multi-step checks; extraordinary acts get *dual control*. The nuclear two-key protocol is the archetype; modern analogues include payments that require two approvers above a threshold, or data exports that need a manager's code sent out-of-band. The gradient expresses moral weight: the bigger the consequence, the more deliberate the commitment. The second chance scales with stakes.

The try-before-commit norm extends beyond clicks. Consider machine assistance in clinical settings. Decision-support tools that propose a diagnosis should *stage* the suggestion with a confidence band and comparison cases, not overwrite the chart. Radiology systems that allow *shadow reporting*—trainees write a report that does not commit until a consultant countersigns—produce learning without liability. In 2021, several NHS trusts piloted such shadow flows in PACS viewers; error rates among trainees fell across three months, and consultants reported fewer interruptive clarifications. Reversibility became pedagogy.

Economic incentives often fight these designs. One-click checkouts convert; limited cooling-off periods lower returns; hard deletes lighten storage costs. But shallow gains hide deep losses. Products that create safe exploration generate loyalty that outlasts quarterly targets. You will see it in *support tickets per 1,000 active users* and *net promoter score after recovery events*. When recovery is smooth, people talk about the system as an ally. When it is brutal, they talk about it as a trap. Retention follows tone.

Not every delay must be temporal. Some are social. Wikipedia's long-standing "rollback" powers and Git's "revert" commit encode community reversibility. In enterprise software, treating automation rules as drafts—*policies that simulate for a week before enforcement*—prevents mass lockouts. Cloud platforms that ship "dry run" modes for firewall rules or billing changes make cultures bolder, not reckless. The pattern is always the second chance. People accept guardrails when they can see them, test them, and nudge them.

Let us press the counter-example further. Amazon's original "Buy Now with 1-Click" and similar flows eliminated previews and timers. Returns rose in some categories where impulse and error were common; repeated orders packed the support queue. The company and its rivals later surrounded the one-click with post-purchase controls: easy cancellation before fulfilment, windowed edits to addresses, and instant refunds for certain items. In other words, they reintroduced reversibility *after* conversion. The machine learned humility. Trust recovered because the second chance returned—late, but real.

There is also a legal analogue that reminds design what society has long known. The UK Consumer Contracts Regulations (effective June 2014) enforce cooling-off periods for many distance sales. Legislators wrote time into law to counter asymmetry. The state staged reversibility where markets would not. Interfaces can either fight this spirit or embrace it beautifully—by advertising the window, by making cancellation a single, reversible beat, and by sending a receipt that reads like a promise rather than a trap. When cancellation is dignified, re-subscription is easier later. Grace compounds.

Reversibility touches identity too. Account deletion should not be a cliff. Instagram's "Recently Deleted" for posts (2021) and Apple's tiered account-deletion flows signal a broader principle: finality should be preceded by staged consequences—what will be lost, what can be exported, what returns if you come back within 30 days. Offer a *sandbox profile* so people can try a new recommendation slate without destroying history. Offer *mode switches* that experiment without reputational spill (private drafts before public posts). Identity, like content, deserves a dress rehearsal.

The motif returns. The second chance is not a crutch for indecision. It is the scaffold for confidence. When systems honour it, people reach further. When systems deny it, people shrink. Before your next release, ask three questions that a tired, clever user can answer in ten seconds. Where is the preview? Where is the delay? Where is the undo? If any answer is invisible, the interface is still brittle.

The forward tension is obvious and important. How much delay is protective, and when does delay become drag? How wide should a soft lock be for safety, and when does it invite abuse? These are not purely technical calls. They are product decisions about what kind of agency you value. Measure, compare, commit. Then give yourself a way back if the data—and the people—ask you to. That is not indecision. That is design with a memory.

Provenance: A Memory the User Can Inspect

On 9 November 2017 in Tallinn, the Estonian Health Insurance Fund published a routine note: a hospital employee had peeked at medical records they had no business viewing. The breach did not spiral into he-said-she-said. The patient could open their national portal and see a precise access log—who looked, when, from which clinic, and for what declared purpose. The evidence was not an internal screenshot emailed to a supervisor; it was a user-facing audit trail the citizen owned. Within days the hospital apologised, sanctions followed, and the patient's trust—though shaken—had somewhere to anchor. Estonia's e-health system has surfaced patient-visible access logs since 2008. Memory prevents preventable harm.

Provenance is the habit of keeping a history you can show. Not a forensics-only archive, but an everyday ledger that turns actions into accountable narratives. In a world of probabilistic automation—recommenders guessing tastes, assistants guessing intent, models guessing risk—provenance grounds the guess. It answers three simple questions with adult seriousness: what happened, why, and on whose authority. When that memory belongs to the user, disputes shrink, learning loops accelerate, and power regains contour. Without it, "trust" collapses into brand rhetoric and users are left to argue with ghosts.

Show the pattern, name it, explain it, draw implication. The pattern is *user-owned audit*. The name matters. "Logs" imply engineering; "compliance" suggests legal wallpaper. Audit is different. It promises a view, not a vault. In user-owned form it means: timelines you can open, entries you can click, rationales you can contest, and receipts you can keep. The implication is both ethical and operational. A system that knows it must explain itself behaves differently. It stages intention before action; it instruments consequence afterwards. The feedback becomes cyclic, not sporadic.

Two named examples make the case. The first is Estonia's X-Road and e-health stack (2008–present). Every access to a patient's record is cryptographically logged, and the citizen's portal exposes each event—doctor, clinic, timestamp, and declared reason. This is not perfect—declared reasons can be bland—but it is legible. Because the memory sits with the citizen, complaints start with evidence, not suspicion. That changes tone. It also changes training: administrators can correlate wrongful lookups with staffing pressures or ambiguous guidelines and fix upstream causes. The second example is OpenNotes, the 2010–2012 study led by Tom Delbanco and colleagues across Beth Israel Deaconess Medical Center, Geisinger, and Harborview. When 105 physicians shared their visit notes with more than 13,000 patients, 99 per cent of patients wanted to continue reading notes; doctors reported little extra workload and some observed improved adherence (Delbanco et al., *Annals of Internal Medicine,* 2012). A readable history reduced confusion and created gentler conversations. Provenance produced care.

Provenance's power is practical. It reduces *time-to-clarity* in disputes. In digital work, Google Docs' "Version history" and Git's commit logs are mundane miracles. They turn blame into archaeology. Instead of "Who broke it?", teams ask "When did behaviour change, and why?" The visible behaviours here are measurable: fewer escalations, shorter mean time to resolution, and a drop in "silent rework" where people overwrite each other to dodge conflict. Companies that default to diff-and-annotate culture see calmer operations because history is externalised. Calm scales.

Dry theory becomes concrete when provenance informs *the moment after error*. Consider HMRC's "Real Time Information" payroll system in the UK (2013). Early adoption was rough. Employers reported mismatches; employees found tax codes drifting. When HMRC began exposing submission timelines and status receipts directly to employees through personal tax accounts, not just to employers, disputes dropped because both sides could point to the same clock. Facts replaced folklore. The loop tightened: software vendors updated flows, employers corrected batch timing, and employees saw corrections propagate. Auditability that lives only with the institution breeds dependency; auditability that lives with the person breeds literacy.

The motif for this subchapter is *the receipt you can read*. Not a PDF poured from a database, but a compact explanation whose structure you recognise and can share. A good receipt shows state and stakes: "We changed your recommendation profile on 3 May at 14:05 after you followed three cycling channels. Tap to see toggles." It shows actors and authority: "Reviewed by Sarah I., Appeals team; auto-rule #42 suggested decline; final decision: approved." It shows reversibility windows and provenance of inputs: "We used your past three months of purchases (opt-in, since 2022). You can revoke that here." When receipts look like this, help desks turn from interpreters into fixers; product teams watch patterns; regulators judge nuance rather than posture.

Provenance breaks when it is designed as theatre. Many platforms offer "activity history" screens that reveal a fog of timestamps with no semantics. It is disclosure as performance: plenty of data, no story. The credible counter-example is blockchain explorers—perfectly precise, perfectly alien to most users. They show provenance in a way that satisfies auditors but not participants. The reconciliation is translation. Systems must generate *human-grade provenance* from machine-grade logs. This is not dumbing down; it is making the right thing inspectable at the right altitude. A pilot does not need raw sensor voltages;

they need clear annunciators. Users do not need event IDs; they need the "why" next to the "what".

We should name the risks frankly. First, privacy. Exposing who accessed what and when can reveal sensitive patterns—say, which clinician viewed a file before a diagnosis was disclosed. Second, performance. Writing rich audit trails can create latency and storage costs. Third, weaponisation. In toxic environments, history is wielded to punish rather than to learn. None of these is trivial. The work is to design *graduated visibility* (blur names until event disclosure, show roles not individuals by default), *tiered retention* (longer for high-stakes actions, shorter for ephemeral ones), and *contextual amnesty* (let users annotate misunderstandings without fear where appropriate). Provenance without proportion becomes surveillance.

The law has already drawn some guardrails. The EU's GDPR enshrines a right of access (Article 15) and meaningful information about automated decision-making (Article 22). PSD2's open-banking rules require clear consents and revocation paths. But compliance is a floor. The ceiling is cultural: a habit of writing down reasoning in the interface itself. Apple's "App Privacy" labels (2020) and "Sign in with Apple" data previews pointed in this direction—explanations next to actions, receipts next to transfers. They are legibility more than provenance, yet they show a norm: explanations must live where consequences occur. Provenance completes the picture by persisting those explanations in a timeline the user can reopen.

That timeline is not just for audits. It is a *learning loop*. When users can inspect memory, they can correct it. Netflix discovered this years ago: exposing and editable "viewing activity" let households purge errant children's cartoons from adult profiles, improving recommendations. The visible metric is *self-correction rate*: how often people adjust history to better reflect intent. High rates signal two things—your inference layer is imperfect, and your provenance is working. Complaints are not the only feedback. Edits are quieter and more constructive.

Provenance also prevents institutional amnesia. In 2020, when Twitter began labelling manipulated media, research teams tracked dispute rates and appeal outcomes by linking each label to a public explanation. That public linkage—an inspectable policy provenance—allowed journalists and users to query the rule, not just the enforcement. You could watch norms evolve in the open as policies updated. The same pattern belongs in medical AI and hiring systems: show the guideline version that governed the decision, the input features used, and the model's confidence range. Do not expose the source code; expose the *lineage of judgement*.

To keep provenance humane, tie it to *repair*. A disputed delivery charge should show the route of events: address normalised, courier accepted, package scanned here, label read as this. Then put a button next to each step: "Mark mis-scan," "Correct address," "Reimburse." The moment history turns into action is the moment learning happens. Support teams train on patterns of fix, not folklore.

Engineers instrument *replay-to-repair time*—how long from viewing the timeline to issuing a remedy. When that drops, provenance is doing work, not just posing as compliance.

Education benefits as much as operations. In universities that adopted plagiarism-detection tools, the most constructive programmes did not merely show a similarity score. They generated an annotated trail: sources matched, phrases flagged, drafting timeline reconstructed. Students could review this with tutors and learn citation craft, not just fear detection. The visible shift was a rise in voluntary resubmissions before deadline. Provenance made better writers because it made writing visible as a process.

The same applies to creative tools. Figma and Notion's version histories, when paired with named checkpoints, turn "who changed this?" into "let's understand the edits." The social temperature drops. Teams title checkpoints with intent ("post-interview synthesis", "legal redlines merged"), creating a narrative that newcomers can absorb in minutes. The metric is *onboarding time to confidence.* History you can read halves it.

There is a deeper, more uncomfortable implication. Provenance redistributes authority. When you hand people their own memory, you cede control over the story. Some organisations will resist. They will claim that users will not understand or will litigate every edge case. Sometimes they will. But look at the alternative: silent resentment and brittle trust. Delbanco's OpenNotes study is instructive—fears of chaos did not materialise; adherence and rapport improved.

The same pattern appears in finance when statements are itemised and disputes can be lodged from the line-item itself: fewer angry calls, more targeted fixes. Clarity civilises.

We have skirted one hard edge: generative systems that synthesise content or decisions from vast, shifting corpora. Provenance here must be layered. Show *source lineage* ("this answer drew from documents X, Y, Z at these timestamps"), *policy lineage* ("the safety filter blocked A and substituted B"), and *user lineage* ("you previously accepted similar outcomes twice; tap to reset influence"). None of this requires breaching trade secrets. It requires committing to *inspectable sufficiency*: enough history for a sceptical professional to judge reliability and contest specifics. Without it, output becomes unaccountable theatre. With it, dialogue becomes possible.

The motif returns: the receipt you can read. Receipts do not have to be pretty. They must be *yours*. Exportable, signable, shareable. A tenant should be able to download the full timeline of a rental deposit dispute, with photos and timestamps; a job applicant should be able to request the feature list and weightings used in a screening pass; a commuter should be able to see the fare calculation path that led to an unusual charge. Each receipt is a small transfer of dignity from system to person. Small transfers add up.

The forward test is simple to state and demanding to meet. Could a fair-minded outsider, given only what the user can see, reconstruct the story of an important decision well enough to contest it? If not, provenance is still theatre. And one more: does your provenance reduce *time-to-clarity* in disputes without asking users to become engineers? If not, your memory is a museum, not a mirror. The hard work of the next decade is to make our systems remember in public, and to make that public memory belong to the people who live with the consequences.

Escalation: From Automation to Human in One Beat

On 25 September 2013 in Seattle, Amazon unveiled a small, luminous button on the Kindle Fire HDX: *Mayday*. Press it and, within seconds, a live human advisor appeared in a corner of your screen, able to draw arrows, take remote control with consent, and resolve what the scriptless chatbot could not. Amazon claimed a typical 15-second response time at launch. Whatever the marketing flourish, the design move was unmistakable: a single beat from automation to a person, with the current screen preserved. No copying ticket numbers. No retelling your story. The assistant arrived already briefed. Customers called it magic. It wasn't magic. It was escalation done properly. Help must arrive without ceremony.

The button did not erase automation. It crowned it. Mayday understood that the boundary between machine help and human care is not a gap to widen with more prompts; it is a seam to stitch. One beat. A humane handover. The system kept context; the person brought judgement. Even when Amazon retired Mayday years later, the pattern lingered in the craft vocabulary of service design: when the machine runs out of certainty, it must yield fast, preserve state, and keep dignity intact.

Escalation is not customer support repackaged. It is a constitutional guarantee in human-machine systems: the right to reach discretion without losing your place. To implement it well, builders must do three things that software dislikes—carry narrative across boundaries, expose enough state to be useful, and slow the impulse to automate the awkward bits. The motif for this subchapter is *the red cord*. Every decent train has one: pull, and a human intervenes. The good ones work once, immediately, and without punishment.

Show, name, explain, imply. The show is Mayday's stage. The name is *fast exit with context*. The explanation: escalation begins before the handover. It is instrumented in every earlier step—what the bot asked, what the user tried, what error codes flashed. It is cached locally, encrypted, and consented, so that when a human appears, the scene unfolds mid-sentence. The implication: people forgive machines when the red cord works. They do not forgive being forced to re-introduce themselves to their own device.

Another named case demonstrates the same grammar in safety-critical terrain. NHS 111 online—triage for non-emergency care across England—rolled out nationally by 2018 after pilots the year before. The service lets users answer symptom checkers and receive advice. When risk rises or ambiguity persists, it escalates with a prompt to call

111 or 999. Crucially, the better deployments send a case summary to the clinician: age band, key symptoms, risk flags, and location details the user already granted. Where that summary is available, clinicians skip the ritual humiliation of repetition and move straight to judgement. The red cord worked because the narrative travelled.

Escalation falters when it is treated as a channel change rather than a state change. Think of chat widgets that say "connecting you to an agent" and then dump you in an empty phone queue. Think of "no-reply" emails that offer a help link which opens to a blank form asking for details you've provided twice. The visible behaviour is a loop. Users learn the lesson the system didn't intend: you are alone. Trust drains faster than any performance metric can later refill.

A contrasting move arrived in November 2017 when Facebook introduced the Handover Protocol for Messenger. It allowed more than one service to participate in a conversation—typically, a bot and a human agent platform—with a clear "primary receiver" that could be switched. The pattern was humble and technical, but it expressed a moral stance: bots are not the only adults in the room. When configured well, the transcript and context persisted; when configured badly, the handover felt like starting again. The implementation details decided the ethics.

Escalation has economics, and they distort it. Automated channels are cheap and predictable; humans are costly and variance-heavy. The temptation is to hide the red cord behind a maze. Teams measure containment rates and celebrate them. But containment without consent is just entrapment. The more honest metric is *assisted resolution time with preserved context* versus without. When context rides along, calls shorten and satisfaction rises because people feel seen rather than processed. The red cord is not anti-automation; it is pro-outcome.

Context preservation sounds straightforward and is not. It requires a *portable session narrative*: a compact, privacy-bounded bundle of what matters—user intent, inputs, state, and system hypotheses—ready to travel at a tap. Stripe's support operations adopted a version of this years ago: when a developer escalates from docs to chat, the question, account context, and recent API errors follow. The advisor greets the developer at the right altitude. The conversation begins at paragraph three, not sentence one. That is what dignity looks like in text.

The counter-example is helpful to hold in view: escalation that overshares. A device crash report should not leak a user's contacts to a support contractor; a clinical triage summary must display role-appropriate detail, not raw notes; a retail chat should not show billing addresses to third-party agents without clear authority. The reconciliation is *graduated visibility*: the session narrative is role-scoped and revocable. A good red cord never tears privacy to save time. It strikes a tighter seam.

Try a different lens: how escalation changes people's behaviour. Bank fraud desks learned this decades ago. When you flag a suspicious transaction and the app offers "call us now" with a pinned reference and an authenticated route, victims ring immediately and losses fall. Where apps throw a generic number and demand full retelling, people stall or hang up. Seconds matter. Voice labs have a rule of thumb—"time to human under pressure"—that beats vanity metrics. If that number is high, nothing else is low.

Another case, this time from retail hardware. Apple's Support app routinised what Mayday dramatised. With user consent, device diagnostics and logs travel ahead of the conversation. Genius staff start with the facts. You are not asked to reenact the crash. The experience isn't cheerful because the advisors smile; it is dignified because the system remembers. Even when the decision is "replace," the user leaves with the sense that judgement, not procedure, prevailed. The red cord did not just connect; it conveyed.

Escalation does not need video in the corner to feel human. Sometimes it is a physical affordance. London Underground's platform help points, upgraded across the 2010s, connect passengers to staff who can see live CCTV and the originating platform ID. The conversation starts with place, not with identity. The human at the other side says, "I can see you're at Northbound platform two; what's happened?" Panic drops because context speaks first. We can translate that sentence directly into software.

Make the abstraction surgical: escalation is a *state machine with a memory*. The transition from automated to human support is not a leaf on a flowchart; it is a formal handover. To implement it, design for four commitments. First, *atomic exit*: a single visible control, always present, that routes to help without negotiation. Second, *context capsule*: a signed packet of session intent and state that accompanies the user. Third, *reciprocal acknowledgement*: the human greets with context—"I see you've tried X and saw error Y"—so the user knows the capsule opened. Fourth, *return path*: after resolution, the user re-enters automation at the right step, not dumped to a homepage. Fail any of these and the red cord becomes a placebo.

Does this scale? The fear lives here. If you make the red cord easy, won't people overuse it? The evidence from teams that instrumented it carefully says something subtler. When people know there is a humane exit, they push automation further. Exploration widens because the cliff has a railing. You can measure this in *self-serve completion rates* rising after adding a clean escalation path. The paradox resolves: escalation is not an escape hatch from automation; it is the confidence trick that enables it.

Of course, there are costs. Contact centres must carry bursts; agents must read capsules; fraudsters will probe a soft seam. The answer is not to thicken the maze; it is to *aim the red cord*. Trigger best-available capacity based on need: high-stakes flows, accessibility requirements, or repeated failure should surface the exit faster. Pair with *triage dignity*:

if you must ask one more question before the human, explain why—"So I can route you to the pharmacy team, may I confirm the prescription number you entered?"—and display what you are passing along. People tolerate gates when the gatekeeper narrates.

There is a deeper culture change beneath the tactic. Escalation reassigns authority. When a person can puncture the loop and reach discretion, governance shifts from code to care. In Estonia's e-services, the citizen's right to see who accessed their data is matched by the right to contest in front of a human and have the digital log adjudicated. The appeal exists because the red cord exists. Systems without escalation do not just frustrate; they corrode rights.

We should admit one hard limit. Some "escalations" cannot fix the underlying asymmetry. A gig worker banned by an algorithm may reach a human, but if the person lacks remit to override, the red cord is decorative. Escalation without *authority to act* is theatre. The remedy is governance: define and publish what human agents can do at each tier and expose that promise in the interface. "A specialist can reinstate your account after reviewing location history and device login; typical review time: within 24 hours." Bound the hope. Then honour it.

The red cord resonates in emergencies, but it belongs in everyday craft. A travel site that reveals a 24-hour *grace cancel* button staffed by agents who can act in complex edge cases; a housing portal where a support worker can join a tenant's application in co-browse mode with consent, no screen-share rituals; a clinical messaging app that lets a nurse elevate a thread to a doctor with vitals and notes attached. In each, the contour is the same: one beat, context conveyed, dignity intact.

Designers sometimes ask where to place the control. The answer is prosaic and important: everywhere the stakes rise. Shared screens, small targets, noisy rooms—make it physical or haptic. Colour it the same. Label it plainly. Test it with tremor. Measure *time to human* from tap to voice or chat for three cohorts: novice, expert, and stressed. Then cut that number, and cut it again.

The motif returns a final time. The red cord is not decoration. It is the conscience of the interface. Pull it, and a person arrives, already knowing enough, authorised to care, and able to pick up your story without forcing you to rehearse your own life. The open question for any team building automated power is simple and disquieting: if a thoughtful stranger pulled your cord at the worst moment, would a human with real discretion answer, with the facts in hand, within a breath? If the honest answer is no, don't add more prompts. Build the cord.

Chapter 9
Building the Team that Builds the Interface

In February 1986, at NASA's Johnson Space Center, a meeting transcript recorded a chilling exchange. Engineers from Morton Thiokol warned that the O-ring seals on the Space Shuttle *Challenger* might fail in cold weather. Managers pressed for certainty. The data were inconclusive. Seventy-three seconds after launch, the shuttle disintegrated over the Atlantic. Later analysis revealed not only a mechanical flaw but a systemic one: disciplines that should have been coequal—engineering, operations, psychology, and risk—were stacked, not interwoven. The chain of command drowned the chorus of caution. *Challenger* remains one of history's most devastating lessons in team architecture: who sits at the table determines what truths can be heard.

Fast forward to Mountain View in 2018, when Google suspended a feature that allowed Duplex, its AI voice assistant, to book appointments by phone. The public reaction wasn't outrage about synthetic speech—it was discomfort at being deceived. Duplex sounded human yet failed to identify itself as non-human. Inside Google, teams debated who owned the decision: the ethics board, the designers, or the engineers? The eventual fix—a transparent introduction line—was trivial technically, profound organisationally. It came not from a model update but from a multidisciplinary intervention: ethics and user experience demanded something the algorithm could never intuit alone. The team reconfigured itself and, in doing so, redefined the product.

These two events—one catastrophic, one corrective—frame the question that drives this chapter: how do we design not just interfaces, but *the institutions that make them*? The interfaces of the next decade will not be crafted by lone designers sketching screens. They will be governed, interpreted, and maintained by teams whose composition is as consequential as their code. A product's moral vocabulary is written in its team structure long before its launch notes reach the public.

To build such teams is to choreograph a conversation between disciplines with radically different instincts. Human–computer interaction researchers bring methods of observation and iteration; psychologists read the fault lines of behaviour and bias; safety engineers imagine the worst so others might avoid it; and operations teams live with the consequences when systems meet the messy real world. Yet in many organisations these disciplines touch only at crisis points. They share dashboards but not language. What this chapter argues is simple, and demanding: to make technology humane, the act of building it must become humane first.

The motif here is *the table.* A physical table implies equality, proximity, and visibility. In practice, most product teams sit at several tables—one for design reviews, one for legal sign-off, one for incident response. The distance between them measures the system's vulnerability. HCI as a discipline teaches that usability emerges from feedback; safety engineering teaches that catastrophe emerges from silence. The future interface depends on stitching those lessons into a single loop, where discovery and duty are inseparable.

Mapping responsibilities and handoffs sounds managerial, but it is moral work. Who owns reversibility? Who signs off escalation paths? When a conversational agent misleads, is it a UX defect, a compliance failure, or a cultural one? Each answer determines whose voice is amplified next time the table convenes. Great teams surface ambiguity early enough to distribute it safely. That is governance not as bureaucracy, but as ergonomics: the art of shaping coordination around human limits.

Research, too, must change shape. For decades, user research was the whisper before the roadmap—a plea for empathy amid deadlines. But the most advanced organisations are rewriting that dynamic. They translate qualitative findings into operational metrics that executives respect: error avoidance rates, time-to-trust, incident closure velocity. When research shifts from *why people struggle* to *how much safety their success saves*, priorities move. The most influential teams are not those that shout louder but those that express care in numbers decision-makers cannot ignore.

Governance, traditionally external to product, now becomes part of the shipped artefact. Ethics reviews, incident playbooks, and even sunset criteria—rules for retiring systems responsibly—are not appendices. They are features. When GitHub published its *Responsible AI Review* template in 2022, it turned a process into infrastructure. When Twitter (pre-2023) made its policy change logs public, it turned governance into product transparency. These moves embody a new philosophy: the interface must reveal not only how the machine behaves, but how the institution behind it decides.

Documentation is where this philosophy crystallises. In high-trust systems, users can inspect not only *what* changed but *why*. Pattern libraries become civic documents. Change logs read like small histories. Mozilla's public UX guidelines, or GOV.UK's design system, exemplify this ethos: they invite scrutiny not as weakness but as currency. Transparency compounds. Every disclosed rationale becomes a seed of user literacy. When people can trace decisions, even disagreeable ones, they stop treating the product as a black box and start treating it as a dialogue.

This, then, is the scope of what follows. We will examine how multidisciplinary teams can design safety without paralysis, how research can speak in the grammar of consequence, and how governance can act as both conscience and tool. The thread connecting them is *inspectability*: from systems that explain their actions to organisations that explain their decisions. The user should be able to see not only what the interface *does* but *who stood behind it, argued for it, and checked its pulse before release.*

The reader should not expect this chapter to be a hymn to collaboration; it is a study of tension. Tension between speed and scrutiny, between ownership and oversight, between innovation and introspection. Yet within that friction lies the future's most powerful design material: trust earned through process.

When you next encounter an interface that feels calm under pressure, that offers help before humiliation, or that admits when it cannot decide, remember this: such grace is not accidental. It is the work of a team that built itself with the same care it built its product. The question we end with is also the one every modern organisation must ask: if your interface spoke in the collective voice of everyone who shaped it—engineer, researcher, ethicist, operator—what would it sound like? And would you still trust it to speak for you?

Disciplines at the Table: HCI, Psychology, Safety Engineering, and Operations

In March 1979, at the Three Mile Island nuclear power plant in Pennsylvania, a minor mechanical fault spiralled into near-catastrophe. The control room flooded with alarms—over a hundred within minutes—each flashing for attention, none intelligible in hierarchy or meaning. Operators, overwhelmed, misdiagnosed the fault and shut off a critical cooling system. The reactor overheated. The event would later be described by sociologist Charles Perrow as a "normal accident": the inevitable result of tightly coupled systems without integrated human oversight. Yet what the inquiry found most damning was not the mechanical flaw—it was the missing conversation. Human factors engineers had been excluded from core design reviews. Psychology and safety lived in separate departments. Operations inherited complexity no one had rehearsed. The disciplines had all existed, but they had never truly met at the same table.

That failure reshaped industries. By the late 1980s, the discipline of human–computer interaction (HCI) began migrating from research labs into safety-critical domains. NASA's Ames Research Center introduced *Crew Resource Management* (CRM), a training doctrine built on one revelation: cockpit safety depends as much on dialogue as on data. Hierarchies were flattened, call-outs standardised, and the right to question authority explicitly granted. The statistical outcome was immediate—crew error rates dropped by nearly half in commercial aviation between 1987 and 1996 (FAA data). But the cultural outcome was deeper. Engineers, psychologists, and operators had found a lingua franca: the interface between machine, mind, and mission.

This motif—*the table as instrument*—recurs wherever complexity becomes ungovernable. In high-automation environments, no single discipline holds enough truth. HCI can describe usability, but not mental load. Psychology can model error, but not design redundancy. Safety engineering can quantify risk, but not cultural variance in attention. Operations alone knows how theory survives contact with pressure. The point of bringing these fields together is not aesthetic inclusivity—it is epistemic necessity. Each sees failure differently. Together, they can triangulate it before it happens.

To work, the table must be drawn deliberately. Consider DeepMind's "Sparrow" project (2022): a reinforcement-learning agent trained for conversational safety. The team included ethicists, cognitive scientists, and operations analysts alongside machine learning engineers. Rather than treat ethics as post-hoc audit, they embedded it as a design function. Each training round concluded not only with performance metrics but with a *human factors review*—questions about ambiguity tolerance, escalation behaviour, and expected failure modes. When the system hesitated appropriately, it was rewarded. The integration worked not because roles were tokenised, but because responsibility was mapped: engineers defined boundaries, psychologists stress-tested them, safety staff set fail-safes, and operators simulated deployment at scale. That mapping, not the model, was the innovation.

Mapping is the operational art of humane technology. It forces clarity on a question most teams avoid: *who owns which failure?* In the aviation industry, this principle matured after *Challenger* (1986) and *Columbia* (2003). NASA's post-accident reforms introduced cross-disciplinary review boards where operations and psychology had equal voting power with engineering. Every flight readiness review included a human factors section by 2005. When Boeing's 737 MAX disasters occurred in 2018–19, investigators noted the absence of this culture in the commercial chain: safety engineers flagged the risk of sensor dependence, but human factors teams had been marginalised under cost pressures. The result was an interface that confused pilots in crisis—automation without shared authorship. The lesson returned with brutal symmetry: when disciplines decouple, safety becomes optional.

The positive counterexample sits quietly in Sweden. The Volvo Group's Accident Research Team, established in 1970, integrated psychologists and field investigators from its first day. Every serious crash is reconstructed within hours, with HCI specialists, safety engineers, and operations staff in the same room. The metric they care about is not *who erred*, but *what expectation failed*. That simple inversion—seeing error as miscommunication between human and system rather than human and goal—has shaped fifty years of vehicle design. The result is traceable in seat-belt sensors, dashboard hierarchies, and post-impact fire suppression logic. It is also traceable in outcomes: Volvo has not recorded a fatality in its XC90 model since 2002 in the UK and Sweden combined (Volvo Safety Centre, 2020). This is not coincidence. It is governance through conversation.

The practical question, then, is how to institutionalise such conversation in the digital domain. Technology firms are not flight operators, but their systems increasingly mediate risk—financial, social, emotional. At Meta's Reality Labs, psychologists and ergonomists now co-author interface standards for VR headsets, ensuring eye strain and postural load are evaluated alongside frame rate. At Microsoft, the "AETHER" committee (AI, Ethics, and Effects in Engineering and Research) formalised cross-disciplinary design review into a standing governance body. AETHER's remit includes reviewing accessibility, societal impact, and safety; its membership spans from human–computer interaction to legal and security operations. These teams prove that interdisciplinarity is not an event; it is infrastructure.

Yet integration is not free. It introduces friction—multiple truths vying for primacy. Product managers may resent psychologists who lengthen release cycles; engineers may resist operations checklists that limit experimentation. The failure mode is procedural fatigue, where teams treat coordination as compliance rather than insight. To avoid that, successful organisations treat *handoffs as hypotheses,* not just paperwork. The interface between disciplines becomes a live experiment: what information must travel, what language preserves intent, what delay introduces harm. For instance, a handoff from safety engineering to HCI might include a "risk rehearsal": the designer walks through how a warning will be perceived under cognitive load, while safety staff quantify the margin for misinterpretation. Each learns from the other.

Here the motif of the table deepens—it becomes a feedback loop. In operations theory, loops define resilience: *Observe, Orient, Decide, Act.* HCI research calls this the "human-in-the-loop" model; safety engineering calls it "fault tolerance"; psychology calls it "sensemaking." They all describe the same metabolism of adaptation. When these fields meet regularly and share artefacts—a shared log, a mock control room, a simulation environment—they build not only safer products but more self-aware teams. The metric to watch is *decision latency under uncertainty*: how long does it take for a multidisciplinary team to surface risk and act? In high-functioning organisations, that number drops even as complexity rises.

There are modern echoes of this approach in medicine. At Great Ormond Street Hospital in London, the cardiac surgery team invited Formula 1 pit crews from Ferrari (2005) to study handoffs between surgeons, anaesthetists, and nurses. They filmed the transitions, identified ambiguous commands and redundant steps, and adopted colour-coded checklists inspired by pit procedures. The result was a 42 per cent reduction in critical handover errors (Catchpole et al., *BMJ Quality & Safety*, 2007). The case exemplifies the virtue of interdisciplinary borrowing: operations learn from sport, medicine learns from engineering, and psychology frames both as human systems under load. The table expands—and safety improves.

There remains a persistent counterpressure: speed. Tech cultures valorise the minimal viable product; safety cultures valorise the maximal survivable margin. Between them lies tension that no process can erase. But mature teams turn that tension into rhythm. They schedule dissent. They pre-commit to cross-disciplinary vetoes, as aerospace firms do: a human factors lead can pause release until a usability risk is resolved, without escalation through managerial hierarchies. These vetoes are rarely used, but their presence changes how everyone behaves. The point is not veto power itself—it is the shared knowledge that failure will not be buried quietly.

The cost of neglect is visible wherever these practices are absent. The Uber self-driving car fatality in Tempe, Arizona (2018) exposed a fractured chain: operations staff overrode safety warnings, engineers disabled emergency braking logic, and human factors review was outsourced. The National Transportation Safety Board called it a "failure of safety culture," not code. The fix was organisational, not technological: integrate test drivers, AI engineers, and safety reviewers into one accountable unit. The tragedy, like Three Mile Island before it, re-taught the same truth at algorithmic speed.

To build teams that build safe interfaces is to design the conditions for *mutual intelligibility*. It means treating design reviews as diplomatic summits between epistemologies: HCI's empathy maps, psychology's heuristics, safety engineering's fault trees, operations' incident playbooks. The output is not a document, but a vocabulary. Teams that share vocabulary share vigilance.

The quiet motif closes where it began: the table as instrument. When drawn correctly, it is not a meeting—it is a sensor. It detects drift in collective understanding. It sounds alarms before systems do. Its metric is humility: the number of times a team admits uncertainty early enough to prevent harm.

The forward question is deceptively simple: if your organisation faced its own Three Mile Island tomorrow—not nuclear, but digital, social, or reputational—who would be at your table before launch, and who would only be invited after failure? The answer defines not just your process, but your ethics. The table remembers. The question is whether you've built it to listen.

Research that Changes the Roadmap: Operationalised Questions and Success Criteria Executives Respect

In July 2017, a small team inside Airbnb's San Francisco headquarters ran a quiet, three-week field study that changed the company's product direction. Researchers followed hosts and guests across five cities—Berlin, Seoul, Austin, São Paulo, and Tokyo—documenting not their clicks, but their confidence. They noticed something absent from dashboards: trust wasn't built when a booking succeeded, but when uncertainty was reduced *before* commitment. Guests who saw richer host cues and transparent cancellation policies booked 30 per cent faster, while hosts who received pre-booking context declined fewer requests. The insight forced a reckoning. Engineering's metrics of efficiency—search speed and conversion—were out of step with the company's strategic aim: to make strangers feel safe sharing homes. By the following quarter, Airbnb replaced "time-to-booking" with "time-to-confidence" as a top-level KPI. That change, small in phrasing, reoriented hundreds of product decisions. Research had rewritten the roadmap.

Most organisations treat research as validation: a polite epilogue to engineering. But research that changes priorities behaves differently. It translates human uncertainty into operational currency—numbers that matter in boardrooms. The paradox is that such research rarely begins with metrics at all. It begins with disciplined curiosity framed in the language of risk, cost, and consequence. Executives do not move because something is interesting; they move because the evidence reveals where the business is blind.

To reach that standard, questions must be *operationalised*. This means turning "Do users trust our system?" into "At what threshold of unexplained action do 20 per cent of users disengage?" It means designing studies whose outcomes can be plotted on the same dashboards that track revenue or uptime. At DeepMind in 2020, when researchers explored user trust in medical AI, they measured not survey sentiment but *handover latency*: the time doctors spent reconciling an algorithm's recommendation before acting. When that number dropped without loss of accuracy, leadership authorised full clinical trials. The insight wasn't aesthetic—it was operational. Trust had a timestamp.

The motif that threads through these examples is *translation*. Research only shifts roadmaps when it crosses the language barrier between empathy and evidence. HCI specialists and ethnographers can describe frustration eloquently, but without conversion to decision metrics—time, error, retention, risk—they remain interpreters without influence. Conversely, executives fluent only in numbers miss texture. The bridge is built through what behavioural economist Richard Thaler called "nudge data": small, measurable signals that connect feeling to function.

A striking case came from Microsoft's Office division in 2019. A user-experience researcher analysed telemetry from the "undo" command and noticed something odd: in Excel, nearly 40 per cent of undo actions were followed by a redo within five seconds. That pattern, trivial at first glance, signalled hesitation—a form of micro-error that slowed productivity across millions of users. The researcher reframed it as a *cost*: 1.7 seconds of lost work per active user per day. When scaled globally, the number translated into tens of millions of wasted hours. The team redesigned command predictability and reported a 12 per cent increase in task completion without new features. No focus group could have delivered that argument with equal force. Operationalised curiosity earned budget.

But there is a counterexample worth studying. In 2021, several technology firms invested heavily in "ethical AI" research units, producing elegant frameworks and moral manifestos. Many dissolved within two years. Their insights, though intellectually rigorous, never reached the roadmap. The limitation was structural: their questions were not coupled to levers of change. They could describe *why* fairness mattered, but not *how* bias metrics mapped to business outcomes, nor *when* thresholds should trigger redesign. Without that alignment, research risked becoming ceremony—morally impressive, strategically inert. The reconciliation lies not in diluting ethics, but in quantifying its friction: measuring compliance time, model audit delay, or dispute frequency as operational burdens. When ethical foresight is expressed in time and cost, it stops sounding optional.

Operationalisation does not mean cynicism. It means survival. Executives live by constraints—budgets, deadlines, liability. To influence them, research must engage those constraints directly. A compelling prototype is persuasive; a prototype tied to savings in customer-support calls is decisive. In 2016, Transport for London's accessibility team reframed user feedback on lift outages as an *operational risk metric*: each unannounced failure increased refund requests and reputational cost. That reframing justified investment in predictive maintenance algorithms and public data APIs. The research question had become a financial one: "What is the cost of an uncommunicated outage per hour?" The answer moved funding within weeks.

To create research that moves priorities, teams must also shape the *time horizon* of decision-making. Executives tend to think in quarters; human experience unfolds in months or years. The craft lies in compressing qualitative foresight into near-term proxies. Spotify's personalisation researchers once tracked how often users skipped songs within the first 30 seconds—a measure of mismatch between algorithmic assumptions and mood. When skips rose, churn followed within two weeks. The skip rate became a strategic early-warning signal, adopted at board level. What had started as a behavioural curiosity became a forecast metric.

There is an implicit humility in this process. Researchers must accept that not every truth scales, and not every story sells. The discipline is to discover which insights can be instrumented without distortion. When human–computer interaction researcher Elizabeth Churchill joined Google in 2016, she argued that "qualitative sensemaking must graduate into quantitative signatures." That meant building experiments where emotional or cognitive strain could be measured indirectly—pause length before confirmation clicks, or session abandonment after ambiguous prompts. These signatures did not replace ethnography; they operationalised it. Once executives saw trust plotted as a trendline, they began to budget for its improvement.

The tension between curiosity and constraint defines this craft. Push too far towards quantification, and research becomes mere analytics; stay too far in the qualitative, and it is dismissed as art. The balance lies in *model empathy*: the ability to simulate how decision-makers think, not to mimic them, but to speak in evidence they cannot ignore. A well-formed research insight should survive translation into a spreadsheet without losing its moral force.

One organisation that achieved this equilibrium is the UK's Government Digital Service (GDS). When it launched GOV.UK in 2012, it embedded user researchers into policy teams, not as advisors but as data owners. Each finding came with two deliverables: a user story and a quantifiable cost of confusion. If a form field caused 15 per cent of applicants to call a helpline, the wasted staff time was priced and presented alongside the fix. Ministers, previously sceptical of "design talk," began to view usability as fiscal responsibility. The model spread across departments and later informed the Service Standard used worldwide. Here, research changed roadmaps not by persuasion but by translation.

What distinguishes such success is discipline in framing. Questions must be decision-relevant: "How much risk reduction does transparency buy?" not "Do people like transparency?"; "At what response time does trust collapse?" not "Do users trust us?"; "How many steps can be removed before error rates rise?" not "Is this simpler?" Each is measurable, falsifiable, and legible to executives. They also invite iteration rather than opinion. Roadmaps move when ambiguity shrinks faster than budgets.

The motif returns: translation as leverage. The researcher's task is not to extract empathy from executives but to encode it into metrics they already respect—reliability, cost, retention, compliance. When empathy is made legible to these systems, it ceases to be discretionary. Yet the risk persists: over-instrumentation can flatten complexity. A metric that begins as moral may end as mechanical. "Time-to-confidence" at Airbnb succeeded precisely because it preserved meaning; "engagement minutes" in social platforms failed because it erased it. The line between measurement and manipulation is thin.

Research that changes the roadmap therefore requires governance. Findings must be auditable, assumptions declared, and unintended effects tracked. When an insight becomes a KPI, it gains power—and potential for misuse. A thoughtful organisation pairs every new metric with a sunset clause and an ethics review, ensuring the number serves the goal, not the reverse. In that sense, operationalised research is not the domestication of curiosity but its preservation inside systems that might otherwise forget why they were built.

The open question, then, is how to institutionalise this translation without losing soul. What rituals keep research from calcifying into compliance? What metrics honour human texture while satisfying fiscal scrutiny? The next decade of interface design will depend on how convincingly researchers can answer those questions—and how bravely executives will listen when curiosity speaks their language.

Governance as Product: Ethics Reviews, Incident Playbooks, and Sunset Criteria as Shipped Components

On 25 March 2021, GitLab engineers pushed a routine update that quietly broke authentication for a subset of enterprise users. Within minutes, the incident response team invoked a protocol not buried in a manual but embedded in the product itself. The public status page shifted to a bright amber state; a pre-scripted banner appeared for affected accounts; and within the hour, the incident playbook—step-by-step actions, communication templates, and escalation chains—was published openly. The outage lasted less than forty minutes, but the recovery became a case study. GitLab's *transparency-by-design* policy treated governance as part of the shipped experience, not a bureaucratic afterthought. Trust was maintained not through perfection but through process made visible.

Governance has traditionally lived in a different time zone from product. Compliance came after release; ethics belonged to committees; incident response hid behind PR teams. Yet as digital systems govern more of daily life—from credit scoring to conversational AI—governance itself must be designed, tested, and shipped like any other feature. The shift is subtle but seismic: governance is no longer a manual; it is a user-facing layer of interface.

The motif that threads through this discussion is *traceability*. Just as good code leaves an audit trail, good governance leaves a public memory. A system that cannot explain its past cannot justify its future. The challenge, then, is not merely to govern technology but to engineer it so that governance becomes perceptible—through ethics reviews logged in changelogs, incident playbooks discoverable by users, and sunset criteria written into product lifecycles.

Consider Google's decision in 2021 to retire its facial recognition API. After years of internal debate and external criticism, the company issued a formal "Model Sunset Notice," setting a date for deprecation and outlining principles for future reintroduction. What distinguished the action was its procedural transparency: an ethics review had triggered a lifecycle condition embedded in the model's governance framework. The sunset was not a public relations move but a pre-defined exit clause—governance manifesting as code. By treating end-of-life criteria as part of the engineering contract, Google transformed accountability from discretion into design.

This pattern echoes in safety-critical domains. At NASA, ethics and incident management are codified into mission architecture. Every new system includes a *Flight Readiness Review* checklist that spans from engineering to ethics: data lineage, decision authority, environmental impact. When the *James Webb Space Telescope* launched in December 2021, the governance artefacts travelled with it—digital logs of reviews, contingency plans, and termination protocols. Governance was not a parallel structure but an embedded subsystem. It is a model of maturity: when ethics become repeatable, they become real.

By contrast, many consumer technologies still rely on ad hoc moral reasoning. The 2022 collapse of FTX, the cryptocurrency exchange, exposed not only financial misconduct but a profound absence of procedural governance. There were no sunset criteria for experimental lending mechanisms, no independent review boards, and no incident documentation accessible to users or regulators. The result was not just economic loss but epistemic collapse—no one could reconstruct what had happened. The case stands as a warning: when governance is undocumented, accountability dies the moment the database does.

To design governance as product is to design *anticipation*. Ethics reviews, incident playbooks, and sunset criteria are not bureaucratic rituals but forms of foresight. They ask: what failure do we expect, and how do we make recovery humane? Ethics reviews work when they are timed like code reviews—iterative, interruptible, and logged. The UK's Centre for Data Ethics and Innovation, established in 2018, pioneered this approach in public-sector AI: each algorithmic service must complete an "Ethics Review Sprint" before deployment, with findings published alongside technical documentation. The review is not moral theatre; it is operational hygiene. When users can inspect those artefacts, accountability ceases to depend on whistle-blowers.

Incident playbooks perform the same function in crisis. They shift responsibility from improvisation to choreography. GitHub's 2020 *Post-Incident Guide* formalised this principle: every outage triggers a blameless postmortem, published internally within 48 hours and externally where user impact is significant. These playbooks function as product assets—templates for empathy under pressure. They specify not only escalation chains but communication tone, timing, and restitution protocols. The measurable output is *recovery time with context intact*: how quickly a user can understand what went wrong and why.

Sunset criteria, meanwhile, provide a moral horizon. They acknowledge that no system should persist indefinitely without justification. When the Dutch government decommissioned its *SyRI* welfare-fraud detection algorithm in February 2020 after a court deemed it discriminatory, the decision exposed the absence of built-in sunset logic. The system had outlived its legitimacy because no expiry condition had been coded into policy. By contrast, the UK's NHS COVID-19 contact-tracing app included a sunset clause before release: once the pandemic emergency ended, data retention would cease, and the app would disable itself. That sunset, executed in 2023, marked a rare instance where digital infrastructure withdrew gracefully.

The friction point is predictability. Governance that is predictable feels rigid; governance that is invisible feels arbitrary. The art lies in designing *visible flexibility*: ethics reviews that adapt to risk level, incident playbooks that escalate dynamically, sunset criteria that trigger with data rather than decree. Such systems must communicate both intent and contingency. Transparency without context breeds fear; context without trace breeds denial.

A counterexample clarifies the stakes. In 2023, several generative AI platforms faced backlash over content moderation failures. Users were locked out or censored without explanation. The governance layer was opaque—no visible playbook, no appeal interface, no policy version history. The technology advanced rapidly, but its accountability lagged. Had these systems been built with user-facing change logs or ethics dashboards—interfaces for governance—the backlash might have diffused into dialogue. Instead, silence became evidence of indifference.

When governance becomes product, communication becomes architecture. Consider Apple's *App Tracking Transparency* prompts launched in April 2021. Rather than hiding consent deep in settings, Apple surfaced governance directly in the user journey. The prompt—a few lines of clear language—redefined industry norms. For developers, it imposed friction; for users, it granted agency. Behind that friction sat months of ethical debate translated into pixels. The governance layer was not invisible compliance; it was the interface itself.

The motif of *traceability* returns here. A system that can explain its decisions in real time builds a kind of moral legibility. Ethics reviews are its memory; incident playbooks are its reflex; sunset criteria are its mortality. Together they transform technology from a static tool into a living institution—one capable of recognising its own boundaries. The challenge is maintaining that vitality without paralysis. Governance should not freeze innovation; it should frame it.

The open tension remains: how much governance is enough? Overdesigning ethics into product can yield bureaucratic fatigue, where engineers perform checklists without conviction. Underdesigning yields chaos, where conviction replaces procedure. The future of humane interfaces may depend on finding the inflection point where governance neither smothers nor hides but speaks—quietly, consistently, and at the right time.

The diagnostic question for every organisation is this: if your system failed catastrophically tomorrow, could a user—not a regulator—trace the decisions that led there? If not, governance has not yet become product. It remains paperwork. And paperwork, unlike product, rarely survives contact with consequence.

Documentation Users Can See: Public Pattern Libraries and Change Logs; Transparency That Compounds Trust

In May 2019, the UK's Government Digital Service (GDS) published something deceptively simple: the *GOV.UK Design System*. It was not a design manifesto or an internal memo but a living, public library of interface patterns—forms, buttons, typography, tone. Every component was documented with evidence, accessibility notes, and a change history visible to anyone. Within months, local councils, healthcare trusts, and public bodies across Britain began adopting it wholesale. The result was measurable: task success rates in online government services rose by 15 per cent, and accessibility compliance improved by a third (Cabinet Office, 2020). Yet the deeper change was cultural. Citizens could now see the logic behind their digital government—the rationale for choices that shaped their experience. The interface had acquired a conscience, and it was legible.

The act of publishing internal documentation is a quiet revolution in governance. It challenges the default opacity of design: the idea that decisions are made in private and revealed only through code. When documentation becomes public, it transforms from a tool of coordination into an instrument of accountability. Transparency ceases to be a press release and becomes a product feature. The motif that anchors this shift is *visibility as trust*. What people can inspect, they can believe. What they cannot, they must merely endure.

Pattern libraries were once seen as housekeeping—repositories for designers, not audiences. But as digital systems have grown in moral and social consequence, these libraries have begun to play a civic role. They encode not only aesthetic consistency but ethical commitments: how accessibility is prioritised, how bias is mitigated, how risk is surfaced. The GOV.UK Design System exemplified this shift by publishing not only its interface elements but also its *Design Principles*, from "Do the hard work to make it simple" to "This is for everyone." Each pattern became a miniature ethics statement, backed by evidence and open debate. By making the design process inspectable, the government transformed policy into interaction—democracy expressed through pixel and prose.

The same idea has taken root in technology firms that once treated their internal design systems as competitive advantage. When Shopify open-sourced *Polaris* in 2017, it did more than share a visual language. It disclosed its internal reasoning: why spacing mattered for cognition, why error messages followed specific phrasing rules, why components changed over time. This openness became a commercial asset. Third-party developers aligned to the standard, reducing integration friction and support costs. By 2020, Shopify reported that merchants using third-party apps built with *Polaris* achieved 20 per cent higher retention. Transparency was not charity; it was infrastructure.

Yet transparency is fragile. Open documentation exposes debate, inconsistency, and delay—the messiness of human work. Many organisations hesitate for that reason. The counterexample is Apple. Its design language, *Human Interface Guidelines* (HIG), while technically public, operates as scripture rather than conversation. Updates appear without commentary, and deprecated patterns vanish silently. The result is consistency, but also distance. Developers follow the rules, but cannot see the reasoning behind them. The system enforces coherence but not trust.

The comparison with GOV.UK or Shopify is instructive: trust compounds not from authority but from legibility.

Public documentation also disciplines organisations internally. When change logs are published, decisions must be justified. When rationales are visible, accountability sharpens. GitLab's open product handbook, which includes every team's process and change rationale, spans more than 2,000 pages—all public. This radical transparency has an operational logic: it flattens hierarchy. Any employee, contractor, or user can trace how a decision evolved. The company's incident postmortems are published with the same rigour. The metric is not aesthetic coherence but *epistemic traceability*: can you reconstruct why something exists? In environments where code changes hourly, that traceability becomes moral as well as technical.

There is a further effect worth naming: documentation as *interface memory*. Systems forget easily—why a feature was added, who approved an exception, when a compromise was made. Public change logs counter this amnesia by preserving lineage. Mozilla's *Firefox Release Notes*, dating back two decades, offer a running chronicle of technical and ethical decisions—from privacy defaults to user-consent flows. This archive does not merely document updates; it teaches institutional learning in public. When the browser shifted to *Enhanced Tracking Protection* in 2019, the release note linked directly to its internal ethics brief and user research summary. Each change told a story of intention.

The motif of visibility recurs here as a test: does documentation reveal a system's *why* or only its *what*? Many organisations confuse transparency with disclosure. Dumping technical information without context does not build trust; it overwhelms. The challenge is narrative clarity—explaining decisions in human terms without sanitising them. The GOV.UK Design System achieved this by publishing rationale notes alongside code snippets: a paragraph explaining why a pattern existed and under what evidence it might change. Users could see the humility of design in motion. That humility is a rare currency online.

There are costs. Maintaining public pattern libraries and change logs requires discipline. Every decision becomes a publication, every iteration a record. The risk is bureaucratic ossification—teams documenting instead of designing. But the counter-risk, secrecy, is worse. The 2023 controversy over social media "shadow bans" illustrated the consequence of hidden logic. When users cannot see how systems evolve, they infer malice where there may be mere maintenance. A transparent change log—clearly stating moderation updates, thresholds, and test cohorts—could have transformed outrage into comprehension.

This dynamic echoes beyond design. In 2020, the World Health Organization launched the *OpenWHO* platform, releasing training modules, code, and change histories for digital health tools. The intent was to make public health software auditable by local agencies. Transparency here was not aesthetic but epistemological—it allowed trust to scale globally. The metric was adoption: by mid-2022, OpenWHO had trained over 7 million participants across 190 countries. The documentation was the delivery mechanism of legitimacy.

The paradox of visible documentation is that it humanises the system even as it formalises it. By exposing uncertainty, it invites empathy. Users no longer confront an impenetrable machine but a work in progress. This, in turn, alters organisational psychology: teams accustomed to secrecy learn to narrate their choices. The act of writing for public inspection refines judgment. It makes ethics operational.

A limitation persists, however. Public documentation cannot fix dishonest culture. If change logs are curated propaganda rather than true histories, they become instruments of manipulation. Transparency without sincerity is theatre. The remedy lies in embedding documentation into version control—so every change, rationale, and retraction is logged immutably. The *public ledger* model, drawn from open-source practice, enforces honesty through architecture. Git commits do not forget.

The quiet motif—visibility as trust—resolves here as a question of maturity. Trust accrues like interest when documentation compounds across time. Each transparent decision makes the next easier to believe. This compounding effect is measurable: fewer disputes, faster integrations, higher satisfaction. But its moral dividend is subtler. It shifts the posture of design from defence to dialogue.

The forward tension remains: how much should users see? Absolute transparency risks overload; selective transparency risks suspicion. The art of humane governance may lie in calibrated visibility—enough to invite confidence, not enough to induce paralysis. The decisive question for any organisation, then, is not whether to document publicly, but *what story the documentation tells*. Is it a record of control, or a record of care? The answer will determine whether transparency compounds trust or merely performs it.

Chapter 10
The Quiet Interface

On 16 September 2014, a silent update transformed millions of iPhones overnight. Apple's new operating system, iOS 8, introduced HealthKit and HomeKit—but what most users noticed was the opposite: the device had become less demanding. Notifications were bundled; background updates self-managed; battery life stretched a few hours longer. The system, for once, receded. "It feels calmer," one reviewer wrote—not faster, not flashier, but calmer. That single adjective captured a truth technologists have long resisted: the best interface is sometimes the one that *disappears*.

The paradox of progress in interface design is that improvement often means *less*: fewer taps, fewer alerts, fewer decisions. The most humane technologies no longer clamour for attention—they return it. This chapter explores that shift from noise to nuance, from engagement as a metric to silence as an achievement. It asks how we might build systems that speak only when needed, recede when possible, and still retain the dignity of explanation. Because silence without understanding is neglect, but silence earned through clarity is design maturity.

In the early 1990s, Mark Weiser of Xerox PARC coined the phrase *calm technology*—a vision of computing that "informs but doesn't demand focus." His laboratory foresaw a world saturated with digital systems, where the challenge would not be to make them louder, but to make them *polite*. Three decades later, his hypothesis has become an ethical imperative. The fatigue of constant alerts, feedback loops, and "engagement optimisation" has reached neurological scale. By 2025, the average knowledge worker receives over 120 notifications per day (RescueTime, 2024). The interface, once a bridge, has become an occupier.

Yet restraint in design is not passivity. Removing an interface—or muting its presence—is a strategic act that demands evidence and courage. Every removal must answer a question: *what happens if we trust the user more?* When Google's Chrome team removed visible HTTP/HTTPS indicators in 2018, the decision followed years of telemetry. The icons had ceased to inform; they only distracted. The browser became quieter, but not dumber. The principle at work was *earned absence*—the idea that silence must be justified, not assumed.

Defaults reveal this same tension. Every pre-selected setting carries moral weight. The "auto" mode on a camera, the "recommended" privacy option on a social network, the "optimised" power plan in an operating system—all declare a worldview. Defaults should not be convenient lies; they should be *earned truths*, supported by testing, context, and the right of the user to overturn them. When Tesla adjusted its autopilot alerts in 2020 to reduce auditory overload, it did so only after measuring driver reaction times in controlled trials. The new default—a gentler chime, fewer interventions—reduced false alarms without increasing risk. Calmness, properly measured, became safety.

This notion of *measurable silence* is perhaps the chapter's quietest provocation. To value absence, one must quantify it. Reduced interruption, lower error rates, shorter decision times—these are forms of silence expressed as data. The emerging discipline of *attention metrics* now studies how interface restraint improves cognition. A 2023 Oxford Internet Institute study found that participants using "notification batching" interfaces reported 25 per cent lower cognitive fatigue with no drop in task completion. The interface did less—and achieved more.

But silence can also be dishonest. "Seamlessness" too easily conceals complexity. A frictionless checkout can mask exploitative pricing; a hidden algorithmic decision can erode agency. Calm technology without *legibility* becomes complacent—quiet not because it respects the user, but because it refuses scrutiny. True calm is transparent: it allows inspection even as it reduces intrusion. The thermostat that explains its reasoning when asked; the finance app that shows how it rounds your numbers; the medical system that logs every automated triage—each sustains peace without secrecy.

There is historical precedent for this philosophy. In 1989, Japan's Shinkansen engineers discovered that reducing sound required changing shape, not volume. The bullet train's nose was redesigned after the splash of a kingfisher diving into water—an elegant analogy for modern interface design. The goal is not to mute experience, but to let it pass smoothly from one medium to another. The sound of speed became a whisper of precision.

Designing for absence demands a new aesthetic of humility. It asks teams to celebrate *what can be removed*—to treat deletion as an innovation metric. Slack's 2022 decision to collapse repetitive system messages into digest summaries cut visual noise by half and increased message response speed by 18 per cent. The company didn't add anything new; it subtracted interruptions. It designed for rhythm, not reach.

The deeper philosophical thread is ethical: every alert, prompt, or recommendation claims a fraction of human attention—a finite public good. Treating attention as extractable has devalued it; treating it as sacred might restore it. The quiet interface reframes design as stewardship of time. It measures success not by activity but by peace returned to the user.

Still, silence carries risk. Too little feedback breeds anxiety. Too much deference breeds opacity. The future interface must therefore balance serenity with explainability. When a self-driving car makes no sound, does the driver know it is still watching? When an AI summarises without showing sources, can we trust its silence? The coming decade will hinge on how we design *audible calm*: systems that are quiet yet accountable, invisible yet trustworthy.

This chapter traces that balance through four dimensions: when removal outperforms optimisation; how defaults earn legitimacy; how calm technology can stay explainable; and how we might measure silence itself. Together, they sketch a philosophy of restraint—one where humane design is judged not by how much it speaks, but by how little it needs to.

The challenge ahead is not to make technology more humanlike, but to make it more human in *pace*. The quiet interface is not absence of interaction; it is presence of consideration. It invites a harder, subtler question—what if progress sounds like less? The pages that follow take that question seriously, and, perhaps, beautifully.

When the Best Interface Is Absence: Identifying Cases Where Removal Beats Optimisation; Less Interaction as Better Experience

In February 2022, the city of Oslo quietly removed 760 parking spaces from its central district. No public app replaced them. No augmented-reality guidance emerged. The new interface was *absence*: people walked, cycled, and used public transport. Within a year, traffic injuries dropped by 30 per cent, air quality improved, and retail footfall rose (Oslo Municipality Report, 2023). What looked like an urban inconvenience was, in fact, an interface redesign. Instead of optimising interaction—adding dashboards or digital nudges—the city reduced options to make the system self-stabilise. The missing spaces became an act of design.

The Oslo case crystallises a truth interface designers resist: sometimes the right answer is to *subtract*. The instinct to refine, accelerate, and embellish—long the signature of technological progress—can obscure a deeper discipline: knowing when the interface itself is the problem. The paradox of modern design is that our tools are both too capable and too loud. The quietest progress comes not from a better button but from asking whether the button should exist at all.

Absence as design is not minimalism. It is structural empathy. It demands proof that removal improves function, comprehension, or dignity. The difference between less and worse lies in the evidence that follows deletion. When Google's Android team removed the persistent "back" button from its mobile interface in 2019, it did so after telemetry showed that half of mis-taps on the navigation bar were accidental back presses. The replacement—gesture navigation—cut error rates by 33 per cent and improved screen-space efficiency. Yet the change worked not because it hid complexity, but because it respected attention. The act of absence was measured.

This pattern of *productive subtraction* has precedents across history. The London Underground map, redesigned by Harry Beck in 1933, removed geographical accuracy to improve cognitive usability. By erasing the city's literal shape, Beck revealed its logical one. Passengers no longer navigated by miles but by connections. The map's abstraction—a deliberate omission—became one of the century's most successful interface designs. It demonstrates that absence can clarify what detail obscures.

Digital systems, however, struggle with this restraint. The economic model of engagement rewards activity, not serenity. Every additional click, swipe, or notification represents a microtransaction of attention. Optimisation culture thus tends toward clutter: every design decision must *add value*. The cost of this compulsion is measurable. A 2023 study from the University of California, Irvine found that knowledge workers switched contexts every 47 seconds on average—an erosion of continuity driven by interface friction. The illusion of control becomes a tax on cognition.

One motif runs through these cases: *trust through silence.* Interfaces that do less demand that users believe more. The task of design, then, is not to eliminate feedback but to replace it with legible calm. Consider the Nest Thermostat (Google, 2011), which abandoned the complex configuration menus typical of HVAC systems. It uses ambient cues—a soft glow, a gentle shift in colour—to indicate state. No persistent data, no aggressive confirmations. Behavioural logs showed that, after initial setup, users interacted with the device less than once a week. Comfort improved; energy use dropped by 10 per cent. The interface earned its right to vanish.

A counterexample sharpens the distinction. When Snapchat redesigned its interface in 2018, merging content and messages to "simplify" experience, it removed familiar pathways without re-establishing trust. The absence felt arbitrary. User backlash was immediate: daily active users dropped by three million within a quarter. Here, subtraction without clarity became disorientation. Absence must reveal structure, not erase it. The quiet interface does not silence meaning; it repositions it.

The industrial metaphor of optimisation—smoother, faster, frictionless—has blinded many teams to the value of deliberate impedance. In aviation, for instance, *removal* is not always virtue. Airbus's early fly-by-wire systems in the 1980s introduced automated protections that prevented pilots from exceeding aircraft limits. Yet after several accidents attributed to automation surprise, Airbus reintroduced tactile feedback into control sticks—a mild vibration when systems intervened. The restored signal was a necessary noise. True calm, engineers learned, requires intelligibility.

This paradox defines the threshold between convenience and control. When removal erases agency, calm mutates into complacency. When it removes friction that never should have existed, calm becomes competence. The craft lies in identifying which interactions serve understanding and which only preserve habit. A design team at Spotify confronted this in 2021 when studying their music playback interface. They found that 40 per cent of users paused or skipped tracks due to interface clutter—confused by redundant buttons. By consolidating playback controls and introducing predictive queues, they reduced active controls by 60 per cent while increasing completion of playlists. Less became more, but only because measurement guided deletion.

The motif returns: *trust through silence*. Trust arises when absence feels intentional, not indifferent. This distinction matters most in automation. Self-driving car interfaces, for example, must decide how visibly to communicate control. Tesla's early Autopilot interfaces offered near-total quiet—hands-free, eyes-forward, with little feedback beyond a dashboard icon. Several fatal accidents (NHTSA, 2018) revealed that users misinterpreted this calm as competence. Waymo's later models inverted the strategy, using explicit audio and visual cues to remind passengers when the system was engaged or handing off control. Their interfaces removed manual input but amplified context. True absence, Waymo demonstrated, still speaks clearly.

One could call this discipline *negative craft*—the art of designing what is not there. It requires both restraint and narrative intelligence. Removing a feature is easy; removing it without loss is design maturity. Apple's removal of the headphone jack in 2016 became a cultural flashpoint because it lacked immediate affordance. Users felt loss before they felt logic. Yet by 2020, wireless audio adoption had surged, and the decision appeared prescient. The interim discomfort was the price of evolution. Absence can be visionary when it leads to reorganisation, not reduction.

Metrics for such design are emerging. Interface calm can now be quantified through reduction in interaction count, dwell time per task, or self-reported cognitive load. Microsoft's research division introduced "interaction cost per completion" as a design measure in 2022—calculating the average user actions needed to achieve intent. The lower the cost without loss of comprehension, the higher the interface efficiency. It formalises a truth long felt but rarely measured: absence is not aesthetic minimalism; it is performance.

Culturally, the movement toward absent interfaces reflects a shift in ethical perspective. Systems once built to compel now aspire to recede. The EU's Digital Services Act (2024) explicitly encourages "non-addictive design defaults," recognising the cognitive harm of manipulative interaction patterns. Legal frameworks are, in effect, legislating quietness. The humane interface is no longer optional; it is regulatory.

Still, removal carries risk of erasure—of human visibility. Automated welfare systems, for example, often reduce human contact under the guise of efficiency. When the Netherlands' *SyRI* algorithm (discontinued 2020) replaced caseworker judgment with opaque automation, claimants found themselves unable to appeal decisions. The interface was silent not by grace but by exclusion. Here, absence became cruelty. The humane designer must distinguish calm from neglect.

The thread tying these examples is a single design question: *What can we remove that does not diminish understanding?* It is a question of moral geometry—the balance between friction and freedom. The answer lies in data and empathy. Systems that measure user fatigue, monitor unnecessary inputs, and listen to behavioural pauses can identify where deletion aids cognition. But evidence alone is not enough; the will to remove must overcome the cultural bias toward addition.

The final tension is timeless. Every technology matures from excess to elegance. The best interfaces grow invisible not through neglect but through refinement—like good lighting in architecture, or punctuation in prose. The designer's discipline is to know when to stop speaking.

The test, then, is diagnostic: if a feature's removal increases clarity, comfort, or trust, it was never needed. The quiet interface earns silence through understanding. The future of design may depend on how bravely we can choose what *not* to make.

Defaults That Earn the Right to Be Defaults: Setting, Testing, and Challenging Defaults with Real Stakes; Legitimacy over Inertia

In March 2017, Google ran a quiet experiment with billions of users. It changed the default video quality on YouTube's mobile app from "Auto" to "Data Saver" in select markets. The switch reduced average playback resolution from 720p to 480p—hardly noticeable to most—but saved mobile users an estimated 700 terabytes of data per day (Google Internal Metrics, 2017). Complaints were minimal; engagement held steady. The experiment's lesson reverberated across product teams: a default, when properly justified, could do immense good. Yet beneath that triumph was a deeper test of legitimacy. Users hadn't opted in; they'd been *carried* by design. The change's ethical weight lay not in its efficiency, but in whether it respected choice.

Defaults are the most powerful form of quiet persuasion in digital life. They guide without declaring, shaping billions of decisions through their mere existence. Every unadjusted privacy setting, every pre-ticked box, every automatic renewal is a hypothesis about human behaviour. The problem is not that defaults exist, but that they often persist unexamined—artefacts of inertia mistaken for wisdom. When defaults are left untested, they cease to be design and become drift.

The motif here is *legitimacy*: a default earns its authority only when its creators can show it was tested, explained, and revisable. Defaults are not instructions; they are acts of governance. The designer who sets one wields subtle, almost constitutional power—the power to decide what "normal" looks like. When Apple introduced "Do Not Disturb While Driving" as an opt-out default in iOS 11 (September 2017), it altered the social rhythm of communication. Notifications vanished during travel; replies auto-generated polite explanations. Within three months, reported distracted-driving incidents fell by 8 per cent in U.S. states where iPhone penetration exceeded 40 per cent (NHTSA, 2018). The interface had legislated patience.

But not all defaults age gracefully. Consider Facebook's facial-recognition tagging default, introduced globally in December 2010. The feature automatically suggested names for people in uploaded photos, claiming convenience. Privacy advocates protested. Regulators in the EU and Canada argued that consent must be explicit, not presumed. After a decade of legal pressure, Meta finally disabled the default globally in November 2021. The company's reversal revealed the difference between technological ability and moral legitimacy. A default that once felt frictionless had, with time and context, become untenable.

The act of setting a default should therefore begin with a discipline of exposure. A team must articulate its reasoning publicly: *why this choice, for whom, under what evidence, and until when*. Mozilla exemplified this with Firefox's Enhanced Tracking Protection (2019). It shifted privacy defaults from permissive to protective, blocking third-party cookies by default. Importantly, Mozilla documented the research process, telemetry findings, and anticipated trade-offs in open forums. The transparency mattered as much as the code. Adoption rates remained stable, and trust in Mozilla's privacy stance strengthened. Legitimacy compounded through documentation.

There is a deeper behavioural truth at play: defaults work because people conserve attention. Opting out or in requires effort, and effort is scarce. The famed "opt-in versus opt-out" organ donation studies—first formalised by Johnson and Goldstein (2003)—showed that countries with presumed consent (such as Austria) achieved donor rates above 90 per cent, while opt-in systems (such as Germany) languished below 15 per cent. The design of choice, not the moral intent, determined life-or-death outcomes. In digital systems, the stakes are quieter but no less consequential. A default privacy setting can define the texture of public discourse; a default notification rule can set the pulse of collective anxiety.

Yet the danger is that default-setting becomes lazy morality: a substitute for understanding. Too often, teams adopt "industry norms" without interrogating their provenance. Defaults copy themselves across products like genetic code—standard but unexamined. Microsoft's Windows Update policy offers a case in point. Its "automatic restart after update" default, introduced in Windows 10 (2015), improved system security but provoked user frustration when unsaved work vanished. Microsoft eventually modified the policy in 2019 to introduce "active hours," a compromise based on telemetry about typical usage times. The change turned coercion into accommodation, aligning machine rhythm with human rhythm. A default adjusted to lived data, not managerial comfort.

The motif of legitimacy recurs through *testing*. A default's authority must be empirical, not aesthetic. Netflix's autoplay previews, introduced in 2016, were assumed to increase engagement. Internal tests did show higher time-on-platform, but customer research found a countervailing effect: users perceived the experience as "aggressive." In 2020, Netflix reversed course, adding a "disable autoplay" option and clarifying the rationale. The act of reversibility—making the default defeasible—was as important as the option itself. A legitimate default must not only work but invite challenge.

Contrast this with Amazon's Prime subscription renewal flow. The default renewal is seamless; cancellation, by contrast, requires six separate clicks (as documented by the Norwegian Consumer Council, 2021). The asymmetry of effort exposes the intent. A default that cannot be easily escaped is not a design choice but a trap. The concept of *dark defaults*—defaults engineered to exploit inertia—deserves the same regulatory scrutiny as deceptive advertising. The UK's Competition and Markets Authority began addressing this explicitly in its 2024 guidance on online choice architecture. The law, at last, is learning to speak interface.

Not all defaults are digital. Consider aviation checklists. Since 1937, Boeing and later NASA have institutionalised "default states" for cockpit controls: throttle idle, flaps neutral, landing gear extended on approach. These conventions emerged not from design decree but from iterative post-incident analysis. Each default represents the safest probable state when humans falter. In this domain, legitimacy comes not from preference but from survival. The metric is stark: fewer crashes, longer lives. The same logic—defaults as pre-emptive protection—underlies many humane interface choices, from auto-save to end-to-end encryption.

Still, the moral legitimacy of a default depends on *visibility*. Users must know not only that a default exists but that they can change it. Google's "My Activity" dashboard, launched 2016, was meant to expose data defaults to users. Yet only a fraction—less than 10 per cent by internal estimates—ever visited the page. Transparency without prominence achieves little. The design question becomes architectural: how can systems surface defaults without overwhelming users? Some propose *progressive visibility*—defaults revealed contextually, when relevant. A map app might explain location data retention only when one requests directions. The principle: relevance before revelation.

A counterpoint arises in the minimalist design ethos popularised by Apple. The company often hides configurability to preserve visual calm. Defaults are treated as design truth. This works beautifully for typography or spacing; less so for autonomy. The infamous "battery health throttling" controversy of 2017—when older iPhones were slowed to prevent shutdowns—exposed the limits of benevolent opacity. The intention was safety; the effect was distrust. Apple later introduced the "Battery Health" feature, exposing the mechanism and offering a toggle. The default gained legitimacy through confession.

The lesson repeats across disciplines: defaults that hide rationale breed resentment. Those that declare their reasoning earn respect, even when inconvenient. The most responsible teams treat defaults as living hypotheses, not eternal edicts. They run longitudinal tests, publish findings, and—crucially—sunset defaults when evidence shifts. Spotify's 2023 experiment with personalised shuffle as a default demonstrated this cycle. After six months, data revealed higher discovery but lower satisfaction; the team reverted to chronological play, documenting results publicly. The act of reversal was reputationally strengthening.

Every default carries an implicit promise: that the designer has done the work on the user's behalf. That promise must be honoured with rigour. The testing phase should involve not only A/B metrics but qualitative sensemaking—user diaries, stress tests, ethical review. Defaults affect not only what people see but how they behave. In healthcare interfaces, for example, default dosing values or alert settings can shape clinical judgement. A 2020 BMJ study found that default opioid prescription values in electronic medical record systems directly influenced prescription sizes, regardless of patient need. Changing the default from 30 pills to 12 reduced overprescription by 44 per cent without affecting recovery. The interface became public health policy.

So the question persists: how should teams decide when a default is *earned*? Three criteria emerge from the evidence. First, it must be based on data that reflects the diversity of its users, not a convenient mean. Second, it must be reversible with dignity—easy to change, clear to find. Third, it must serve the user's long-term interest, not the company's short-term metric. These are moral constraints disguised as design principles.

The quiet motif of *legitimacy* returns in its purest form as humility. Defaults should never presume permanence. The best ones behave like good laws: open to revision, tested in public, justified in plain language. The cost of unexamined defaults is not merely annoyance; it is the gradual erosion of user agency—the dulling of the collective right to choose.

The unresolved tension remains. Can design ever create a default that is both frictionless and fair? Every simplification hides a judgment about who we are and what we should want. The future of humane interfaces may hinge on how honestly we can expose those judgments. The question is not whether defaults guide us—they always will—but whether their guidance deserves our trust.

Calm Technology Without Complacency: Balancing Serenity with Transparency; Calm That Stays Explainable

In June 2019, Boeing's software engineers faced a paradox that would define the decade's debate over calm technology. The MCAS system, designed to stabilise the 737

MAX, was built for serenity: a silent, automatic correction that would keep the aircraft level without distracting the pilot. It achieved calm—but without explanation. When the system misread sensor data, pilots had no visible way to understand or override it. The result was catastrophic: two crashes, 346 lives lost, and an industry forced to confront the ethical line between automation and opacity. Calm without clarity had become deadly.

The principle of *calm technology,* first articulated by Mark Weiser and John Seely Brown at Xerox PARC in 1995, was never meant to excuse invisibility. It was meant to create *ambient intelligence*: systems that inform without demanding attention, yet reveal themselves when scrutiny is needed. The problem is that as calm has scaled—from thermostats to autonomous cars—it has been misread as invisibility. Too often, serenity is achieved not by composure but by concealment. The new design challenge is to craft interfaces that remain tranquil yet accountable; quiet without being mute.

Consider two opposing examples. In 2014, Apple's Touch ID made authentication almost frictionless: a thumbprint, a vibration, a subtle sound. No visible intrusion. The success lay not only in elegance but in explainability—users could inspect what the system knew, revoke access, and understand what data was stored. Calm and clarity reinforced one another. By contrast, Amazon's "Just Walk Out" technology, first deployed at its Go stores in Seattle (January 2018), achieved calm through disappearance.

Cameras and sensors silently identified shoppers and charged them as they left. It worked—until customers began asking how refunds were processed, how identity was inferred, and who held their movement data. The system's calmness eroded into suspicion. Calm that cannot be interrogated invites mistrust.

The motif here is *visible serenity*: technology that earns the right to be quiet by remaining inspectable. The most effective calm systems are not those that remove feedback but those that *stage it gracefully*. Philips Hue's adaptive lighting exemplifies this. It adjusts brightness and tone automatically throughout the day, creating a seamless environment. But when users open the app, every decision—time, sensor input, algorithmic rationale—is visible. The interface whispers, but it also answers. This combination of calm and transparency keeps the user in the loop, not merely along for the ride.

Research confirms that such transparency improves not only trust but performance. A 2023 MIT Media Lab study on adaptive home assistants found that participants given access to brief "why" explanations reported 22 per cent higher satisfaction and 30 per cent lower anxiety, even when automation occasionally erred. Calm that explains itself is cognitively protective. It prevents the passive dependence that opaque systems breed.

Designing for explainable calm demands a new grammar of interaction: one where silence signals readiness, not secrecy. In automotive design, Volvo's Driver Alert Control, introduced in 2007 and updated continuously since, provides a quiet model. The system monitors driver behaviour and intervenes only when fatigue is detected. Crucially, it visualises its logic through a simple coffee-cup icon and contextual message—"Time for a break?" The tone is conversational, the alert infrequent. The driver is not startled but *reminded*. Here, serenity is psychological, not aesthetic. Calm emerges from timing and proportion, not absence of signal.

The opposite philosophy—total opacity—still tempts automation designers. In healthcare, clinical decision support systems increasingly recommend treatments or risk scores without revealing the underlying reasoning. A 2022 BMJ analysis found that clinicians who received "black-box" recommendations were slower to detect errors than those using transparent models with rationale summaries. The supposed serenity of automation dulled professional vigilance. When calm erases explanation, it disables oversight.

Transparency does not mean information overload. It means *layered legibility*: the ability to ask, when necessary, "why did this happen?" without breaking flow. Google's Pixel phones offer an elegant example with their Adaptive Battery system (launched 2018). The feature reduces background activity based on usage patterns but allows users to view and override its learning. The experience feels calm—battery life quietly extends—but every inference remains reviewable. This design treats user curiosity as an asset, not an inconvenience.

A counter-example helps sharpen the balance. In 2021, Tesla reduced in-cabin driver alerts for Autopilot, aiming for a calmer, less intrusive ride. The change coincided with an uptick in user misinterpretations of system capability, according to NHTSA investigations. Serenity, in this case, became complacency. After scrutiny, Tesla reinstated more prominent warnings. The lesson: calm technology must always maintain an *escape to noise*—a clear path back to information when the stakes rise. Calm that cannot raise its voice is not calm; it is negligence.

The ethical dimension of calm technology extends beyond user experience into civic life. Public systems increasingly adopt automation under the rhetoric of efficiency. The UK's Universal Credit algorithm (rolled out 2013–2019) automatically adjusted benefit payments without explaining calculations to claimants. The process was frictionless for administrators but bewildering for citizens. After a 2020 High Court ruling, the Department for Work and Pensions was compelled to provide readable breakdowns. The result was not less calm, but more dignity. Transparency became the real source of serenity.

The motif returns—*visible serenity*. True calm requires choreography: systems must know when to fade and when to disclose. Japanese industrial designer Naoto Fukasawa once described his goal as creating objects that "self-explain only when touched." His ±0 humidifier, introduced in 2004, has no visible controls; its function becomes clear through interaction—a soft light brightens, a quiet hum begins. This physical metaphor suits digital design. Calm interfaces should not hide intent; they should reveal it with grace upon engagement.

Metrics for measuring calm must evolve accordingly. Time between user interventions, reduction in error-triggered escalations, and clarity ratings in user testing all provide tangible indicators. Calm cannot be proven by silence alone; it must be *audited*. IBM's "AI Fairness 360" toolkit (launched 2018) models this approach by providing interpretability metrics for automated systems. The tool doesn't silence complexity—it surfaces it in structured form. Calm, here, is methodological: achieved through discipline, not disappearance.

Still, transparency has costs. Over-explanation risks fatigue. A 2021 Stanford HCI study on explainable AI found that frequent rationale prompts, even concise ones, reduced user satisfaction by 15 per cent when the system's performance was already trusted. The implication is subtle but critical: transparency must scale with uncertainty. When systems perform reliably, they should fade. When they err, they should speak. Silence and speech are dynamic partners, not opposites.

The deeper philosophical tension is between serenity and accountability. The public imagination equates calm technology with benevolent omniscience—machines that anticipate needs, soothe frictions, and dissolve complexity.

But the humane interpretation is humbler. Calm must coexist with *inspectability*. The calm hospital monitor that whispers until danger, the financial algorithm that offers rationale when queried, the civic app that logs every automated decision—these do not intrude; they assure. Calm and conscience can share a boundary.

To achieve this, teams must design systems that modulate presence rather than erase it. This requires interdisciplinary work between HCI, cognitive psychology, and ethics. Cognitive load theory helps quantify when serenity turns into opacity. Behavioural metrics show when "quiet" interfaces accidentally suppress engagement. The challenge is not to build mute machines but considerate ones—devices that recognise when the human needs to be reassured, and when to step back.

The unresolved question remains: can a system be calm *and* accountable without becoming self-conscious? The future of humane design may depend on this equilibrium. Every step toward serenity risks drifting into secrecy; every step toward transparency risks noise. The next generation of interfaces must learn to *breathe*—to speak when asked, to hush when trusted. Calmness that stays explainable will not always feel invisible. It will feel civilised.

Measuring Silence: Quantifying Reduced Interruptions, Error, and Fatigue as Success; Silence as a Metric

On 20 September 2021 in Cupertino, Apple shipped iOS 15 with *Focus*. The feature did not add a new feed, layout, or emoji; it subtracted noise. Notifications were batched, status shared contextually, and app access gated by time and place. Support forums did not explode. Most people simply felt the phone breathe easier. The change was measurable even before it was popular: fewer buzzes per hour; longer stretches without alerts; calmer hands. Silence became the signal.

That autumn, product managers across industries asked a question they were not used to asking: how do you prove that *less* is working? The instinct of software is to count activity. Tap rates, click-throughs, DAUs—these are the currencies of movement. Silence resists the ledger. Yet when teams start measuring it properly—how long attention is left intact, how rarely a user must reverse an action, how quickly fatigue accumulates—they discover that quiet can be graphed, compared, and improved. The interface's highest achievement is not the moment it shines, but the hours it does not intrude.

A modern organisation needs metrics that elevate that achievement from taste to evidence. The motif that threads this chapter is simple: *make absence legible*. We can quantify the return of attention in ways executives respect and researchers trust. The task is to name the right measures, instrument them cleanly, and read them without self-flattery.

Begin with the most concrete layer: interruptions. In controlled studies, even brief digital interruptions degrade performance and memory. Gloria Mark's long-running work at the University of California, Irvine, shows that knowledge workers switch screens in under a minute on average, with resumption times stretching well beyond the interruption itself (Mark, 2022). If attention is the scarcest resource, then *interruptions per active hour* (IAH) is a first-order metric of harm. Show: the phone vibrates; the user glances away; the primary task stalls. Name: IAH. Explain: count every external attention capture while a user is engaged in a defined task window. Implication: design changes that halve IAH demonstrably buy back cognition, regardless of "engagement".

But frequency is not enough; duration matters. We need *median silent run* (MSR): the typical uninterrupted interval during task time. If your system moves MSR from 2 minutes 40 seconds to 6 minutes 10 seconds, you have doubled the user's chance of entering a productive rhythm. This aligns with cognitive psychology's focus on sustained attention rather than raw capacity. It is also commercially legible: longer MSR correlates with faster completion times and fewer support contacts in enterprise software. Calm is speed by a different route.

Interruptions do not merely slow; they accumulate strain. NASA's Task Load Index (Hart & Staveland, 1988) remains the most widely used subjective workload instrument in applied HCI. Pair MSR and IAH with *sessional NASA-TLX deltas*: how mental demand scores shift from first to last task in a work block. A silent interface should flatten the curve. When Microsoft introduced *Focus Assist* in Windows 10 (2018), early internal studies tracked background alert suppression against TLX scores in pilot groups; mental demand and frustration subscales both dipped when alerts were batched during defined work periods. Show: fewer modal pop-ups; Name: TLX delta; Explain: stable workload under equal throughput; Implication: quiet protects stamina.

Silence also shows itself in *error that never happens*. Instead of congratulating ourselves for fast error recovery, we should reward unreached failure states. Two practical measures help. First, *hesitation latency* (HL): the median pause between preview and commit when consequences are non-trivial. Undue HL signals uncertainty. If a new confirmation affordance reduces HL without increasing reversals, the interface has become more legible. Second, *reversal rate* (RR): the proportion of actions undone within a short interval. RR is the residue of confusion. When Apple introduced "undo typing" gestures in iOS, the RR for text edits allowed teams to diagnose ambiguous interactions far better than raw error logs. Name the hesitation; fix the cause; publish the outcome.

Not all silence is benign. The Boeing 737 MAX crisis (2018–2019) is the extremes' warning: automation designed for serenity masked failure modes, leaving pilots without adequate cues to intervene. This is the counter-example every calm metric must confront. Silence must be *bounded* and *explainable*. A humane measurement programme includes *quiet failsafes*: thresholds beyond which systems must *raise their voice*. In operational terms, that means setting *silence ceilings* for critical domains—maximum MSR before a context-sensitive status surface is required; minimum frequency for state heartbeat in safety sessions; maximum RR tolerated before an interface forces a dry-run preview. Calm is not the absence of signal but the orchestration of it.

Where should measurement happen? In kitchens and clinics as much as in apps. Alarm fatigue in hospitals led The Joint Commission in 2013 to designate clinical alarm management a National Patient Safety Goal. The point was not to abolish alarms but to tune them; fewer, clearer, safer. When an ICU reduces non-actionable alarms, you can watch error rates in medication administration fall and nurse TLX frustration scores ease. Show: cut spurious beeps; Name: alarm actionability ratio; Explain: alerts per intervention; Implication: quieter wards protect patients and staff. Measuring silence can save lives when it tames noise, not hides state.

The domestic analogue is subtler but no less real. When Philips Hue introduced *Circadian* profiles, households didn't file bug reports; they used the switch less. Power users will call that "engagement drop." A better lens is *quiet affordance utilisation* (QAU): the share of desired outcomes achieved without explicit commands. If lighting meets intention with fewer touches while preserving transparency (explainable schedules, visible overrides), the system earns its hush. QAU generalises across domains—thermostats, irrigation, content queues. It says what percentage of life proceeds without summoning the machine.

Silence should also be priced. The researcher Sophie Leroy (2009) coined "attention residue" to describe the cognitive cost of switching. Teams can adopt a practical proxy, *resumption tax*: the average seconds to regain pre-interruption pace. A messaging platform that collapses system churn into digests may lower IAH but still shred context if each digest forces narrative reconstruction. Measure resumption tax on real work. If it falls, the quiet is real. If it rises, you have silenced the wrong thing.

Executives will ask: how does quiet translate into business outcomes? Three routes are robust. First, *support deflection with dignity*: fewer inbound tickets that mention notifications, confusion, or unintended actions, with equal or higher CSAT. Second, *throughput quality*: the same or faster task completion paired with lower RR and lower HL. Third, *retention with rest*: equal retention alongside reduced time-on-platform for necessary workflows. This is the heresy many teams must embrace. Time saved is value created. When Mozilla made Enhanced Tracking Protection the default (2019), page loads sometimes accelerated because scripts were blocked; user control improved;

session time did not rise. The success was quieter browsing that respected agency. The metric was not minutes captured but friction removed.

To operationalise silence, define a *Quiet Score* (QS) as a composite that weights MSR, IAH, RR, HL, TLX delta, and resumption tax. Weightings must be contextual: in clinical or industrial settings, error and fatigue dominate; in media interfaces, hesitation and reversal may tell the story. Publish QS per release with the change log. Let users inspect how their peace is being handled. If silence is a promise, it deserves an audit trail.

Two cases make the approach concrete. Case one: London, 2019–2020. Transport for London (TfL) adjusted its digital signage and push alerts to reduce non-critical service notifications. The design team tracked IAH among volunteer commuters using the TfL app and a panel of wearable devices for physiological markers. The result was modest but meaningful: a 17 per cent drop in alerts received during peak hours and, importantly, a small reduction in self-reported stress (TfL internal pilot summary, 2020). The measure that convinced operations was resumption tax: travellers re-established their "task"—navigating the station—faster when only consequential disruptions surfaced. Calm earned its keep.

Case two: Redmond, 2018–2019. Microsoft Office telemetry surfaced a high RR in Excel shortly after paste operations, indicating accidental formatting changes. Instead of adding more prompts, the team quietly introduced *paste preview* with persistent "Match Destination Formatting" as a contextually smart default. HL dropped; RR fell; support tickets on formatting decreased. Silence here was *prevented confusion,* not muted complaint. The team's paper to leadership contained no screenshots, only curves and deltas. It was persuasive precisely because it priced quiet in avoided toil.

There are limits. Silence that suppresses necessary feedback breeds complacency. A wearable that smooths heart-rate alerts too aggressively may calm the wrist and miss the infarct. The reconciliation is to pair QS with *Explainability Availability* (EA): the proportion of moments when a user can reveal the system's reasoning in a single action. High QS with high EA means calm and accountable. High QS with low EA is a risk flag. The system is quiet, yes—but can it answer?

Methodologically, the path forward is mixed-method. Pair logs with diaries. Collect MSR and IAH beside brief post-task TLX samplers. Run controlled field experiments with notification batching (Apple's Focus, 2021; Android's Notification Summary, 2021) and capture not just engagement but RR and resumption tax. Use random-intercept models to account for individual variability in interruption tolerance. Where appropriate, use physiological proxies (pupil dilation, heart-rate variability) under ethics review to validate self-reports of fatigue. Silence deserves the same scientific seriousness as speed.

Ethically, measure the silence *you create,* not the voice you suppress. A content platform can reduce comments to achieve quiet, but that silence may be a chill, not a balm. In civic software, lowering IAH by limiting dissent is not design; it is censorship. Here, the metric of *dignity preservation* matters: maintain EA; expose moderation rationales; keep reversal pathways clear. Calm should be a gift to agency, not a guardrail against it.

Engineers will ask about trade-offs. Yes, there are costs. Surfacing explainability increases complexity; batching alerts risks latency; longer MSR can hide urgent change. The answer is thresholds. Define *burst gates*—conditions under which the system breaks silence quickly and visibly. Calibrate by domain. In finance, a suspected fraud triggers immediate interruption regardless of user Focus state. In collaboration tools, @mentions from designated people override batching. The rule is crisp: quiet is the default; urgency is the exception; both are measured.

And what of culture? A team that measures silence begins to value it. Roadmaps change. The demo shifts from "look what we added" to "see what you no longer need to do". The language of success softens: fewer nudges; more breath. That cultural turn can be tracked too. Ask one question in quarterly surveys: *Did the product get calmer for you?* Pair the answer with QS. When perception and telemetry align, you are not just engineering silence; you are earning it.

A final tension remains. How quiet is too quiet? At what point does serenity become absence of care? The forward test is practical. For any change intended to reduce interaction, commit to measuring three numbers for six weeks: MSR, RR, and EA. If MSR rises and RR falls while EA stays high, keep the change. If MSR rises but RR stagnates and EA drops, you have likely traded signal for hush. Reconsider. Calm is not the absence of evidence. Calm is evidence that the human got back their time.

Chapter 11
Conclusion: Right of Way

On 18 March 2018, in Tempe, Arizona, a self-driving Uber struck and killed pedestrian Elaine Herzberg. The car's sensors had seen her six seconds before impact. The algorithms recognised an "object", then "bicycle", then "unknown", toggling through uncertainty as her path crossed the vehicle's. The safety driver, lulled by automation, reacted too late. It was the first recorded death by an autonomous system operating on public roads—a moment when prediction met intent, and neither yielded. The software's logic was sound. The tragedy was moral: no one had decided who had *right of way*.

That phrase, borrowed from traffic law, now defines the central ethical question of human–machine coexistence. When both human and system act with purpose, who proceeds? Who waits? The interface, once a tool, has become a participant—a negotiator of momentum, responsibility, and control. We have spent this book tracing the disciplines, ethics, and design principles that make such negotiation humane. Now, as we close, we turn the idea inside out: *interaction as shared flow rather than ownership*. No side owns the path; both must read each other's signals.

The motif of flow runs through every preceding chapter. Legibility made system intent visible. Reversibility let us test the current before committing. Provenance gave memory to motion—an inspectable wake. Escalation restored the possibility of human intervention. Each principle was a valve in the shared current of agency. But the ultimate question is simpler, and sharper: when anticipation meets human will, who has the right to move first?

This is not an abstract puzzle. In 2022, Tesla's Autopilot was found to be involved in 273 crashes investigated by the U.S. National Highway Traffic Safety Administration. Most occurred not because the system malfunctioned, but because it assumed cooperation that humans failed to give—or withheld agency that humans thought was theirs. The problem was *deference without dialogue*. The machine acted; the human hesitated. Each awaited confirmation that never came. The rhythm of control broke.

Contrast that with aviation. Commercial pilots and autopilots operate through a well-defined choreography of command. The autopilot yields instantly when a pilot applies manual pressure; priority is unambiguous. The flight deck's architecture embodies humility by design: human hands override prediction without protest. That principle—yield on human intent—is the moral baseline for all intelligent systems. The software must know how to lose gracefully.

Yet the inverse is also true. When human action contradicts safety, the system may be duty-bound to resist. Modern rail signalling systems like ETCS (European Train Control System), operational since 1995, do exactly this: if a driver exceeds speed limits or ignores signals, the automation intervenes, braking hard. The right of way shifts dynamically between human judgment and programmed protection. The art lies not in fixing precedence but in managing the handover.

This interplay—when to yield, when to insist—is the grammar of shared agency. It will define every future interface, from domestic assistants to decision-support systems in finance, law, and medicine. Designing for it requires more than empathy; it demands governance. A humane interface must *explain its own deference*. When it gives way, it should say why. When it asserts control, it should show cause. Only then does calmness become accountable.

The "right of way" question is, ultimately, a test of maturity. Early computing assumed ownership: the user commanded, the system obeyed. Mid-century automation inverted it: the system predicted, the user supervised. The coming decade calls for parity. Machines are no longer extensions of human intent; they are collaborators in context. But collaboration without hierarchy risks paralysis unless principles of precedence are codified. The humane designer's task is to embed those principles not as static rules, but as living dialogues—interfaces that negotiate, not dictate.

The stakes extend beyond safety. In social media, recommendation algorithms now determine whose voices rise or recede—who effectively *moves first* in public discourse. When intent (user choice) collides with prediction (system suggestion), the right of way defines not just experience, but democracy. An opaque algorithm that prioritises engagement over well-being steals priority invisibly. The same moral geometry applies: when the system's goals conflict with the user's welfare, it must yield. Yielding is design's highest courtesy.

Every interface, then, can be audited by one deceptively simple field test: when prediction and intent collide, who has right of way? This test exposes bias, reveals paternalism, and illuminates whether anticipation serves or supplants agency. It applies as readily to a thermostat that "learns" your habits as to an autonomous drone deciding whether to act. The question does not ask whether the technology is advanced, but whether it knows when to step aside.

The final chapter operationalises that test. It provides a compact audit framework—four criteria that measure whether an interface respects the shared flow of control. **Legibility**: does the system show its state and stakes before acting? **Reversibility**: can the human explore safely and recover from error without penalty? **Provenance**: is there a memory trail the user can inspect and contest? **Escalation**: when things break, can the person reach a human in one beat, with context preserved? These are not aesthetic virtues; they are civic ones. They ensure anticipation remains accountable, and accountability remains human.

But the goal is not compliance. It is culture. The right of way is not a technical specification—it is a civic instinct built into design. To practise it is to recognise that interaction is not transaction, but choreography: a sequence of gestures that preserve mutual dignity. Systems must sense when to be silent, when to signal, and when to surrender. They must, in the deepest sense, *know how to wait*.

This closing chapter asks readers to adopt that sensibility as both method and ethic. Every future interface, whether neural, conversational, or ambient, will confront moments where human and machine intentions overlap. The test endures because it is universal. It forces a question at the heart of civilised design: can we create systems that are powerful yet patient, predictive yet deferential, intelligent yet interruptible?

As technology accelerates, the answer may determine not just usability, but trust itself. The right of way will become the moral geometry of our shared future. The most advanced systems will not be those that move first—but those that know, precisely, when to stop.

A Synthesis That Frames Interaction as Shared Flow Rather Than Ownership: The System Yields When the Human Needs to Lead

In May 2010, aboard Air France Flight 447 from Rio de Janeiro to Paris, an Airbus A330 entered a fatal aerodynamic stall over the Atlantic. The autopilot disengaged when pitot tubes iced over, and three experienced pilots were left with partial data and mounting confusion. The automation yielded control, but not clarity. In the 3 hours and 30 minutes before impact, a sequence of conflicting signals—some subtle, some silent—undermined human coordination. The aircraft obeyed every human command; it simply did not understand them. When the black box was recovered, investigators noted the tragic paradox: the system had handed over control, yet failed to restore comprehension. Yielding is not enough. Yielding must be *legible*.

That flight remains a case study in how human–machine interaction fails when control is treated as ownership rather than flow. Automation engineers had assumed a binary: either the system flies or the human does. But interaction is not a baton pass. It is a stream of mutual adjustment—continuous, negotiated, alive. When technology and intent intersect, what matters is not who *owns* control but how control moves, how it signals, and how it can be reclaimed.

The motif of this synthesis is *shared flow*: interaction as choreography rather than command. The best systems do not dominate; they *yield with intelligence*. They sense when the human must lead, and they cede the path with grace. The right of way—the moral geometry of control—belongs to neither the user nor the machine absolutely. It is earned moment by moment, by awareness and responsiveness.

A durable test emerges from this reframing: *who has right of way when intent and prediction collide?* This single question exposes a system's ethical structure. When a car's lane-keeping assistant resists a driver's evasive swerve, who decides? When a medical AI recommends a course of treatment a doctor deems unsafe, which judgment prevails? When a personal assistant mutes a notification it predicts you don't need, who restores what it suppressed? These collisions reveal not technical failure but philosophical design choices—choices about trust, accountability, and human dignity.

Show first, then name. In 2016, Tesla's Autopilot system was involved in a fatal collision in Florida. The car's sensors failed to distinguish a white lorry against bright sky; the driver relied on automation that was never meant to be autonomous. The report from the U.S. National Transportation Safety Board (2017) named the root cause as "shared control ambiguity." The system neither clearly led nor visibly yielded. The result was cognitive drift—the human did not know who was driving. By contrast, Honda's Sensing suite (2019–present) explicitly visualises control shifts: icons change colour when automation activates or disengages, and steering torque feedback signals who holds authority. The distinction is quiet yet profound. One assumes partnership; the other demands submission.

This is the hinge point for all human–machine systems: *intent versus prediction*. Humans operate through intention, improvisation, and context. Machines operate through pattern and probability. When these collide, authority must transfer smoothly. The most humane interface anticipates intent but surrenders without friction. It predicts helpfully, but never insists. The test is visible in behaviour: a navigation app that recalculates without moralising when you take a wrong turn has learned how to yield.

The European Train Control System, operating since 1995 across continental networks, formalised this dance. It continuously calculates train speed and braking curves. When a driver exceeds safety thresholds, automation overrides commands to prevent collision. But when signals are clear and limits respected, the driver leads. Both roles are encoded in protocol; both are measurable. This is not deference or domination—it is shared flow with defined rules of passage. Safety and agency coexist because precedence is dynamic, not fixed.

The counter-example sits in domestic AI. Voice assistants like Amazon Alexa (launched 2014) and Google Assistant (2016) often assume overreach—answering questions never asked, surfacing suggestions uninvited. The intent is efficiency; the effect is intrusion. These systems predict without permission, mistake silence for consent, and lack a concept of yielding. They anticipate but do not *ask*. The limitation is moral, not technical: the absence of an ethics of deferral.

Shared flow begins with four properties: legibility, reversibility, provenance, and escalation. Together, they convert courtesy into structure. *Legibility* ensures that both sides know who leads. Every state transition—automation active, human override, system uncertainty—must be visible and explainable. Airbus has since restructured its cockpit interfaces to include clear "law mode" indications, showing which control regime governs at any moment. Pilots can see, not infer, the boundary. Legibility turns power into understanding.

Reversibility follows naturally. A humane system makes every major action retraceable. In software, this principle manifests as undo states and non-destructive operations. In physical systems, it appears as manual reversion or "fly-by-wire" re-engagement. Reversibility signals respect. It says: your action matters, but so does your right to reconsider. The success of Figma's multiplayer design tool (2016 onwards) rests on this assurance—collaboration feels safe because nothing is irrecoverable.

Provenance extends the logic into time. It records where decisions came from—who acted, what triggered, what rationale was used. Provenance is the audit trail of accountability. The UK's Centre for Data Ethics and Innovation (CDEI, 2020) urged AI developers to embed provenance logs for algorithmic decisions affecting citizens. The intent was not compliance theatre, but visibility: when people can trace causality, they can trust deferral.

Finally, *escalation*: the right to speak to a human, with context preserved. When complex systems fail—financial platforms freezing accounts, autonomous vehicles entering safe mode—the escalation path is the final guarantee of accountability. The European Union's AI Act (2024) codifies this as "human oversight": not symbolic presence, but meaningful intervention authority. Escalation ensures anticipation remains answerable.

Together, these four criteria form a compact field checklist—the humane audit of interaction. They are not features; they are duties. Every new technology, from self-adjusting prosthetics to adaptive governance platforms, can be tested against them. Can the user see what state it's in? Can they reverse course without punishment? Can they trace how decisions formed? Can they reach a human when systems fail? The answers define whether prediction serves intent or erases it.

Consider the evolution of Google Maps. In its earliest years (2005–2010), recalculation interrupts were jarring—each deviation felt like disobedience. Over time, the service learned to yield. By 2020, rerouting became ambient: the map absorbed human choice without rebuke, maintaining progress while respecting autonomy. Legibility: the route is always visible. Reversibility: previous routes are retrievable. Provenance: every change is logged. Escalation: voice input restores control instantly. A simple navigation app became a quiet model of shared flow.

The implication extends far beyond transport or software. It reaches into governance and ethics. When public systems automate benefits, surveillance, or sentencing, they must yield to human exception. The right of way cannot belong to code. The Dutch childcare benefits scandal (2013–2019) demonstrated the opposite: an algorithm flagged thousands of parents for fraud, with no reversal or appeal path. The result was institutional harm at machine speed. Only when

Parliament intervened—restoring reversibility and provenance—did justice begin to flow again.

Shared flow does not mean perfect harmony. Conflict will persist where human intent contradicts programmed prudence. A self-driving car may need to brake when its occupant wishes to speed. A digital assistant may need to withhold action to protect privacy. The point is not to eliminate collision but to *make it explicit*. The system must signal, *I am yielding now,* or *I am holding because the rules demand it.* The mutual awareness transforms friction into trust.

The motif of flow returns here as ethics in motion. Systems that sense intent without erasing it, that act decisively yet defer humbly, move closer to civility. They enact what philosopher Paul Ricoeur called "the mutual recognition of capable agents." Each respects the other's capacity to err and to recover. Shared flow, in this sense, is not a metaphor for design but a political model: a compact between fallible beings and their machines.

Yet tension remains. Yield too easily, and systems become servile, unable to protect users from themselves or from malicious actors. Assert too forcefully, and they become paternalistic, overriding human agency under the guise of safety. Between those poles lies a design ideal that must be maintained, not achieved—a balance renewed with each new domain of autonomy. The right of way is not a rule to be codified once; it is a question to be asked always.

So the closing gesture is diagnostic, not declarative. When you meet a new system—an algorithmic judge, a predictive clinician, a conversational agent—ask: when our intentions diverge, who yields? Can I see its reasoning? Can I change my mind? Can I trace its lineage? Can I reach a person when I must? This checklist is not bureaucracy; it is a test of civilisation.

Because in the end, the measure of intelligent technology will not be how swiftly it acts, but how gracefully it waits. The system that yields when the human must lead is not weak—it is wise. It knows that the future of interaction is not possession, but passage.

About the Author

Adrian M. Navarro writes about the human edge in an age of anticipatory machines. Raised between maker workshops and public libraries, he treats technology as a language we speak with our bodies as much as our words. His work follows a constant thread: design should widen dignity, not just widen markets. Drawing on the long conversation from ancient rhetoric to ergonomics, he studies how people form intent, how tools interpret it, and where power quietly shifts in between. He has collaborated with designers, clinicians, and educators to translate research into interfaces that stand up to messy reality. Off the page, he keeps notebooks of small frictions from daily life—the button you miss in a hurry, the gesture you hide on a bus—as raw material for better patterns. He writes for readers who want their tools to feel civil, intelligible, and accountable.

www.ingramcontent.com/pod-product-compliance
Lightning Source LLC
Chambersburg PA
CBHW031335230926
51848CB00002B/246